A Man Called Raleigh

By W. Horace Carter
Pulitzer Prize Winning Journalist

Published By:
W. Horace Carter
ATLANTIC PUBLISHING CO.
P.O. Box 67
Tabor City, N.C. 28463

All rights reserved. This book, or parts thereof, must not be reproduced in any form without permission.

Copyright 1988 by
W. Horace Carter
First Printing 1988

Library of Congress Card Number 87083704

Printed in the United States of America by
Atlantic Publishing Company
Tabor City, N.C. 28463

Published By:
W. Horace Carter
Atlantic Publishing Company
P.O. Box 67
Tabor City, N.C. 28463

ISBN 0-937-866-15-6

FOREWORD

Almost every person who walks down the street is a story and you only have to stop and talk with him to find experiences and philosophies worth recording with ink and paper.

My father Walter Raleigh Carter was just a common man from an humble birth and throughout a lifetime that might have been routine except for his unusual wit, story telling acumen, travel and experiences that he so enhanced as to make them classics. It's a real tragedy that he did not have an education for I sincerely believe he would have been another Will Rogers.

While he didn't even know the meaning of the word "journalism," his faith in me and my goals played an important role in my successful pursuit of a newspaper and writing career. Dad and my mother never questioned my ability to earn a UNC Chapel Hill degree in journalism and determination to go on to writing for a living. I most certainly would not have written these stories here had they not had confidence.

Fear was not in Dad's vocabulary. I often wondered if what Paul said to Timothy wasn't appropriate for his life: "God has not given us the spirit of fear, but of love, power and a sound mind."

He had no great power except with his own offspring but he was without fear, had plenty of love and a mind that was always sharp.

I am grateful to have had a father like Walter Raleigh Carter whose raw intelligence and humor rubbed off on all who knew him. I thank God for the privilege of calling him my Dad.

ACKNOWLEDGEMENTS

This book would have never been written had it not been for my wife Brenda who insisted that I do it. She believed that my Daddy had such an interesting life that his children and grandchildren, and our grandchildren deserved to hear about it and if the book weren't written, they would never know about this interesting ancestor.

Much credit must also go to my sister Betty Herlocker who remembered many of the little stories told here and who had the pictures that helped make the book fully illustrated.

My brother Mitchell also was a good source of some of these chapters and many of the experiences reported here happened to both of us, along with various neighbors in the Endy Community.

Others deserving honorable mention for their encouragement to write **A MAN CALLED RALEIGH** are my daughters Linda Burleson and Velda Kay Hughes and my son Rusty Carter and his wife Susan.

ABOUT THE AUTHOR

W. Horace Carter is an outdoor magazine writer and author of the non-fiction book, **Land That I Love**, that tells the story of the life of Dr. John N. Hamlet, the naturalist who captured the monkeys used to research and perfect the polio vaccine. Before he began full time magazine and outdoor writing, he edited and published weekly newspapers in the Carolinas for more than three decades. One of those weekly newspapers was **The Tabor City Tribune**, Tabor City, North Carolina. On July 26, 1953, he was notified he had won the Pulitzer Prize for Meritorious Public Service, the first weekly newspaper ever to win that coveted award. And he did it in a town of less than 2000 people and a circulation of only 1100. He still owns that paper and is editor-emeritus.

He is also the author of **Creatures and Chronicles From Cross Creek, Wild & Wonderful Santee Cooper Country, Nature's Masterpiece At Homosassa, Return To Cross Creek**, and co-author of **Hannon's Field Guide For Bass Fishing, Typewriter Soldier**, the story of Ernie Pyle's death, and **Hannon's Big Bass Magic**. He edited several other books.

In 1954, Carter was named "One of Ten Most Outstanding Young Men in America" by the United States Junior Chamber of Commerce for his continuing crusade against the Ku Klux Klan in his Eastern North Carolina and South Carolina community. He also was recipient of the Sidney Hillman Foundation Award, the President's Award from the National Editorial Association, the B'nai B'rith Award, and more than 20 other state, regional and national honors.

He is 67 years old and is a talented fresh water fisherman. He helps others catch fish and has written about his expertise in this field for every major national and regional outdoor magazine.

He founded **The Tribune** in 1946 after getting his journalism degree from the University of North Carolina in Chapel Hill and serving in the U.S. Navy during World War II. He founded Atlantic Publishing Company, a printing, die-cutting, wholesale paper distributing company that is a major business in Southeastern North Carolina. It is now being run by his son, Rusty, and associates.

Carter was raised humbly in Stanly County, N.C., and graduated from Endy High School. He trapped cottontails and hunted squirrels and quail to supplement the food supply during the big Depression when his father lost his $18.00 a week job.

He entered college at Chapel Hill with $112 he had saved working the graveyard shift at an Albemarle cotton mill for $10.37 a week. He worked six to eight hours a day as a student assistant at the University News Bureau in Chapel Hill to pay his way through college. He was elected editor of the student newspaper and tapped into the Golden Fleece at U.N.C.

In Tabor City where he has raised his family of three children he has served as mayor, president of the Rotary Club, Baptist Sunday School teacher, charter president of the Recreation Commission, charter member and later chairman of the Columbus County Industrial Development Commission, charter president of the Carolinas Country Club, and a member of the county library board, among other positions.

He is a director of the Outdoor Writers Association of America, three time past President of the Florida Outdoor Writers Association, and past President of the Southeastern Outdoor Press Association, a 11 State organization. He has sold more than 1,000 magazine stories.

This book is a compilation of stories told by his father or experienced himself as he grew up in the Endy community during the Great Depression and thereafter.

Dad's Conflict With His Father

It was a tough September Saturday afternoon. Dad had worked and sweated washing a half a dozen big elephants for a circus on the outskirts of Badin. His reward was a ticket to get inside the big tent so he could see the show, something he had dreamed about all his life. With the task complete at dusk, he walked inside the tent that housed the three rings of entertainment. His heart thumped as he thrilled to trapeze acts, fire eaters, trained dogs, wild animal roars and numerous clown escapades that brought laughter to hundreds under the big top. It was an evening he would never forget, but he had virtually forgotten that his stern father at the crossroads village of Palestine in Eastern Stanly County, North Carolina, some five miles away, had said, "Raleigh, you be home by dark." Having turned twenty-one the previous March, Dad was legally his own man, but he was still dominated by a father who held a tight rein and demanded unquestioned obedience.

It was nearly 9:00 p.m. when Dad walked out the tent door and headed for home. It was 10:00 when he stepped on the front porch of the old log house that had been home for him and eight brothers and sisters since birth. He was breathing hard from the fast walk over the rocky dirt road and was startled when his father, Tom Carter, a tall mustached farmer, rose from his homemade rocking chair where he had sat in the dark awaiting Dad's return. "I told you to be back by dark," he said in a sober, threatening voice.

"But, Papa, I got a chance to see the circus. I had to wash the elephants to get a ticket and that took all afternoon. But then they let me inside for nothing. That's why I am late," Dad pleaded his case.

"That has nothing to do with it. You disobeyed and I'm giving you a licking," his father said and he proceeded to turn his twenty-one year old son over a straight chair and lashed him severely with his leather belt. Dad uttered no whimper. He just stood up after the frailing, walked through the house to his bed and plopped down without taking off his soiled overalls. He could not sleep nor did he ever again go to bed in that ancestral home.

He sat up on the bed at the first streaks of daylight, unsteady from a nervous night of dozing and thinking. He had never been given a chance to go to school. "I don't know what grade I got to in school but it was whatever grade you can get to in three months. That's all I ever went," Dad often said years later. His father had controlled him like a slave.

He thought some more. He had been sent to work in a textile mill in Albemarle when he was seven years old. He worked twelve hours a day Monday through Friday. "Then we had a short day on Saturday and got off at 4:00 in the afternoon," Dad recalled. He worked those seventy hour weeks as a child from the age of seven for seventy cents a WEEK, a penny an hour. And then morning and night he had to walk the six miles to the job and back.

"My father took sixty of my seventy cents when I got home each Saturday evening. That was my board and keep. He left me with a dime for the week. Then he stole that out of my pocket after I went to sleep and gave me a whipping for losing it on Sunday morning," Dad told with chagrin years later. He probably exaggerated a bit, but basically the abuse was real. He was being held in peonage.

What would he do now that it was daylight? Dad pondered his life to date. "I didn't even know they made little shoes until I was seventeen years old. I thought they just made them for big people," he often said later.

After he grew out of the child labor hell in the mill, Dad had got a job chopping out railroad crossties with an axe from hardwood logs at New London, a hamlet just north of Albemarle. The pay was better, a full dollar a day for ten hours hard labor. Most of what he had earned was taken by his father each week, like toll to a miller. But he had pigeonholed a few bucks. His father didn't know he had them or he would have taken that too.

Dad stood up from the bed. The die was cast. He had made a decision. His father would never whip him again. He dressed with the only Sunday school shirt and pants he had, stuffed his few other clothes into a paper bag and walked out of the bedroom. His mother stood over the old wood cookstove in the kitchen. You could see that she was worried and had been crying.

"Where you going, son?" she questioned when she saw him dressed with the humble bag in his hand.

"I'm leaving, Mama. I can't stand it here any more. I love you with all my heart, but I can't take Papa's beatings and abuse any more," Dad told her as he hugged her with tears in all four eyes, and he walked to a corner closet and picked up an old .16 gauge shotgun. "You have been a good mother and I'll always miss you," he said in a choking voice.

"The gun was the only thing that my Papa ever gave me. I wanted to take it with me. Perhaps it would sell for four or five dollars and help me buy a train ticket. I stepped off the porch and was almost out of the yard when I heard Papa's gruff voice.

"Where you going with my gun?" he said in a threatening tone.

"You gave me this gun. It's mine," Dad answered without any semblence of fear this time.

"It's my gun. You ain't taking it nowhere," he said, demanding obedience.

"I walked back to the porch and laid the gun on the steps. I didn't say another word to my father. I was again being victimized by an uncaring parent whose only interest in me was for what I could earn and bring to him on Saturday night. I didn't look back when I walked away from that old farm and headed for the Southern Railroad Depot in Albemarle," Dad recounted the events of the day that he left home. He would never again show any friendship with his abusive father, but he did see him a few minutes nearly a decade later when his mother was dying. Occasionally, thereafter he visited brothers and sisters in the neighborhood and spoke to his aging father but there was no love between them. The wounds of childhood never fully heal.

At the train station, Dad asked about the price of a coach ticket to Terrill, Texas. That's where his mother's family had moved some years before. His plan was to go there and work with his Grandfather Mason and his offspring. The ticket cost was more than Dad had in his hidden kitty.

"How far can I get on $18.00?" he asked the clerk.

"Let's see, that will get you to Mobile, Alabama," the railroad attendant said.

"O.K. I'll take a ticket to Mobile," he said and he handed over his hard-earned cash.

He arrived in Mobile the following morning, hungry and tired. He went to the Western Union office and with his last dollar, sent a message to his grandfather asking for help so he could get to Texas. The money came quickly by wire and a joyous Raleigh Carter stepped off the old coal-burning train at Terrill, near Forth Worth, late that afternoon. Two of his cousins and his grandfather met the train and were happy to see him.

"How's your mother?" Grandfather Mason asked Dad about his married daughter.

"She's kind of sickly but she sends you her regards and hopes you'll let me stay with you," Dad replied.

Texas was a dry, hot, cotton-growing flat country at Terrill and that crop was what had brought the Mason family from North Carolina. Dad was happy as the old buggy pulled by a beautiful quarter horse moved across the prairie to the Mason homestead.

"Why did you leave home?" Grandfather Mason asked Dad.

"I just couldn't get along with Papa. He took everything I earned and then whipped me like I was a child. That's why I'm here now. Last Saturday night he beat me for getting in late from the circus at Badin," Dad told somewhat sorrowfully.

"Why were you late?" the old grandfather asked.

"I had never seen a circus and I had to wash the elephants to get in. Then I had to see the night show and I didn't get back home until about 10:00. But I'm glad I got to see the circus. There were some ladies in the show that were as pretty as a speckled pup under a red wagon. I'll never forget that show," Dad said with enthusiasm as he remembered the circus entertainment.

"Well, you are a man here and on your own. You can work on the farm for your room and board but I'll give you some acres so you can grow a crop of cotton for yourself. I think you'll get along fine with us," Mason said, as the buggy stopped in front of a moderately attractive and functional stucco house with not a tree in sight. It was a barren prairie.

Grandmother Mason walked out on the porch and the constant Texas wind tugged at her long hair. "Raleigh, is that really you? I haven't seen you since you were a little tot. You had anything to eat?" she asked, her maternal instinct showing.

"Not a bite except two ham biscuits that Mama put in my bag when I left the house two days ago," Dad said, "But hungry or not, I'm as happy as a dog in a meat house to be here." Dad's cleverness with words and phrases was apparent even then.

Food was not a scarcity at the Mason home. Water was. There was no well and no lake or stream. The only drinking water was caught in barrels from the house roof drain-off during infrequent rains. Those rains made the dirt like putty and it stuck to your feet like it was glued, caking up in clumps too heavy to walk with.

"The water was always full of little wriggling animals but you had to drink it. There wasn't any thing else," Dad remembered." I shut my eyes and held my nose when I drank.

During the next year, Dad worked with his cousins and grandparents growing cotton. It was hard work, and while Dad never picked a bole of cotton in North Carolina, he had to pick it in Texas. There were no machines then that made the job easy.

Picking sacks in this big cotton-growing state were eight or ten feet long. You could put a passel of cotton in one sack before you had to empty it and even with the long rows of most fields, you could make a round without going to the dump. Back in the Carolinas, cotton was picked in a sack that swung from your shoulder and the strap bit into the skin and bone from even a little weight. The rows were short and you emptied your cotton into burlap sheets on the ground at one end of the field each round. Even good cotton pickers could jerk out no more than about 200 pounds of cotton a day in the Carolinas. Texas pickers didn't have the weight of their cotton on their shoulders and didn't suffer from the back-breaking bending required back east. They put pads on their knees, usually pieces of old automobile tires, and picked cotton as they moved along in this kneeling position.

"I worked just as hard as my cousins and when it was picking time, I picked a row every time they did. But strangely, at the end of the day I would have between 200 and 300 pounds and they would have 400 to 500. I suppose those boles they reached over and harvested from my rows every now and then when I was getting behind made part of the difference. But then I picked my cotton pretty clean like people did at Palestine. They just grabbed and if the bole came loose from the stalk, it went into the bag. The gin got the trash out anyway and they saw no reason for keeping their cotton clean," Dad recalled his Texas experience.

"People traveled on horseback most of the time in Texas in that era. One Sunday morning my cousins wanted to know if I would like to go to church. I was interested and they went out and hitched up three of the riding ponies. I dressed with the only good clothes I had. We mounted and headed for the church. You could see it in the distance and it looked like it was just a few miles away. Actually it was twenty country miles away and it was a long ride.

"My cousins spurred their mounts and all of us left the house at a pretty fast trot. A mile across the prairie they picked up speed and when they reached a three wire fence, their ponies gracefully jumped and didn't miss a step. I noticed they were looking back at me as my pony approached the fence at a fast clip. He didn't make any effort to jump. He had never been trained. He just saw that barbed wire, threw out his front feet and stopped in his tracks. I went head first right into the wire and was cut, scratched and bruised all over. My devilish cousins came back laughing. They knew my pony wouldn't jump. It was their idea of a practical joke. It wasn't funny to me. My clothes were ruined, and I was hurting all over. I gave them a cussing, caught my pony and went back home. I never did see the inside of that church and the cousins didn't either," said Dad.

One year of Texas cotton growing was enough for Dad. When he sold the harvest from the five acres that his grandfather had given him, he thanked his generous relatives, rode to the station on the same old buggy again, and boarded a train for Cleveland, Ohio.

"I never want to go back to Texas. It was windy, hot, dry, uncomfortable and the water was wiggling. Once was enough for me," he said.

A stranger in Cleveland, but with energy and some mechanical ability from his experience with the railroad, on the farm and in the textile mill years before, he found a machine shop job. He worked it and a moonlighting job as an usher in a theatre. He made a lot of friends and accumulated a little financial nest egg. He learned about another job in Pennsylvania and left Ohio.

It was in Pennsylvania that he met the Anderson family with whom he lived for four more years. He didn't leave until he was called by the draft board for a physical examination pursuant to service in the armed forces. He failed the exam because of the extra thumb on his right hand, but the board suggested that he go somewhere and get a job helping with the defense buildup. He went to Newport News, Virginia and began his boiler making on the battleship Maryland.

Dad with cotton bales in Texas

Dad, right, with friend Leslie Turner in Ohio

Dad, standing, with Horace Mann, in Ohio

Dad's Extra Thumb

Dad was at the prime age for the draft when World War I broke out. He was working as a machinist in Pennsylvania when he got the "greetings" call from his draft board. Now Dad had no great desire to go into the Army during the big war but he was a good citizen and would always comply with any draft law. He reported to the draft board for his physical examination on time.

Doctors were looking and listening for physical defects in a whole room full of draftees when Dad reported. When his place in the line reached the examining physicians, he was sure they would accept him quickly. He was not a big man, but he was tough and strong at 145 pounds. He had never been in a hospital and was a fine physical specimen.

The doctor examined him carefully, finally taking a look at his right hand. He focused on Dad's hand with disbelief.

"What's this?" he asked, looking at Dad's unique hand.

"It's my extra thumb," Dad said.

"Well, it sure is unusual. Most people born with a defect like that would have had it cut off when they were infants. No one would have ever known about it. But yours is normal size," the doctor noted.

"Yeah, I had it all my life. I was born at home. There was no doctor at my birth to cut off an extra finger," Dad acknowledged.

"That's too bad. We just won't be able to use you. Gloves issued in the Army wouldn't fit and that extra thumb might cause other problems too," the examining physician said, almost sorrowfully, regretfully.

"I acted like I was really hurt that they couldn't use me. It was such a shame that I wouldn't be able to get in the service and be shot at, gassed and bombed all over Germany," Dad

Dad, right, with friends in Ohio

grinned. "But he did have a suggestion for me. In that I was a machinist, the doctor suggested that I do my part for the war effort by reporting to one of the defense industries where they needed trained craftsmen."

Shortly after that rejection for the army, Dad took a train to Newport News, Virginia, where ships were being made for the war effort. Shipyard workers were serving their country well.

Dad always had something to say about jobs he applied for. Work was scarce and wages low. I recall once when he was looking for a job and he came home telling about it.

"The boss told me he had a job that would pay me $20.00 a week now and $25.00 a week in six months. I told him I would come back in six months," Dad recounted. There was some humor then even in adversity.

Money was easier to make during war times than in the Depression but many people rationalized that you would buy just as much with a little money then as you could with a lot more money now.

"That may be true," Dad said, "But I like to have more money. It makes it seem like I get something for my work. When I get $30.00 rather than $18.00, even if it does buy the same amount of groceries, I had rather get the $30.00. But I recall that a Coke was 5 cents during the war and 5 cents during the Depression. Chewing gum was a nickel both times. I'll take those times when you get more money.

"Some people won't work in good times or bad times regardless of how much they could get paid. They act like they are asleep and play dead, waiting for someone to feed 'em. I think you have to want to get ahead even if it seems impossible. You got to have ambition. That's the mother of dissatisfaction and you are not going to have much happiness until you are tired of treading water and decide you want to amount to something more than your training conditioned you to," Dad often observed. It was good thinking then and now.

"I looked at a big bulletin board at the entrance gate at the shipyard. There was a long list of job openings with what the pay scale was for each position. The highest paying job on the board was boiler maker. Right then I decided that I was a boiler maker. I walked inside, applied for the job and got it. They needed me. I worked there during the rest of the war and drew my good pay as a boiler maker. I had some assistants who knew a lot more about the blueprints and drawings for the boilers than I did. But my experience with air hammers and other tools got me by. I stayed until we completed the battleship Maryland. My extra thumb didn't bother me but the noise working in that big boiler cost me the hearing in my left ear. I never regained that. When the war ended, I quit the job and went back to Stanly County.

"I got married after I met Waulena Lowder, a tiny little woman who grew up on the outskirts of Albemarle. It was kind of love at first sight," Dad recalled. "We got married in a few months."

He used that extra thumb that sprouted out from his normal thumb, just like it was supposed to be there. He would screw on taps on bolts when he was working on cars and it never seemed to get in his way. It was almost like people were supposed to have two thumbs on the right hand.

"But the thumb was the handiest when it got me out of the army. If I hadn't had it, I might never have made it back to North Carolina," Dad said many times as we talked about his unusual appendage when we were growing up. In later wars, it certainly would not have disqualified him for the armed forces. But it did in WWI and it made Dad happy.

Mama, left, and her sister Alice when Mom was nine

After seven years of wandering and working in Texas, Ohio, Pennsylvania and Virginia, Dad returned to his native Stanly County in North Carolina, late in 1918. Unmarried, he wasted only a few months before meeting a petite little lady Waulena Lowder Carter, of the Albemarle section. A kind of whirlwind courtship followed for three months and they were married in 1919. They moved into a two bedroom, frame house in the Efird Mill housing development in West Albemarle. I was born there January 20, 1921 and Mama weighed just 102 pounds at the time. When I was three years old and Mitchell an infant, the family moved to Endy where Dad had bought twelve acres of land and built a $1200.00 house on credit. The house, renovated many times, is occupied today by my sister Betty and her husband J.A. Herlocker.

Dad posed with this lady, who is unknown

Mitchell and I were born in this West Albemarle house

Our Endy home - now occupied by the Herlockers

Dad Must Have Been A Teacher's Pain In School

Like he often said, Dad never knew what grade he reached in school. He only knew it was whatever grade you could reach in three months. That's all he ever got to go to school and this was a sore subject with him because some of the older children had a chance to get to high school.

School must have been a play time with him because he had pranks on his mind that must have made him a problem for his teacher in a one room school house.

Students had desks, one behind the other in neat rows, and Dad sat about half way down one row with a kind of sissy youngster directly in front of him. It was early winter time and Dad was still barefooted, often saying he didn't know they made little shoes until he was 17 years old. He thought they were for grown people. By going barefoot virtually all the time, the skin on his feet and toes was tough, almost like leather. With a kind of natural dislike for the boy in front, he devised a scheme for playing one of his tricks. He took a straight pin and stuck it through some tough skin on his big toe. With that sharp weapon secured, he kicked the calf of the youngster's bare leg.

"That boy came right up out of the seat hollering and grabbing his leg like he was snake bit," Dad laughed years later when he told it.

"What's wrong with you, Percy?" the teacher asked.

"Something bit me," the boy said half sobbing and rubbing the leg.

The teacher looked around for a spider or mosquito and, of course, found nothing. I was busy studying my spelling book and didn't even look up," Dad said.

As soon as things quieted down a bit, Dad said he jabbed

the pin in the boy's leg again and it was like instant replay, he popped up in his seat screaming that he was bitten again. Needless to say, the teacher could locate no insects in the area and suspecting Percy was trying to play a trick on her, she was more stern when she told him that time to sit down, stay down and quit disturbing the class.

Moments later, Dad stuck that pin in the same leg and Percy reacted just as he had the first two times. The teacher had lost her patience. She grabbed Percy by the arm and marched him right outside where a long pile of stove wood was stacked for use in the pot bellied stove.

"I'll teach you not to disturb my class all morning again," she said, stripping off a yard-long switch from a piece of hickory wood that was on top of the pile. "She frailed him all over his pin-stuck legs and buttocks for several minutes and had him yelling and crying so you could hear him all over the school yard," Dad recalled that event as he chuckled out loud.

"Finally, she brought Percy back in the room and told him to get his books and move to a front seat, one usually reserved for the girls. He moved right in front of her desk and a pretty little girl took his seat in front of me. That ended my pin trick. I didn't want to see her get a whipping. I took the pin out and Percy never knew what bit him. Come to think of it, he got a raw deal out of that teacher but all of us do at one time or another, one way or another, get a raw deal in life. We just have to take it, suck it up and keep going. All the breaks won't be bad breaks," Dad said, with only a touch of chagrin for his prank that got Percy a beating.

Some people make their own bad luck.

Dad And Politics

I never saw Dad very concerned about politics except one time. That was in 1928 and Al Smith was running against Herbert Hoover for President of the United States. Smith was a New York Catholic. Dad, like many Southerners of that era, had no use for Catholics, any Catholic. He had boarded with a Mrs. Malone in Cleveland who was a Catholic but aside from giving her credit for going to church in good weather or bad, night or day, he had no good words for her religion. He had been conditioned from birth not to like Catholics.

Dad firmly believed that if Al Smith were elected, he would try his best to make everyone in the United States a Catholic. He would force us all to be Catholic. He felt that was Smith's reason for running for the presidency and that all Catholics had one great objective -- to make Catholicism the religion of everyone throughout the world, by force if necessary. Dad felt Catholics had the same objective as communists. He believed it so strongly that he asked Mama to go vote that election. She had never voted in her life. Dad was a Republican and Mama was a silent Democrat. After some urging, she agreed to vote for Hoover. I believe that is the only time in her life she ever cast a vote for a national candidate. And she may have regretted that. Another Catholic presidential candidate did not come along until John F. Kennedy.

Dad's lowly conception of Catholics changed only slightly in his old age. He conceded that people everywhere are generally what their parents are, especially Catholics. Religion is a thing you are conditioned to by your guardians and you fall into that denomination most of the time because you are led there by your peers, not an independent choice. Baptists are much the same.

"I don't think any religion is all right or all wrong but I believe you have to be something. I don't think you can struggle through this life and not have any religion and expect to get any reward. Those people who have no religion and want to keep the kids from hearing about God in the schools ought to leave the country," he said with conviction many times.

It reminded me of my departed friend, Dr. John N. Hamlet. He lived all over the world with more than one hundred religions. He said every one of them thought he was right and he was never smart enough to choose which one was.

"But even the apes get up in the morning, face the sun and beat their chests," said the great naturalist who captured the cynomulgus monkeys used in the experiment that perfected the polio vaccine.

Four years following the Hoover election when Franklin D. Roosevelt was swept into the presidency in a landslide, Dad was running a country store. It was Depression time.

Jackson Whitley and Ceph Blalock were the leading Republicans in our end of the county. Whitley stopped to buy gas the morning after the election. He was distraught. I never saw anyone before or since so upset over an election, not even candidates who lost.

"Raleigh, the Republicans have won our last election. There will never be another Republican in the White House," the old politician said with pain on his countenance. As it turned out, it did take a long time. World War II had to come along before General Dwight Eisenhower made it to the presidency on the GOP ticket. Since then, Republicans have dominated the White House.

Blalock, our next door neighbor, was a prominent Republican and for a time was the caretaker of the Stanly County Home on the Old Salisbury Road. That was the facility where the poor went when they had no families to look after them. They lived there like in a nursing home today and the Blalocks were in charge of the facilities and the farm where they grew many of the crops that fed the welfare occupants. There were little or no welfare give away programs that are so numerous today.

The county home job was a political plum. The Republicans frequently won the local elections in Stanly and after one of those victories, Blalock was rewarded with the county home job. After handling it for a few years, the Democrats went back into power and his family returned to Endy and were our neighbors again for the rest of their lives.

Ceph was a kind of hot head Republican who would get mad at the drop of a hat when politics was argued. Robert (Bob) Doughton was the Congressman from our district for many years and he served as Chairman of the House Ways and Means Committee for decades. One Saturday morning Mr. Blalock met Doughton on the streets of Albemarle and a lively discussion quickly started that grew hotter and hotter. Eventually, Blalock could not stand it any longer and he floored the Congressman with a sharp roundhouse to the jaw. I never knew what came of the case. He was indicted for fighting and paid some kind of fine. But he never seemed apologetic for having his fisticuffs with the political celebrity. It seemed he had finally made his mark in the political arena, even if it was a street brawl.

Dad thought it was funny.

Dad Learned Many Lessons During His Three Months In School

There were no kindergartens when Dad was a child at Palestine. Even if there had been a kindergarten, he would have had no opportunity to attend. What little schooling he got, and he often said it was for only three months all told, he put to good use and it was amazing how he learned the basics of reading and writing in such a short time while absorbing so many of the real values of life.

"I learned that wisdom isn't always found just in college graduates. Little kids can learn things that shape their lives, as mine was. I was taught that I should play fair with others, share things that I had and not to hit people when we disagreed. I learned that things should be put back where I got them and when I made a mess, I had to clean it up. I shouldn't take things that were not mine and when I hurt somebody, I should be sorry for it. I needed to wash my hands before eating anything, drink plenty of milk and get a nap in the middle of the day. I never had time for this, but it made good sense.

"I learned that birds and rabbits live and die and plants grow from tiny seeds that push roots downward instead of up. These too die and we die too. There's nothing here forever.

"Then I learned about the Golden Rule. You consider the things that I learned during those few short months and you'll find they are good messages for the country and all people today. We must live sane lives, stop making a mess and clean it up when we do, stop taking things from others, and share what we have. It's going to be a better world when we hold hands rather than drop bombs," Dad said.

Some Humor In The Tragic Civil War

Many of Dad's close relatives died fighting for the Confederacy in the Civil War. Dad didn't know much about it except what he had heard first hand from some of the survivors who still lived in his area when he was a boy growing up at Palestine.

What impressed him most was the way the South fought on when the troops were starving and had almost nothing to fight with. Ammunition was scarce and while they had some old cannons that they pulled into position to shoot at the Yankees, often they had no projectiles to put in the gun. A big gun without projectiles is a liability, like food to a soldier with no teeth.

"I heard that sometimes they had gun powder but no big bullet to put in the cannon. They gathered up all the metal they could find around some of the Southern farms and crammed it in on top of the powder and fired. Now wouldn't you hate to be out there in the field fighting and see a big log chain come whipping through the air toward you? I just wouldn't want to get killed by a log chain shot from a cannon," Dad found a bit of humor even in the tragedy of that horrible conflict.

Come to think of it, I wouldn't want to get hit by a log chain shot out of a cannon either.

"If you are having a street fight with no holds barred, try to get in the first punch. If you loosen a few front teeth, the fellow might decide he doesn't really want to fight you."

Tidbits That I Remember

In 1934 after Mama had recovered from a long siege of kidney trouble and we had lost our little sister at birth two years earlier, the family packed up for a trip to Ohio and Pennsylvania. Dad wanted to go back to visit the Anderson family that he lived with after he left Texas and before he was married. We all climbed in the 1929 A-Model and Randall Burleson, a school teacher, scoutmaster neighbor who was unmarried, had been invited to make the trip with us. He would help do the driving. Mama couldn't drive and we weren't old enough.

We made the 2,000 mile trip in about ten days and for the first time we saw some of the country that had seemed so far away. I remember the woodchucks in Pennsylvania that had dug holes all over the pastures and the Andersons wanted them shot because the horses and cattle stepped in their burrows and broke their legs. Wild cottontail rabbits were seen everywhere early and late in the day as few people hunted them like we did in the South. We used high powered rifles for the first time. The woodchucks would dart in their holes, then poke their heads up. That's when we shot them.

The Ed Anderson family, a son of the elder Andersons who was about Dad's age, was a carpenter and he had sold his house. The family was living in a two-car garage until he found time to build again. We spent several nights sleeping on the floor in the garage.

My sister Betty remembers one detail of the trip better than any other. We had shredded wheat for breakfast. It was the first time we ever saw that kind of cereal. We had eaten oatmeal and Post Toasties, but shredded wheat was something different and it was good.

I recall going through the mountains of West Virginia when the old Ford started steaming. The water was out of the

My Mother, Waulena Lowder Carter

radiator. Dad walked a short distance to a service station, got a bucket of water and started back to the car. The station attendant hollered, "Hey, mister, don't get run over. You might mess up my bucket." Dad just nodded agreement.

It was in the same era when I managed to have ten cents to attend the first talking movie that ever came to Albemarle. I do not recall who acted in the old black and white film, but I know the title was "Sunnyside Up." We were amazed that you could have sound and pictures telling a dramatic story. We had to read the graphics on the screen prior to that. I do recall that children under twelve could get in the movies then for ten cents. Adults had to pay a quarter. But I was so little, weighing 102 pounds at age sixteen when I got my first driver's license, that I got in for a dime until I was ready to go to college.

This was also the time frame when we got our first electric refrigerator. It was a Westinghouse that ran more than 25 years without any maintenance.

Our first running water was put in the house then too. Prior to that for a long time we had to draw the water out of the deep drilled well by hand with a rope and windlass. Sometimes the well rope broke, and we had to fish the bucket out of the well with a two-way hook on the rope. Later we had a hand pump that made getting water much easier. Finally, with electricity, we got an electric pump that put water in the house, and we had a bathroom with a tub. It was years later when we got a shower. When we got our first electric power, Dad had to pay for the two light poles that brought the line from the highway to the house. As I remember, they cost him $100.00, a lot of money in the early 1930's. The light bill then ran between $3.00 and $5.00 a month. But about all the electricity we used before the refrigerator and water pump was for the two or three naked light bulbs that hung in the kitchen and bedrooms. We had bought some gasoline lamps just before the electric lights were introduced and they were many times brighter than the old kerosene lamps used earlier. I still blame my eye problems to reading hundreds of Smith & Wesson Wild West Weekly magazines with no light except the kerosene lamps. It was about like Lincoln's reading by the light from the fireplace flames.

I almost didn't live through my outdoor experiences as a teenager. Mitchell and I were climbing hickory trees one fall

30

and shaking off the nuts. We harvested these goodies for cracking during the winter when we sat around the fire. I never saw a pecan until I was grown. The hickory nuts were hard shelled and it took a hammer to crack them. But the little bit of meat inside was tasty and interesting to pick out. One day I was in the top of a 60 foot hickory when a limb I was holding broke. I fell eight feet or so and the oversize overalls I wore with about six inches of extra denim in the straddle, hooked on a broken snag in an uppermost fork of the tree. I dangled there a few moments looking down on a three foot high rock wall that made a pasture fence below me. That could have been my death bed but the surplus of cloth in the crotch of the oversize overalls saved me.

We usually had a few acres of corn to harvest in the fall. It was not easy like it is today. You pulled the ears off the stalk by hand and piled them up. These piles were about a dozen steps apart and you threw the ears in a harvest row from about three rows on each side. Then you came back with a mule and wagon, picked up the ears, hauled them to the barn yard, where it was dumped in waist-high piles. Later you shucked it, often with the help of neighbors who had corn shuckings in the fall that were highlighted by a big supper feast after all the corn had been shucked. We also had to cut tops out of the corn about where the ears grew. You cut these tops for the animals a few weeks before pulling the ears. The tops were tied in bundles and stored in the barn loft where they were mixed with hay and fed to the milk cows all winter. Combines changed the corn harvesting but not until I had left home for good for school in 1939. I missed that revolution.

There was no one in our family who could carry a tune in a water bucket but every time there was a singing school at our church, we all went and tried. I did take piano music for seven or eight years, but that was a time when you didn't want anybody to know about it if you were a boy. Music lessons were for girls. Mama wanted me to take the lessons and I did learn to play a few hymns. But my heart wasn't in it. When she was hospitalized for more than a month in 1932, I didn't sit down at a piano a single hour. And I never have since. I'm a firm believer that music and art are traits born in people and without it, you waste your time taking lessons.

Dad broke his arm several times cranking old Fordson

tractors by hand when he was mechanicing. Once someone asked him how he managed to break his arm that was then in a cast.

"I was cranking this tractor when it backfired, the crank stuck in my hind end, threw me over the engine and I broke my arm when I landed on a rock," Dad said and he never told the questioner any different. He never liked to repeat anything he said, not even when the listener asked "what" time after time. When he did answer a what, it was usually with a different answer from the first.

Dad and Mom, second and third from right. Dad's father Thomas is standing next to him.

Mitchell, Dad, Me, Mom and Betty in front

Conversations Around The Winter Fire

With little else to do, families sat around the fire on winter nights and talked. The conversation often turned to ghosts and ghouls, a subject that seemed to intrigue listeners. I suppose that's because there was always some tinge of the unknown, the unexplainable.

A few miles from us, a Russell family lived a good distance from town. Many years ago they had a son killed in a fall from a horse and the family still grieved over the loss of the loved one. But according to the winter stories around the fire, he wasn't really gone, you just couldn't ever see him.

"Every full moon night around 11:00, you can hear a horse plodding up the road and stopping in front of the Russell house. Someone ties the reins to the bannister, you hear footsteps on the porch and the clatter of stirrups when the saddle is hung on the wooden peg in the hall. Footsteps are heard from the hallway to the dead son's bedroom and all is quiet again. The next morning his bed is unused. There's no saddle on the peg. There are some horse footprints in the dirt on the road. But the ghost has gone again," Dad used to tell the story. We were all ears. Old and young are caught up in mystery that defies solution. To know these noises came from the winter wind that fought through the cracks of the old frame house would not have been worth recounting to kids grasping for a bedtime story.

- - - - -

Mama fussed with Dad for not wanting to go to funerals. She would tell him no one was going to his.

"I don't want the people whose funerals I go to coming to mine," he said.

That would have been a bit strange.

Dad's Favorite Brother

Growing up on the small rocky farm at Palestine where the land was so poor that "it wouldn't grow anything but turnips," Dad had a slightly younger brother who suffered from epilepsy, called "fits" by almost everyone then, and there was little or no medicine or treatment for the affliction.

"He was a young man who liked to work. There wasn't a lazy bone in him and he was always doing something even though his ailment made life pretty miserable for him. We kind of grew up together and we were real close all of our boyhood lives," Dad recalled.

"One summer he picked up a gallon bucket and went off into the woods to pick blackberries (also called brier berries) along the shoreline of a small branch that ran through the farm. He didn't come in for lunch but we thought perhaps he was having trouble filling his pail and he would be back soon. But supper time came and he was still missing. We trotted off through the woods in the direction he had left looking for him. We found him lying in a brier patch, his bucket half full of berries. He had suffered a long time with one of his seizures and then choked on his own tongue. It was one of the saddest days of my life," Dad recounted with chagrin that day in his life before he left the family home.

There was a house full of both brothers and sisters growing up at the same time but Spurgeon was his favorite and it hurt to lose him.

"Spurgeon could pick more blackberries than anyone in the community and he liked to work. But that sad day he didn't return from the brier patch. We found him dead," Dad remembered his favorite brother who was born in 1895 and died in 1912 at the age of seventeen.

The Day That Betty Was Born

I was only five and didn't know anything about how babies were made or born. I did know that June 10, 1926 was different from other days. Dad had come home from work in the middle of the morning. Mama was not comfortable and had gone to bed. We had an old lady in the house who was cleaning and cooking, and I had never seen so many pumpkin pies. She had a whole pie chest full and we didn't eat pumpkin pie very often. Then, to make the day even more unusual, Mama told me that I should go over to the Blalocks and play a while with Jennings. Heretofore, I had to ask for permission to go play with him, and she would sometimes give me an hour or an hour and a half to play and be back home on time. This time, she didn't tell me when to come home. She just said Dad would come after me when it was time for me to come home and she grimaced as if she were in pain.

I ran across the meadow to the Blalock's house on the other hill, and I remember that Jennings and I played in the old dirt road that connected their farm with the highway, several hundred yards away. I believe we were rolling old car tires and racing up and down the incline. I did notice that two cars drove up to our house in the early afternoon and at 3:00 they were still there. I wondered what was happening at our house. My brother Mitchell was about three years old and he was still at home with the temporary housekeeper and Dad.

It was almost dark and we had gone into the Blalock home where Jenning's older sister Thelma Lee was helping her mother around the supper table. Mrs. Blalock had been at our house and had come home. I sat down to eat with the neighbors at about the time there was a knock on the door. Dad had walked across the meadow and was there to take me home.

35

"You ready to go home, son?" he asked in a kind of tired tone.

"Yeah, yeah, I'm ready," I said.

He took me by the hand, thanked the Blalocks for looking after me and said "It's a girl. They are doing fine. It was born right after you left."

I still didn't know what was going on. But back in Mama's bedroom, I knew. Lying there beside Mom was a black haired little baby. It was my sister Betty.

I believe that Mama had the assistance of a Dr. Hall from Albemarle in giving birth to Betty but the ordeal may have been the work of the midwife old lady who was visiting. I know Mama and Betty got along well with the childbirth and Mama was on her feet and working around the house a couple of days later.

Mitchell and I had been born at home too. But that was in the tiny Efird Mill frame house in West Albemarle where we lived until I was three. Dr. Hall had delivered us. Few people in that era went to hospitals for birthing children. It was a do-it-yourself occasion right in the bedroom.

I know we were mighty happy to have a baby sister in our house for the very first time. And Dad was proud of his little daughter and Mama.

The saddest day in our young lives was April 29, 1932. Mama was near death in the hospital. We had been farmed out to neighbors for days. A baby sister was born but died after a few breaths. We never saw her alive. Glenn Efird, a neighbor, built a tiny pine box casket for the deceased infant and April 30, 1932, the following day, she was buried in the cemetery at Canton Baptist Church. There were no dry eyes in our family.

Dad often talked about growing old but then spiced it with a bit of philosophy: "If you didn't know when your birthday was, you wouldn't know how old you were. Then you would only be as old as you felt," he said.

Mitchell and I pose in front of the house with the wooden fan rack that often was covered with roses

I sure stretched my fingers for this picture

The Classic Shiner

The Grange was an active farmer organization in the Endy Community when I was growing up and the group got together at the school house every month for its business meeting that was generally followed by a covered dish feast. Children of the Grange members had a youth organization auxiliary that met upstairs in a classroom above the auditorium. It had its own opening business and closing ritual to go through, but it didn't take the youngsters as long to go through the functions as it did the adults. Once the routine was over, the kids were their usual loud and rowdy personalities.

Endy school had been built years ago. The floors were tongue and grooved pine boards. To make this floor last longer and keep down dust it was saturated with oil once or twice each year. Right after it was first oiled, the long hallways made the best skating rink that Endy children ever saw. When a Grange meeting was over and the freshly oiled floors were inviting, we frolicked up and down the halls seeing how far we could skid along. If you had rubber soled shoes, you could slide the entire length of the 150 foot halls.

We were having a ball sliding on the oily floors one night after the official meeting ended. Normally there was a single naked light bulb hanging from the ceiling in the middle of the hallway that gave us some light. It was before the time of public electricity and the power that lit the bulbs came from a Delco gasoline generator in a tiny room downstairs that stored electricity in a whole wall full of big batteries. Unfortunately, some one had failed to crank the generator and the only light we had at the meeting was an old kerosene lantern. The adults downstairs likewise had to use lamps and lanterns for their shindig.

With the children's meeting over and the skating taking place in the unlit hallway, the lantern in the classroom where the meeting took place barely gave enough light to see where you were sliding. Alas! Someone went into one of the other classrooms and came out, leaving the big heavy door ajar. It was half open into the hall. I had already slid the length of the hall several times and was again skidding along merrily in the dark. I met the half opened door at full speed, my feet straddling it. I bounced back about five feet as the door was much stronger than I was. My nose, forehead and right eye had taken the brunt of the blow. I got up crying and bleeding. It broke up the adult meeting downstairs and I went home to get cleaned up and a bandage put on my forehead. My eye was puffing up and hurting but we certainly had no beef steak to put over the eye and perhaps stop it from turning black.

The next day the eye was black and blue both above and underneath. I had to go to school anyway. The shiner was the talk of the class.

"Who hit you in the eye?" was the beginning question.

"I skated into a door," I said.

"Yeah, yeah, that's what they all say," my cronies taunted.

"How does the other guy look?" was another frequently asked question.

"There was no other guy. I ran into a door," I kept pleading.

Such was much of the talk for about a week until the shiner slowly disappeared. It was the only real shiner I ever had and I had to get it by accident in the classic manner often depicted in the comics---running headlong into a door.

There were some other accidents at the school that still are vivid recollections. I recall a day when one of the heavy, six-pane wood windows fell on the fingers of a high school girl. It pinned her fingers tightly to the frame, so tight I couldn't get the window up off her fingers as she screamed in pain. Some help rushed in and the window was pushed up enough to get her fingers free. Three of them were bloody messes as the window crunched skin and bone. That accident took a bit of medical attention and the young lady had a sore hand for weeks.

On another occasion, one of the high school boys was bounding down the stairway toward the half glass doors at the bottom. Instead of opening the door by pushing on the wood frame around the glass, he slammed his hand against the pane while running at full speed. The glass gave way and he stuck his hand and arm through the broken window. It cut long gashes from the palm of his hand to his shoulder and bled like a stuck hog. He went into Randall Burleson's first aid room and got the blood stopped. Randall washed it out with alcohol and bandaged up the wounds. He didn't go to a doctor but he had a bad arm for weeks.

Now torn down, this was the Endy School house just a stone's throw from our house

School Attendance A Must

While neither Dad nor Mama had much education, barely enough to read and write, they were firm believers that life is better for those who do have good training. We lived in the Endy School yard, our land joining the school's with the old red brick building no more than 500 yards away. That close proximity made it possible for us to attend school, at least for a few hours, even when we weren't feeling very well. And if we could walk and talk, Dad and Mama made sure we didn't miss any school days.

In that era, the Endy School had a first, high first, and on through the eleventh grade. State law demanded that students attend school eight months a year, not six months as the Endy facility did after I reached grade four or five. We would go to school six months one year, then two months the next, and all would be promoted. Then you would get four months in the new grade the balance of that year and four the following year to advance to a higher grade. It was a kind of mess but that's the way it was in the six months school until I got near high school.

We kept school teachers at our house in those early years. They roomed and boarded there, and as I recall, they paid $20.00 a month for room and board. While it might not have been a great economic boost, it was a real blessing to me. The teachers made sure I learned my lessons in those early grades and were determined that I get perfect attendance records. That's where I excelled. During the almost 13 years that I attended Endy, I started at age five, I missed only four days of school. All those were in the so-called high first, my second year in school. Everyone had to go to both first and high first. There was no kindergarten. I went to class on Monday and got sick about noon. The teacher sent me home with a high fever, but gave me credit for attendance. I missed the rest of the week with a severe case of measles. But I never missed another day. I was proud of the record but chagrined a bit because my closest friend, Keith Almond, went from the first through the eleventh and never missed a single day. We had great competitive spirit, and I so wished he would get sick and miss at least four days. But he never did. What a shame!

Competition in academics, attendance or any other facet of school life, or any life, I believe, is great for the individuals. I know I worked harder to achieve good grades and perfect attendance because of my constant desire to get ahead of my best friend. Winning those report card battles meant more to me than what Dad and Mama and the boarding teachers thought about the grades, but it was good to know that they appreciated an all "A" monthly report too. Once when I got a "C" in Randall Burleson's sixth grade in math, a subject I still do not know, it was a disaster. It was the first one I ever had on my report card. But it probably made me work harder than ever.

Aunt Myrtie's Husband Mack

Dad's youngest sister was Myrtie and she was still at the Palestine home after Dad returned from his years in Texas, Ohio and Pennsylvania. She was the baby of the family and I think Dad had a little niche of love for her, at least for awhile. But he lost that when Myrtie met a motorcycle-riding, black leather jacket-wearing man named "Mack" whom she married after a brief courtship. He was just the type that this free spirited lady from Palestine wanted, but instead of having money, as she first prophesied, he was flat broke. Knowing that Dad worked hard all the time, Myrtie came to him one day and asked him to sign a promissory note for $300.00. I'm surprised that he did it. Signing a note in more than half the cases results in the signer having to fork over the money. It's more like a gift than a loan.

Dad put our house up as security for the note and Mack and Myrtie got the money. They immediately left town and when the note was due, they were nowhere to be found. The bank called Dad and he had to either pay it or lose the house. He didn't have that much money and rarely ever did. But he financed the $300.00 by the month and eventually got the lien off the house.

From that moment on, he was no friend of his baby sister, who never even thanked him, and his attitude was about par for the course. He didn't like to talk about the signing and subsequent call on the note. But he disliked Mack so much that occasionally the subject popped up.

"Mack was so ugly that you had to tie a bone around his neck so the dogs would like him," he often said. He was a robust physical specimen, but he wasn't that healthy between the ears except he did know how to marry a pretty woman and get her to borrow some needed bucks for their livelihood.

Years later, after I had gone off to school at UNC Chapel Hill, I got a beautiful silk bathrobe, called a house coat today, in the mail. Aunt Myrtie had sent it. I don't know how she got the money but at that time she was a kind of nanny to a wealthy family's children in North Miami, Florida. She handled that job for years and somehow sent me the beautiful robe, the most expensive one I ever owned.

A few years after that, I wrote her while I was in the Navy and stationed at Fort Pierce, Florida. She urged me to visit her in Miami, a short train ride to the south. I got a ticket and met her and my cousin Lucile Stoker, my Aunt Attie's daughter, at a restaurant in the big city. Lucile was living with Myrtie in a tiny frame house a few blocks from her work. I was not a drinker, but we went to a bar and ordered drinks. I sipped something that she ordered for me and we talked for an hour or more. She still remembered that she owed Dad that $300.00 and she was going to pay him when she got the money. She never did, and when I left her and Lucile that evening after a rather brief visit, I never saw her or Lucile again. She died in Miami.

I did take time to thank her for the nice bathrobe; I suppose it was the only remittance the family ever got for the much-needed $300.00 Dad lost by investing in her and my Uncle Mack. Mack died a few years after the marriage and I never saw him after he and Aunt Myrtie roared off down the dirt road at Palestine for the bright blue yonder with the $300 bucks. That was some pair! If there is a lesson in that experience, it is don't ever loan money to a relative. That's the best way I can imagine to lose it and make a permanent enemy.

Once we were in Charlotte for some reason and Dad was driving down a narrow street when a motorcycle patrolman pulled alongside and motioned him to stop. He angled over near the curb and rolled down the window.

"Mister, you are on a one way street," the gentle but firm cop said.

"I know. I'm only going one way," Dad said seriously.

I think the cop must have thought he had stopped a nut. He didn't give Dad a ticket but advised that he turn right at the next corner and get on another street. Dad did.

The Sunday Morning Cow Caper

Sunday morning was a hurry-scurry time at our house. It was the day we were all together for breakfast, Dad often cooking the meal that was something special. But then there was little time after eating to get ready to go to church. Sunday school began at 10:00 and it took about fifteen minutes to drive the couple of miles over the often slick, hilly dirt road in the winter that was a dusty pig path in the summer.

Always impatient to get started, Dad often was fully dressed and ready to go half an hour before the rest of us. He would put on his three piece suit, the only one he had, walk outside and pace around the car smoking his cigarettes while he waited for Mama to get three kids dressed, then dress herself for the Sunday church meeting, a highlight of our week as long as I can remember. Considering she had to wash the breakfast dishes, shine our often dirty shoes a little, scrub behind our ears, comb our hair and then put on our best clothes and hers, it's little wonder Mama had difficulty getting ready to go by 9:45 or thereabouts.

One fall morning after Dad had already strolled out to the car for his impatient wait, Mama looked out the bedroom window and saw one of our half-grown heifers break through the wire of the nearby pasture fence.

"Raleigh, that biggest heifer is loose. You better get her back in the pasture or she will do a lot of damage to the corn before we get back," Mama hollered.

Now Dad liked to have as little to do with the cows as possible. He definitely was not a cowboy. He said he had never learned how to milk and that daily chore always fell upon Mama and the children. And we learned to milk without much difficulty at the early age of five or six. It was always a mystery with us. Why couldn't Daddy have learned to milk? It would have been a help in an emergency. But he vowed he

45

didn't know how. Anyhow, after Mama's revelation that the young cow was out and had to be put back in the fence, Dad stomped out his cigarette butt in the gravels and muttered under his breath.

"All right, all right, I'll get her back in the pasture," and he proceeded to open the gate and with a lot of hand motions and a few trotting steps herded the frolicking cow toward the barnyard gate. A few feet from the opening, the cow decided the grass was greener outside than inside and dashed off through the garden and across the back yard with Dad in hot pursuit. He caught up with the now frightened animal when she found herself in a corner between the pig pen and the chicken house. Dad grabbed the cow's tail and proceeded to drag her toward the distant gate. But the cow was really scared now, bellowing and her big eyes rolling. She had different ideas about where she was going.

With Dad hurling some of the best oaths he knew, and he wasn't a man blessed with a lot of fancy cuss words, the cow broke into a full gallop down the hillside toward the meadow in the dell that separated our place from the Blalock farm a few hundred yards away on the top of another hill. Dad was hanging on to the cow's tail with a death-grip, and he wouldn't have turned loose even if that cow had dragged him into an active volcano. He had grit, determination or guts, whichever you prefer, and he would never say "enough" in any fight. That was giving up, and he wasn't about to admit this half-breed, half grown cow could get the best of him. Perhaps admitting defeat that morning would have been the better part of valor but it was not in Dad's vocabulary. He would hang on to that cow's tail until he had her securely fenced in or she nailed him. She would go back to that barnyard gate even if he had to pull her all the way.

The cow must have had some of the Carter determination. She would not go back through the gate, she would just drag her bedeviler until he hollered "chicken" or else let go of her fly-flicking tail that he was stretching.

With Dad still on his feet but making steps far greater than his legs would stand, the cow bounced down the hillside and made a ninety degree turn at the edge of the meadow where a four strand barbed wire fence was the demarkation of the property lines. Dad didn't make the turn, at least his posterior didn't. He was thrown into the fence and then back out as he hung on tenaciously to the tail. Every five or six yards, the racing cow would swerve enough to throw Dad back into the fence and then out again. He held on despite the torture of being fast massaged with sharp barbs on the pasture fence. When the fence turned at the old county road bed, the cow changed course and headed back toward the barn. By then Dad was being dragged more than he was running but the cow went straight to the gate and calmly walked through it. Her escapade was over. Dad turned loose of the tail, looked around embarrassed and fastened the fence gate after turning an evil eye toward his tormentor that had the same idea about him.

"I didn't have a damn thing on but my socks and my necktie. The rest of my suit, vest and pants hung on the fence along the meadow," Dad said.

Mama was about ready to go to church by that time but the phone rang as Dad walked through the door with his necktie and socks on.

"Waulena, why are you hanging out the wash on Sunday?" Mrs. Blalock's familiar voice asked.

Mama just stammered a bit. In that era church going people didn't do any work on Sunday that could be postponed until Monday. It was a day of rest. Certainly washing was not on the approved list. Mama just looked at the bleeding, bruised man in the tie and socks. She had an idea what Mrs. Blalock was talking about but that was no time to be cracking jokes, no time for explanations.

"I'll call you later. I've got an emergency right now," Mama said and she hung up. Mrs. Blalock never did hear the truth about the Sunday clothes-washing experience and it was one of the few Sundays that we didn't make it to church at all. Dad just wasn't in the mood.

That heifer was the first one that went to market that fall.

When a neighbor's son got married to a lifelong sweetheart, Dad had his classic humor. "I wish he had found a prettier wife instead of one that is so smart."

A Carter Reunion with "Dinner on the Ground"

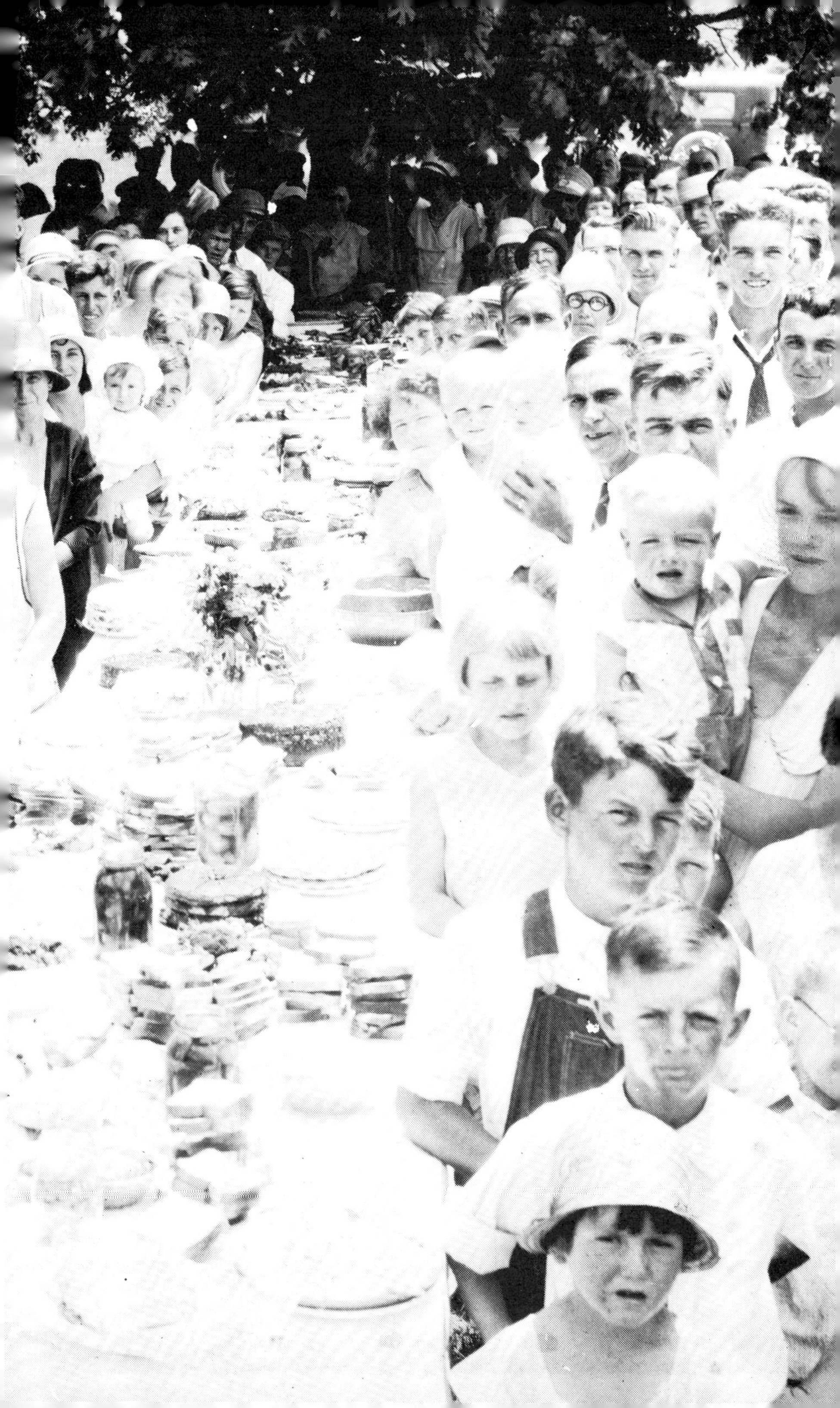

At age 21, Dad posed for this portrait in Texas.

Dad with his Grandfather Mason at Texas State Fair

Church -- Things I Remember

One Sunday morning when we drove the two miles to Canton Baptist Church, an every week highlight of our family, all four tires on the car were going flat when we stopped. Dad looked around and every one of them had from three to five big-headed roofing tacks in them. It was obvious the road was sabotaged. He got someone to drive back down the road while he hung on the fender looking. Sure enough, some prankster had carefully set a row of tacks all across the country dirt road and Dad's tires had picked up their share. As other cars parked at the church, more flats were observed. Some scoundrel had caused a lot of trouble on that Sunday morning.

Folks at Canton by habit usually sat in the same pews every Sunday during the hour long preaching service, more commonly called the "worship service" that followed Sunday School. Dad's spot on the fourth seat from the front was shared by a number of other men from the adult class. Dad regularly went to sleep about midway through the sermon and the man occupying the adjacent seat was a regular there. The pew mate died and Dad seemed pleased.

"I hate he passed away but he always woke me up during the sermon. Now I'll get a pretty good snooze. If I ever have insomnia, I'm going to church. The sleeping there is easier and better than any place I have ever been," Dad said, and he was serious. He told Mama he slept well in church because he had a clear conscience.

One Sunday the preacher was long-winded and was still raving at 12:30. "Where will you be in eternity?" he yelled. As Dad left the church and shook the preacher's hand he said, "In answer to your question about where I would be at eternity, for awhile I thought I would be sitting right there in my pew."

I never knew Dad to be excited about any sermon he ever heard at Canton, except one. We had an interim pastor named Bowers from the First Baptist Church in Albemarle, a much more sophisiticated church than Canton, preach a few Sundays while a pulpit committee was searching for a new pastor. The pompous Reverend Bowers preached a sermon on the subject of how the rain fell on the just and the unjust. There was no earthly reward for being a good Christian. The reward came after death when you went to heaven rather than burn for an eternity in a brimstone place called hell where the fire was seven times hotter than our fire. Preachers agree that hell will be much more heavily populated than heaven.

That didn't set well with Dad.

"I don't want my children to hear any such message. I want them to know this is a better world because of the Christians in it and they will have more satisfaction, happiness and reason for living by being good Christians now," Dad told everyone who would listen.

He might not have always been right but in that instance, I agree. Christians can enjoy life better than most non-Christians. Happiness is the measure of success in the world and a mind that is filled with peace has more room for happiness than one cluttered with sin, lies, thievery, dishonesty, envy and violence.

Each August at Canton, when most of the farm populace was finished with harvesting cotton, corn and other crops, the annual revival was held. It featured dinner on the ground on opening Sunday with both morning and afternoon preaching. Some wag paraphrased the event by calling it all day dinner with preaching on the ground. Anyhow, there was always an abundance of fine country food and every housewife was disappointed if she had to carry home part of her basket of food while other cooks had only empty plates. It made her feel like her preparation was not as tasty as a neighbor's.

Following the Sunday festivities, services for a long time then were held at 10:00 each weekday morning through Friday and an evening session was also scheduled. That meant an even dozen evangelized messages in a six day period. All the services were designed to bring a message to all non-church members that repentance was required and now. The second coming of Christ was near and the sheep would be divided from the goats. It was always this message of hell fire with emphasis upon the need for urgency. I have never believed the preachers or anyone else know whether the second coming of Christ is next week or a million years from now. But it was at one of those midweek revival evenings that I got the feeling I better join the church before it was too late. I went to the altar and accepted Christ. I was twelve at the time. I have never been sorry, whether there is any imminent danger of losing an opportunity to profess Christianity or not. There's no time like the present to do good things. Procrastinators seldom find the right time for their conversion.

Quick Decisions, The Devil's Work

Half century ago there were many more door to door peddlers in the rural communities than there are today. Cars were not owned by everyone and people didn't get to town nearly as often. Peddlers went to the customers instead of the customers going to the merchandise. It was a sign of the times.

Among the most frequent door to door salesmen were pot and pan, lightning rod, patent medicine, herbs and flavoring, gas lamps, steam irons and Bible marketers. As has always been the case, some of the peddlers were uncomfortably persistent and emphasized the once in a life time opportunity that would probably never be offered again. Tomorrow the price would probably go up or the product would not be available at any price, but a check in hand today would guarantee the purchase at great saving.

It reminds you of the sermons we often heard in church then and today about the urgency for repentance now for tomorrow may be too late. The second coming of Christ is near at hand and you cannot wait. It could be true but it hasn't been so far.

It is also remindful of some of the telephone calls and letters in the mail that are received today, urging the recipient to call specified numbers immediately if you want to win valuable prizes or even a free trip to the Bahamas or some other romantic place. To delay making the call is to throw away the chance of a lifetime, the message emphasizes.

Dad was always leery of these hurry up and make a decision peddlers.

"The devil is involved when you have to decide upon something right now. There is deceit or dishonesty when you are pushed to buy something or do something this very instant. God gives you time to make the right decision. He gives you time to think. The devil doesn't want you to think and those cronies of his who push for a yes right now are just carrying out the plan of satan," Dad philosophized.

He wasn't far from the truth. His thinking was pretty accurate. It has made me skeptical of the high pressure salesmen all my life.

Hitchhiker Hailed Dad

Once when Dad was on the way into Albemarle to his job, he passed a man at an intersection who threw up his hand and yelled: "Raleigh! Raleigh!"

Dad hit the brakes and stopped when he heard the man hollering. The man on the roadside raced toward the stopped vehicle and when he got to the door he said, "Going to Raleigh?"

"Oh, hell no! That's my name. I thought you had a message for me," Dad said and he drove off leaving the hitchhiker confused. He was trying to get to the State Capital.

Dad was named for the explorer Sir Walter Raleigh. It was a unique name in his time as it would be today. No one called him Walter. He was Raleigh Carter to all who knew him. I got his first name. I don't like it much either and that's why I have always signed my name W. Horace Carter.

Roasted Sparrow Birds
On A Winter Morning

Our frame house at Endy where I lived from the time I was three years old until I went off to Chapel Hill and college in 1939, was heated with open fire places. We had one in four different rooms but seldom had a fire in more than two at a time. Eventually, we had wood burning stoves fitted into two of the fire places, but most of the time we just started a fire with wood on the "dogs" and managed to stay pretty warm even when we had snow on the ground.

Snow brought some memorable events. With a fire blazing in a combination bedroom-den, we looked for action and Dad taught us how to set deadfalls for birds, little birds not quail. And while it might not be popular today and I would hesitate to do it, we caught many bluejays, sparrows, cardinals and chickadees, among other yard birds, that made some tasty meals for us.

We would put a window screen in the snow and a prop under one end with a string attached that we passed through a window. Then we sprinkled bread crumbs or corn under the screen and watched the trap from a chair in front of the fire. When several birds got under the trap, we yanked the prop out, pinning the birds to the ground. We rushed out excited, caught the trapped birds and picked the feathers off them. Washed and cleaned, we hung these little creatures in front of the fire on a wire and watched them turn and sizzle for half an hour or more. The grease dropped out of the cooking meat and fed the fire. Now there weren't many bites on a little snow bird but every morsel was tasty. We looked forward to the snows each winter and a chance to catch another mess of birds for roasting over the open fire in the house. I never realized that this bird roasting was widespread but years later I saw hawkers peddling cooked finches on a stick in Rome, Italy.

At times, we went out in the snow and tracked cottontail rabbits. They couldn't move around very well in soft snow and it was easy to track one to its hiding place. With one of our dogs, we often caught them without firing a shot, killed them with a rap of our hand across the back of the neck, then skinned, dressed and washed the rabbits before roasting them on the coals. It's a mighty fine meal when properly dressed and cooked either over that open fire, in an oven or fried in a skillet.

Dad wasn't much on rabbit hunting. Cottontails are kind of hard to see setting, particularly in the woods when there is no snow. But some people have the special knack of catching the flash of a rabbit's eye. When you see one like that, it is a shock, almost like some one flashed a beam of the sun into a mirror and then into your face. It stops you in your tracks, and if you have not walked too close to the rabbit, he will stay there in his hiding place and give you time to shoot him with a rifle or even a slingshot if you have the ability to handle one of those homemade weapons. But most hunters could not see rabbits in the nest because they are so well camouflaged and hidden. You generally walked over them, they jumped up and you either tried to shoot them before they got out of shotgun range or you put some beagle hounds on the track. Strangely, a rabbit tracked by a dog will circle and almost always return to within a few yards of where he was jumped. Good rabbit hunters with trained dogs wait patiently for a few minutes while the barking trailing hounds bring the cottontail back. You almost always get a good shot because the rabbit returns hopping along slowly, not running all out like he does when you frighten him from his setting place.

Dad was amazed that some people had the ability to see these bunnies setting in dense cover. He tried to learn that trick but he never did.

But we had an uncle who could see them, Uncle Chester Lowder who lived with us for a number of years.

I remember one winter day when we were rabbit hunting and going down some cotton rows. Uncle Chester suddenly reached down without breaking his stride and came up with a kicking rabbit in his hand. He had seen the setting rabbit and rather than stop and make it run, he just kept right on walking as if he didn't see the animal, then suddenly leaned over and caught it by the hind legs. That's one way of getting some meat without having to look for the lead shot from a gunshell.

We had rabbit "gums" set over many acres of woodlands where we lived and caught cottontails just about every cold morning of winter. Rabbits went into these traps, called "gums" because they were originally made from hollow three foot pieces of blackgum trees. You simply nailed on a board for a back, then rigged a trigger and a front door that would fall when the rabbit went inside and snuggled back to the back of the trap to keep warm. He pushed the trigger out of a slot and the door fell. Later we made these out of one inch thick, six inch wide pine boards and they worked fairly well after the lumber had turned dark. Sometimes we coated new lumber with mud to disguise it. Rabbits were not inclined to go into them when the lumber was bright and new. Rabbits went into these traps to keep warm, not to feed as some people have wrongly guessed. We never put food in our traps. We depended upon mother nature's frosty mornings to put the cottontails in our gums. We set the gums along rabbit paths that were easy to see around briar patches, thickets or small grain fields where the bunnies fed at night. They moved along the same path so frequently that they were a slick route in the pine needle covered ground. They always set in their nests in the daytime and then moved around at night to get food and water. The only exception to that habit was in summer when baby rabbits can be seen early and late in the daytime feeding near cover. They hadn't learned about hunters and predators yet. But we trapped only in winter and rabbits do not feed in the daylight then.

One winter day when Mitchell and I were having no luck finding rabbits and were impatient to have some action, so we could shoot our shotguns, we came across a rabbit gum that some one had set and hadn't checked that morning. It had a fine rabbit backed up in the trap. That gave us an idea for making the day a little more exciting. I reached in and got the rabbit by the hind legs and pulled the kicking critter out. I could have killed the cottontail with one easy lick across the back of its head with the edge if my hand. But that was too easy. We decided to take the rabbit to the middle of a nearby field and turn it loose. The plan was to shoot it when it got a reasonable distance from us. It was a huge field of twenty acres or more. We went to the middle and I dropped the rabbit to the ground. In our hurry to out shoot each other, both of us fired twice at the running bunny with our double barrel shotguns. We didn't cut a hair off that rabbit and it trotted on into the woods to thrill some other hunters on another day. But not because of our conservation attitude. The critter just outfoxed us and escaped. That makes you feel kind of stupid, as it did us that morning.

People are not the only rabbit hunters. Hawks and snakes catch many of the cottontails but a single pair may produce as many as two dozen or more baby rabbits in a single season and where the habitat is plentiful and poisons not scattered indiscriminately, cottontails will thrive.

We had an old house cat named "Snowball" that was a fine rabbit hunter. She stalked even grown rabbits, then pounced on them, choked them to death and dragged them a half mile to the house. You could tell when she had a rabbit, and was struggling under the load she dragged because of the special mournful meow that she had. It was a lonely noise. You could hear her a hundred yards before she came out of the weeds and broom straw. She would bring the rabbit to the yard, and often just drop it, look around and her eyes seemed to say, "Look what I got for you. If you can't find any rabbits to shoot, you ought to take me with you on the next hunt."

It would have been a joke in our day to carry a cat hunting, but at Evinston, Florida, there is an astute squirrel hunter who always takes his cat with him. He says a dog makes a lot of noise and runs the squirrels into holes in the trees. But his cat quietly moves along in front of him, simply makes the squirrel hop up a few feet on a tree trunk and bark at the cat. The hunter then has an opportunity to shoot the squirrel before it realizes the cat is a decoy and the real danger is the two legged predator who follows.

We raised tame rabbits at our house for several years. We had one old doe that was colored exactly like a wild cottontail. But she was larger than the wild species. She was prolific and I remember her giving birth to thirteen little rabbits one day. As soon as they were big enough to move around, they would squeeze out of the wire pen and eat grass in the yard.

"Those baby rabbits kept all the cats fat. Snowball thought these critters were like manna from heaven and the other cats learned to watch for the infant cottontails too. They were great cat food," Dad said.

Dad posed for this trick picture in Ohio after leaving Texas.

Dad's Views On Sports

He never had much opportunity to participate in athletics and wasn't real sure of the rules even when we were playing baseball and basketball at Endy but Dad had an interest in all sports. He never could understand football. "The officials call holding on the players several times during a game. That's a crazy call. They hold all the time from the beginning to the end. That's what the game is all about, catching and holding somebody," Dad opined. It just wasn't clear to him that you could only hold the ball carrier.

He liked boxing, and it was the era when Joe Louis was winning and holding the heavyweight championship for years. Many fans of that era still consider Louis the greatest boxer of all times. It was before the day of television, but we listened to every fight on the radio, our first radio being an antique bit of electronics that had three station selector dials. You had to adjust all three dials to the same frequency to pick up a station. Many people had crystal sets that you could hear only with earphones. WBT in Charlotte was our main attraction.

Dad was intrigued that the boxing champion could make $25,000 and more, chicken feed today, by fighting a match with a contender that lasted an hour or less while he had to mechanic a week to make $25.00.

"I'd sure fight any of them for that much money," Dad said, "But if one of them hit me beside the head, I'd knock the fire out of him." Obviously that's what the boxers were trying to do all the time.

We had an old wood gymnasium at Endy, finally, but basketball was played on a dirt court until I was about through grammar school. You just took a sharp stick and marked the boundary and foul lines. Then with the coming of the WPA, a make-work federal program to give people jobs, we finally got a gymnasium but not without great local effort. Farmers of the community donated the logs for the lumber and a sawmill cut them for nothing. Some farmers helped with the labor free of charge. The Endy Boy Scout troop begged money for the project. I can remember well going into Albemarle on Saturday and soliciting contributions store to store for our gym. We would get mostly nickels and dimes with a few dollar donations and by day's end, we would have collected as much as $20.00. Today schools get more money from taxes than goes to finance anything else, but in that era the community had to want the facilities and put something into it other than tax dollars. The people earned whatever buildings they got and it was not as political as it often is today.

After the gym was completed, Mitchell and I were janitors for several years, keeping the place swept and building fires in the big pot bellied stoves at each end of the building prior to games. I think we got about $8.00 a month for the work. Dad often attended the games and he didn't like for Endy to lose. He was a poor loser; a competitive spirit always burned in him.

"I don't see how anyone can keep from throwing a basketball through a hoop three times as big as the ball. Our team can't get it through an open door but it ought to be easy to shoot a goal," Dad said often.

One night when he walked down the sideline as the teams were warming up, the coach handed him the ball and said, "Mr. Carter, you are always talking about how easy it is to throw a basketball through the hoop, how about you trying it for us?"

Dad was 35 feet from the goal along the sideline. He took the ball and awkwardly heaved it in a big arc toward the rafters. It dropped through the net without hitting the rim. The coach couldn't believe it. His mouth dropped open in amazement.

"Mr. Carter, that was great. Here, let's see you do that again," he urged, trying to hand him the ball again.

"No, once is enough. Like I said, I don't see how your players can miss getting a ball through such a big hoop. I'm tired. Once is enough," Dad grinned and took his seat. He never again showed his expertise that I know about.

62

The Negroes of the county, and they were "Negroes" then and not blacks, with the few liberals referring to them as "colored" and the reactionary population calling them "niggers," played high school sports in a conference of their own. There was no integration in the public schools. There was no integration of blacks and whites in sand lot and semi-pro baseball either. The era of Jackie Robinson who broke the color line in the major leagues, was some years away. The Negroes of Kingville and Badin had baseball teams and they played each other throughout the summer. Unfortunately, they did not know the rules very well, and many whites attended their games just for the humor. Perhaps that was mean but it is the truth. Dad was one of those whites who got a big kick out of watching the Negroes play. It was like a circus sideshow.

One Saturday evening he came in laughing and anxious to tell about the game he had watched at the old Efird Ball Park that afternoon.

"One team had a big burly catcher who was pretty good but his pitcher was having trouble getting the ball over the plate. The umpire wasn't giving him anything and called many pitches balls that the catcher thought were strikes. When the cleanup batter came to bat, the pitcher let loose with his best fast ball and the umpire yelled 'Ball one.' The second pitch came in low and the ump again yelled 'Ball two.' The third pitch was in the same spot and the umpire raised his left hand with three fingers out and said 'Ball three.' The catcher's temper was rising. Then it boiled. He pulled his mask off, reached in his back pocket and placed a tiny black pistol on the ground under his mitt. The umpire looked with fear in his eyes when the catcher pointed to the gun so the ump would know it was there. Then the catcher turned to the ump and quietly said, 'It's time for you to start calling strikes.' The umpire obliged! The first pitch came in and the ump yelled 'Strike one.' The next one was 'strike two' and the third 'strike three' as the batter went down. The catcher pocketed his pistol and the game went on," Dad chuckled at the situation. "That ump didn't even look at where the last three pitches were.

"Later in the game, that old catcher hit a ground ball to the shortstop and he ran down the first base line as fast as he could put one foot in front of the other, but the ball got to the

63

first baseman five steps before the runner. The home plate umpire thumbed the runner out, but it didn't stop the runner. He rounded first and headed toward second, sliding in under the throw of the first baseman to the second sack. There the catcher beat the throw and the ump hollered 'Safe.' The runner kept his base and the teams ignored the play at first base," Dad recounted the strange call as he chuckled.

In that time frame, few teams had an umpire on the field as well as one behind the plate. One official called all the plays, as that ump did from home plate that day. And then and now, officiating was a thankless task, often performed free of charge but it didn't keep players and fans from abusive yells and even fights.

Dad and a friend spar a bit while he was living in the North. Boxing was a popular sport and Dad always said he would fight any of the great champions if they would pay him his share of the gate --- then a matter of $10,000 to $25,000.

The Bitch Was Really In Heat

Once when Dad was running the country store and garage, a pack of dogs kept hanging around the place and sniffing a little mongrel bitch that was obviously in heat and attracting plenty of company. He got tired of the pack running in and out of the open garage and caught the little female as she pranced around among her male suitors.

He reached on a shelf where he had a box of red pepper, lifted the little female dog's tail, and poured a spoonful of the hot pepper on her hind end. She yelped a couple of times and took off out of the garage with all the males in hot pursuit. They caught up with her and again started the tail sniffing that these canines always do when chasing a bitch in heat. One or two sniffs convinced them this was not the thing to do but by one they each sniffed in some of the pepper and even the males began poking their noses around the hind end of other males. The pepper curse was spreading and about that time a customer stopped at the store.

"Raleigh, did you see some dogs come by here chasing a female in heat?" the man asked.

"Yeah, I sure did," Dad said.

"Well they are up that dirt road yonder a half mile or so and I never saw such crazy dogs. They are sitting on their rear ends and sliding themselves along the ground and whining like they are trying to scratch their tail ends. I never saw such crazy dogs and they have lost all interest in sex," the man laughed.

Dad grinned. He said later when the little bitch had pups that all of them had sore eyes.

Things The Weather Did To Us

We didn't have a lot of snow at Endy in Piedmont North Carolina but occasionally a few inches would fall. Often it would be followed by rain and more cold, and this would put a slick coat of ice on top. Those were the times that we enjoyed the cold the most. It usually closed down the school for several days because the busses couldn't run. The dirt roads were muddy, slick and often impassable for days.

At first, we began riding down the slopes of the hills around the house on a wide piece of plank and that was fun but it was not fast enough. No one had a snow sled made for the purpose. We hit upon something novel. We borrowed Mama's big porcelain dishpans, the containers she used to wash dishes in. They were about a foot and half in diameter and big enough for youngsters our size to sit in. Given a little push from the top of a hill, the pans made great sleds as the rider went round and round at breakneck speed to the bottom. It's the one thing I remember the best about snow at Endy.

Hail was a threat to farm crops in the hot months of summer. But it could also damage other property and one August Sunday afternoon when we were farmed out to neighbors while Mama was hospitalized, a sudden thunderstorm dropped balls of ice as big as golf balls over the community. I remember we were playing baseball in a nearby pasture and we had to hustle to a neighbor's barn to keep from getting hurt from the dangerous missiles from heaven. It stopped after a few minutes but it piled up around the eaves of the house where we were staying a foot deep. We scooped it up and made ice cream. In that respect it was kind of like manna from heaven. But it had its vandalizing features. There was no one at home in our house. The hail poured down through the fireplace chimneys, rolled across the carpet and melted. When we got home the next week, the whole house had a smutty, dirty floor and it tooks days to clean it up. It was a real mess. All that glitters is not gold seemed to fit the occasion.

Summer rains are almost always needed when you are gardening or farming. Dad said almost every close neighbor got more rain than we did although he thought we were paying the preacher as much as anyone else. Some old wag had said that you wouldn't get much rain if you didn't pay the preacher. He didn't subscribe to the scripture of the rain falling on the just and the unjust.

On a clear summer day when showers were spotted and rain fell around the community, Dad would look across the hills to the Almond, Blalock or Efird farms and declare he was going to buy an acre or two of land over there where they got a lot of rain every time they needed it. He never did! I suppose we might have had just as much rain as the neighbors and I often wondered if maybe the Almonds, Efirds and Blalocks didn't see the rain on our garden and think like Dad did. Maybe they ought to get a little parcel of land from the Carters to plant a garden. The Carters seemed to get all the nice summer showers.

Many times it seemed the real bonanza spots were somewhere else. Is it really greener across the fence on the other man's place?

Descriptive Expressions

I doubt that the expressions were original. He probably heard them somewhere, but two of the phrases Dad used often when the occasion was appropriate I still remember. If a pretty woman walked past, he would likely describe her as "She's as pretty as a speckled pup under a red wagon."

If an incident made someone jubilant he might say, "He's as happy as a dog in a meat house."

Both expressions always seemed to describe the situation perfectly.

Dad was a cigarette smoker most of his life and never believed it was harmful to his or anyone's health.

Dad's Cigarette and Coca Cola Habit

All of his adult life, Dad smoked. Most of the time it was cigarettes but in later life, he switched to cigars. He also liked Coca Colas, the small bottles. He always said that the company put the same amount of syrup in the 16 ounce Cokes as they did the 8 ounce ones, the only size you could buy until a few decades ago. He got used to the small bottles and despised the larger size, but he may have succumbed to the economy and bought the larger ones when the price soared from five cents to ten cents. He didn't like to be cheated if he could get twice as much for the same money.

"I don't think the stuff in the bottles costs the bottler anything. If they can wash bottles, fill them up, cap 'em, deliver to stores all over the country and sell them for a nickel retail, the ingredients can't be any more expensive than water," Dad used to say, and he had a point.

He almost always smoked Camel cigarettes and when the Marlboro variety was introduced and the TV, newspapers, billboards, etc., were filled with promotional advertisements, Dad said he would never be able to smoke Marlboro cigarettes. He didn't have a horse. All the smokers in Marlboro country wore cowboy hats and rode a horse. He never did.

Mama was forever critical of Dad's smoking and drinking Cokes.

"If you don't quit all that smoking cigarettes and drinking Cokes it's going to kill you," she often pleaded.

"Ah, I'll keep right on smoking and I'll probably have to get run over by a car to kill me," Dad said.

He kept smoking and drinking and indeed did die when a car plowed into him. Prophetic? Maybe.

Mrs. Blalock Took Him Seriously

The Ceph Blalock family were our nearest neighbors and they lived on a hill across the meadow from us, about a quarter of a mile away. Mrs. Blalock was a strong willed, hard working woman and she kind of wore the pants in the Blalock home as it was plain to see when you lived near them.

Late one afternoon Dad walked down the hill, across the meadow and past the barn where Mrs. Blalock was milking a cow. It was near dusk on a summer evening. He had something he wanted to talk over with Ceph.

As he passed near the barn, he heard Mrs. Blalock hollering to Ceph, but she was getting no answer even though she yelled at the top of her voice several times. Dad just spoke to her as he went past and on toward the house.

"I'll tell him you are calling for him," Dad told Mrs. Blalock.

"Good, Raleigh," she replied. "Tell him I need him here at the barn right now to do the feeding."

Dad went on to the house and past the giant oak tree in the Blalock yard that still stands today and measures more than four feet in diameter. He found Ceph shelling some corn in what they called the "old house" and the noise from the machine undoubtedly was what kept him from hearing his wife's beckoning.

Anyhow, Dad and Ceph talked over whatever business they had and Dad left, going back past the barn where Mrs. Blalock was just finishing milking one of the several cows that they had.

"Raleigh, did you see Ceph?" she asked.

"Yeah, I saw him. He said he was getting tired of you always yelling at him and if you kept it up he was going to knock you down again," Dad said without cracking a smile.

"That louse said that?" she said, with a flush of anger. "I'll see if he wants to knock me down," Mrs. Blalock said as she set the milk pail down and headed toward the old house at a fast trot.

We never did hear what ensued when the two got together. But for sure, Ceph Blalock got a roasting, even though he probably never knew what had got his wife so riled up. For sure, he didn't knock her down.

Dad thought the Blalock episode was funny. Dad always said that wives loved husbands who beat them up better than those who were treated kindly and loved.

He had some strange conceptions of humor. Once he took two of our cats and pinned their tails together, then hung them on a clothes line in the yard. The cats each thought the other was hurting his tail and they fought like their lives were being endangered. Finally, the fight was so vicious that the clothes pin snapped off their tails and they both fell to the ground. The cats were almost insane with fright and pain and one dashed toward the house just as I opened the screen door. The cat made about two bounces through the kitchen and leaped right in the middle of the dining table where Mama was entertaining a few of the neighborhood ladies. They all screamed, the cat was again scared half to death and it dashed to the door, pushed it open and disappeared into the woods.

The whole episode was hilarious to Dad and he laughed for a week every time he thought about it. It never was funny to Mama and she let Dad know about it time after time.

The cats didn't think it was funny either.

Dad had another experience with an animal that he frightened that he often told about. He was working in the garage in Albemarle one winter day when he saw a mangy old dog hanging around inside the building, perhaps to get out of the cold or else because some of the mechanics were throwing the old half breed canine some scraps from their lunches. The dog had been there several days making itself at home. Dad thought maybe it was time to get the dog off the premises. He looked around and found a piece of an old rusty muffler and he wired the metal piece to the dog's tail. The dog at first didn't move around and didn't realize it was tied to something. Dad pushed the critter a time or two and it moved a few steps, the muffler rattling and following close behind. That set off the chain reaction. The dog thought he was being followed, and when he ran the muffler bounced against his rump and scared him some more. Frightened at his plight, the dog barked a couple of times and headed for the door. The more the muffler clattered behind him the faster the dog ran and the more it bounced against his rear end the dog barked faster and louder.

The scared animal made a turn down main street and was wide open, headed for West End. By then the sidewalks had people staring at the runaway dog and the police department cruiser was in hot pursuit. Some thought it was a rabid canine. The excitement didn't stop until the muffler came loose and skidded across the pavement on the Town Creek bridge. The dog disappeared in the vicinity of the old Efird Baseball park and hasn't been heard from since.

Later that day, the police car stopped in front of the garage and a big, burly officer came in the garage. Dad knew him.

"Raleigh, someone said that runaway dog came from around this section. Did you people see anything? Do you know anything about who tied that can thing to the dog's tail?" the officer inquired.

"I don't know who did it. I was here all morning. That dog came through the shop like he was shot out of a cannon and ran right on out the front door barking and heading for hell. He sure was scared. I hope you catch whoever put that thing on that old mutt. It was a dirty trick," Dad said and went back to tinkering with the old A-Model engine.

It was his kind of prank that he enjoyed for days.

It's hard to always know whether life is successful or not, especially someone else's life. But Dad seemed to have found happiness in his life, despite years of hard work and little financial prosperity. I wondered if an humble philosophy I have related in numerous public speeches over the years wasn't meant for him:

"We must live lives acceptable to God and pleasing to man. We must reach out for an untenable something called happiness that's always just beyond our grasp. But when mankind puts service above self, he comes closest to reaching that elusive satisfaction with his life."

Most people leave only children. Dad left a heritage of experiences for this and other generations that are spiced with humor and common sense. He will not be soon forgotten.

Checkers, Dad's Store And The Cigarette Theft

For a number of years Dad ran a country garage where he repaired cars, sold a little gasoline, and carried a few staple groceries and snacks. The first of these stores was set on big six foot long, oak pillars to get the floor to highway level. Under the garage grass grew in a pasture.

When Dad wasn't busy working on someone's rundown vehicle, he liked to play checkers with some of the loafers who hung out around the potbellied stove all during the winter months when there wasn't much farming going on. Mitchell and I often got into these games after school and on Saturdays and frankly we learned to play the game pretty well. Playing checkers was a passion of Dad's but he just never really could play the game with any degree of sharpness. He could not see ahead as you must to win. We beat him regularly and unmercifully, often irritating him enough to get him mad. Finally, we just played each other, Mitchell generally beating me fairly and squarely, and Dad played with some of the other hangers-on around the stove.

It took some regular fire chunking to keep wood in the old cast iron stove in the cold weather. The front door of the garage was always open, inviting customers to come in, and you had to keep wrapped up and turn your backside to the stove frequently to keep comfortable enough to survive.

Dad was usually pretty careful to close all the dampers and opening to the stove when he locked up and headed for home about dark each afternoon. But one day he failed. A few minutes after he went to the garage in the morning, he was back home and upset. During the night, a fire had started in the floor around the stove. Miraculously, it burned right through that floor and the stove dropped to the ground but the

Dad ran a country store and garage at Endy for several years blaze went out. He had a hole six feet in diameter in the floor and no stove, but the building had been spared. Somebody had been so intense with the checkers game that no precautions were taken at closing time to keep the fire inside the heater. They patched the hole, brought the stove back up to its original spot and the checkers games were delayed only a few hours.

One fall morning Dad went to the store and unlocked as usual. He was stunned a bit when he discovered that during the night some one had broken in, taken all the cigarettes out of the glass display case, and absconded with them. Now cigarettes then sold for only ten and fifteen cents a pack but even that made them the highest priced products he had for sale by bulk.

Dad looked at the empty case a few moments, then turned back to the door, locked up, got in his car and drove a short distance to a neighbor's house. The man of the house came to the door and Dad asked him if his boy was home.

"Yeah he's here," the neighbor said.

"I'd like to talk to him a minute," Dad said.

Moments later the teenager emerged kind of sheepishly from the house and approached the car where Dad was smoking and apparently unconcerned.

"Son, you broke in my store last night and stole my cigarettes. Go get 'em and bring 'em back to the store before noon or I'll notify the sheriff," he said as he cranked the old A-Model and drove away. Not another word was said.

Within the hour, the youngster came in with a sack full of cigarettes. Leaves and pine needles were mixed with them and he obviously had buried them in the woods under the fallen foliage. Dad never turned him in and as far as I know never told his family. But it remains a mystery as to just how he was so sure this neighbor's boy had been the culprit. Today, making such an accusation would have probably brought a denial and maybe even a court suit for character assassination. But it solved a theft then and, except for the inconvenience, nobody was the loser.

Later we guessed that the thief had left his cap at the scene. That's why Dad was so sure of himself. He recognized the cap.

It Took A Lot Of Pepsi To Fill Him Up

During the years that Dad ran the country store in the forks of No. 27 and the Canton Church road that was a half mile from where we lived, he handled mostly cold drinks, snacks, gasoline and a few canned staple groceries. In the back of the building, he worked on cars and trucks and what money was made usually came from that part of the business.

There was a slightly retarded youngster who lived nearby who spent a lot of time hanging out around the store, particularly in the winter when he couldn't be much help to the farmers in the area. One cold day some other youngsters from the community came by and saw him hanging around. We'll call him Jack, although that was not his name.

"Jack, how many Pepsi-Colas can you drink?" one loafer asked.

"I don't know. About a dozen big 'uns I guess," Jack said.

"I'll tell you what. I'll buy a dozen 12 ounce Pepsis if you'll drink 'em right here one right after the other."

"I'll do it," Jack said, and he pulled the first one out of the old ice box and started gulping it down. Over the next hour and a half he drank the dozen and he looked like his eyes would pop out. His belly bulged.

"I think I could eat some ice cream too," Jack volunteered.

"Go to it. I'll buy as much as you can eat," the same bystander who made the Pepsi proposition said.

Jack ate two pints of vanilla and three icy popsicles. He looked mighty peaked and said he believed he would go home. He made it home but passed out as he went up the backdoor steps. His parents rushed him to the hospital emergency room where they pumped his stomach out and the doctor said he was near death.

That episode kind of stopped the gluttony around the store.

Dad sold Gulf gasoline. The two old pumps had glass tanks at the top that held ten gallons. You could see how much gasoline you bought as it went down when you pulled the handle on the spout. You hand pumped the gas back in the tank after each sale.

Dad always complained about buying gasoline whenever the distributor came and found he was about out. He always swore that he bought a lot more than he sold and often didn't have money to refill the storage tanks. He would wait a few days until he had the money, then get 400 or 500 gallons and be back in the gas business.

Gasoline prices fluctuated then and now but Dad always felt that 20 cents a gallon was the proper price. That would get you five gallons for a dollar and he considered that fair. However, there were times when it dropped to 16 and 17 cents but rarely below that. That price made it harder for Dad to figure and there was no digital read out on the tanks. All the gas was regular.

I recall a time when the rural mail carrier there, Leslie Efird, stopped on his delivery route one day and said, "Raleigh, I'll fill up with gasoline every day except Sunday with you if you will knock off two cents on the gallon. I'll be a regular customer."

Dad came home that night telling about it. "What do you think about it? Should I give him a two cent discount on the gas he buys?" I didn't say anything. I wasn't a businessman then and while the volume would help Dad's business, it was up to him to decide whether he would sell at a discount price. I didn't know what he should do.

The next evening he came in and sat down to supper. "I decided not to sell Leslie the gasoline cheaper than I sell everyone else. He gets paid better than these mill hill folks I sell gas to and the farmers don't make much either. Why should I sell him gas cheaper than everyone else when he makes more money than anyone else?" Dad revealed his decision.

It might not have been a good business judgment but it made sense to me. Still does.

77

Where's The Dog House?

I was with Dad once when he was running the country store and garage when he was talking a trade with a customer. For a few bucks worth of groceries, he was going to bring us a six week old beagle hound puppy and that was exciting to me. They agreed upon the deal and a few days later I was there when the man brought the cute little white and black pup.

He gave the dog to me and I looked around and Dad knew I was expecting something else.

"What's the matter, son?" he inquired.

"Well, he must not have got the dog house fixed," I said.

"We didn't make any deal on a dog house," Dad said, looking at me as if I had been imagining things.

"I thought you did. You asked him if the dog's house broke," I said and it took Dad a moment to figure out how I had tangled up the sentence.

Those Chinese Names

Dad was always amused at the names that the Chinese people had like Chang, Ching and Chung, etc. He said that there were so many of the Chinese that they had run out of names and now when a baby was born, they took a tin can and rolled it down the street. Whatever sound came from the rattling, bouncing metal is what they called the child.

"That's why you have names like Cling, Clang, Clung and maybe even slam, bang, bump. That's the kind of noise the cans make on a cobblestone street when you let it roll along," he said.

He probably never realized that the Orientals would think a name like Carter was strange.

Sunday Morning Breakfast Was Special

Breakfast at our house on Sunday morning was often more than the usual eggs with fatback or ham from our homegrown hogs. It was the one morning of the week when both Dad and Mom were there and that wasn't normal on week days because they both worked at public jobs in town; Dad the day shift and Mom the evening shift.

Breakfast on Sunday became something special and I can remember well that many of those were gourmet meals. Most families might have reserved this for company but it was our family affair.

Mama always made biscuits in the morning and we seldom had store-bought loaf bread. It was for sale, but most country people made their own biscuits from scratch. There were no canned biscuits and even the bought loaf bread was one huge chunk, not sliced as it is today. It was difficult to slice it with a knife. Biscuits made with a spoon full of shortening and buttermilk were great at any meal. But loaf bread was a luxury.

In the spring and summer when we had young chickens running loose in the yard, Mama might fry one of these for Sunday breakfast. Dad often had a hankering for steak and would bring in a big thin-slice of round steak that either he or Mama would fry brown in a skillet and then make gravy that went well with the homemade biscuits. Round steak is the only kind we ever had. I never saw a T-bone, sirloin, or other broiling style steak at our house until long after I had moved out. Steak meant round steak to us and it was good to me, then and now. It is hard to beat. Often it was tough but Dad tenderized it by beating it with the edge of a plate. That made it easy to chew.

I remember along about 1935 when Ed Anderson and his

79

wife from Ohio visited with us. Dad had lived with Ed and his parents in Cleveland when he was out of North Carolina for several years. Anderson drove into Albemarle from Endy and ordered some round steak. After it was cut, he told the butcher to grind it in his sausage mill. The butcher was shocked.

"You want me to grind this round steak and make it like sausage?" he asked.

"Yeah, that's exactly what I said. I want it ground. It's tough unless you grind it but anyone can chew it if it is ground, made into patties and cooked," Anderson told the unbelieving market man.

The steak was ground and Anderson brought it back to our house. It was the first ground steak I ever saw and it was also a first for almost everyone else. Markets made hamburger from pork and scraps of beef but no one in our community had ever heard of grinding pure round steak. It started a trend in Albemarle that grew rapidly and it is common practice to grind steak everywhere now. But that Ohio Yankee started it in our area.

In addition to young fried chicken and steak that was often our special Sunday breakfast, Dad would sometimes bring home salt mullet or spots. They were cured in salt and if you tried to eat a piece the way it was cured in brine, it would quickly turn you off. It was as salty as the Dead Sea of the Middle East. But Mama would take the salt fish, soak them in water over night, changing the water several times. In the morning, you could remove the fish from the water, roll them in corn meal and fry them a golden brown. It was a meal I still remember.

We never filleted those fish. We cooked them bones, skin and all. That's the way I like fried fish. I thought it was great then and it is today, if you can find any salt fish. With freezers and sophisticated canning, curing fish with salt in this country is almost a lost art.

Those Sunday morning meals were delightful and I still have those memories etched in a corner of my brain. It was something that excited us before going to church. It was a happy time.

Helping Hand Not Always Appreciated

We always had a car of some kind at our house even when they were not plentiful everywhere in Stanly. Dad always had to get back and forth to his public job and living five miles out of Albemarle, he had some kind of vehicle to make the daily trip.

People without a car often came to him when there was sickness or a need for getting to town and they had no transportation. Such was the case one Christmas afternoon when a weeping lady came to the door with a crying baby in her arms and asked him to carry her to the sheriff's office so she could swear out a warrant against her abusive husband. He had just come home drunk and beaten her up for the umpteenth time. She could not put up with it another day.

Dad didn't want to leave the holiday atmosphere of home but he didn't want to appear unconcerned either. He asked the lady to get in the car and he carried her to town. It was a holiday and there was no sheriff to be found at the office. After some inquiring, he learned where the sheriff lived and eventually located the officer and the abused lady signed the warrant. He brought her back to Endy where she got out of the car at a brother's house. She thanked him profusely.

A few days later the hearing date arrived and the case came to court. By then the weeping lady was regretting she had taken out the warrant, a normal reaction, and the abusive husband was repentant, also normal. They both went before the judge and pleaded for understanding and begged him to drop the warrant.

"If it hadn't been for that busybody Raleigh Carter who brought me to town I wouldn't have sworn out this warrant to begin with. I'd just have gone back home and we would have settled this dispute without going to court," the lady told the judge.

"I don't know why Carter had to stick his nose in our business to begin with. It's none of his business if I beat my wife up," the husband said. "He got us in this mess."

The judge dropped the case and before long the stories that were told to the judge circulated around the community.

"You would think I was the one who beat up the man's wife. I was the culprit in the whole affair. It sure is strange. I lost a lot of my Christmas holiday, carried the lady to town after her tearful begging and wound up the goat," Dad recalled.

"It proves what I said a long time ago. If you see someone coming who wants help in solving a family squabble, hide under the bed or get lost. You'll be the loser. Abused wives love their husbands better than those who are treated fairly. You can't win when you try to help and always they are ready to be lovey dovey again in a day or two after being beaten and abused," he often said. "They take their hate out on anyone who tries to help."

All is fair in love and war but it seems like such an injustice when you suffer for your own compassion. But that is not unusual in family squabbles. Love osbscures a lot of faults.

Dad May Have Been Part Indian

From the earliest recollection I have of Dad, he had a lot of jet black hair, and eyes as black as the dark side of the moon. He had a swarthy complexion too, and I often wondered if he didn't have some American Indian blood in his veins. He never discussed it and probably didn't know.

But he was conscious of his raven-colored hair and when he got about fifty and it started turning grey, he joked about that.

"I don't care what color it turns as long as it doesn't turn loose," was his remark.

And it never did turn loose. He had a head full of gray hair when he was killed. He was sympathetic with the bald headed folks but didn't want to ever be without some color of hair on his head.

The Dynamite Disaster
And Near Miss

Not far from where we lived at Endy was a Burris family that farmed and one winter they were clearing some woodland for planting. It was a big job in that there were no bulldozers, draglines or any other kind of stump pullers. To clear a new ground, you had to saw the trees down with an old cross cut saw, then either wait years for the stumps to rot or blow them out of the ground with dynamite. It would have taken forever to dig up the hundreds of stumps that were in a new ground of only a few acres after the timber was felled.

Burris punched a hole under a big oak stump and inserted a stick of dynamite, affixed a cap and fuse that would set off the explosion, lighted it and walked away. He took refuge behind a huge brush pile a hundred yards away and waited for the blast. He waited and waited. He knew it was time for the cap to have fired. The fuse wasn't that long. But he waited some more anyhow as a precaution.

"It must have gone out," he eventually reasoned, and he walked back to the stump where the explosive charge was set. But some how that spark was still alive. Just as he reached the stump, the dynamite exploded. The farmer was horribly mangled but lived a few hours in great pain. It was the kind of disaster land clearing workmen suffered in a period before high technology made it easier with powerful equipment. I remember going to the Burris home and hearing the conversations about the tragic explosion that evening after Dad came in from work.

Another near tragedy happened in the community a few years later. A land clearing project was underway and a dynamite was planted beneath a big stump, the fuse lit and the farmer briskly walked away from the charge. His friendly collie dog had been romping around with him all morning and the dog was curious when he saw the curl of smoke spiralling from the lighted fuse. He took it in his mouth and dragged the dynamite out of the hole, the fuse still sputtering moments after the farmer had walked away.

Playfully and perhaps thinking he was helping, the collie trotted along behind the farmer with the dynamite bouncing over the ground. The farmer turned around to see the dog with the explosive charge only a yard behind him. Fear turned him white and suddenly he was as nervous as a pregnant fox in a forest fire. The dynamite might go off any minute and that would be the end for not only the dog but the man too.

"Get out of here!" he yelled time after time and motioned to the collie to get away.

The dog thought his master was playing with him and he pranced around gleefully with the fuse burning shorter and shorter. Over and over the farmer yelled but it only made the collie dance even closer. It was a dangerous game.

Desperately trying to get away from the dog, the man ran as fast as he could toward his house a few hundred yards away, the dog right at his heels. Out of breath and exhausted, he ran to the screen, opened it and dashed into the kitchen. The collie couldn't get in. He gently laid the dynamite on the stone step at the porch and started walking away sorrowfully at having lost his boss. The explosion rocked the whole yard, tore off half the porch roof and shattered the window panes of every room in the house. The dog tumbled over and over for thirty feet and got to his feet wondering what on earth had happened.

It was a close call for the dog and the dynamiter and all were fortunate that some lives were not snuffed out because of the playful dog that didn't know when to listen to his master.

Dad often talked about the misconception some people have about dynamite. Many people believe it will explode when you put a match to it but it will not. Dynamite explodes from shock not fire.

Relating this to some fellow workmen in the Ford garage one time, they were unbelieving until Dad struck a match to the dynamite and they observed that nothing happened. Then to show it took a lot of shock to set one off, he hurled a stick against a nearby brick wall as his kibitzers headed for cover.

That didn't explode it either. But a dynamite cap bursts from fire in a fuse and that cap explosion sets off the much bigger blast. Sometimes a high powered rifle shot or pistol bullet will explode dynamite but you can burn a house full of dynamite and get no explosion.

Dad Liked To See Kid's Eyes Surprised

Dad often made up humorous stories that he told his grandchildren or other youngsters who were always interested in hearing him talk about things that happened to him. I remember a cat story that he told to a myriad of children, and he always got a kick from seeing the surprise look sparkle in their eyes when he related the punch line.

His favorite cat story had to do with a mean old tom cat that was always fighting and biting the little kittens around the barnyard, sometimes strangling them to death.

"I got mad at that cat and decided I'd kill him and stop his meanness. I got him by the tail and hit him over the head with a stick of stovewood. He went limp. I carried him off in the woods a few hundred yards and threw him on a brush pile. The next day he was back in the yard with a lump on his head and as mean as ever.

"I went in the house got my shotgun and got that critter in my sights. I shot him from about forty feet, and he rolled over on his side, kicking. I was sure he was dead this time so I picked him up, carried him back in the woods again and tossed him on the brush pile.

"The very next day, that tom cat was back in the yard. It took some doing, but I finally got my hands on that cat. I carried him to the woodpile, picked up my axe and chopped his head off. Again I took the cat and the head to the woods and threw him on the brush. Would you believe it? The next morning he came wobbling out of the woods to the back door with his head in his mouth," Dad told the story ever so seriously and the children scratched their heads trying to figure it out.

Some Stories Dad Told

A robbery case came up in Superior Court in Albemarle and a teenage Negro boy was a star witness for the prosecution. The youngster said he was on the street the night of the robbery and saw the suspect leave the store and run across the street to a parked car that he jumped into and drove away.

"What time of night was this when you saw my client run across the street?" the defense attorney asked.

"It was about 8:30 at night," the young man said.

"It was dark then except for a few scattered street lights?" the lawyer continued the questioning, "And you have testified you were at least a hundred yards away."

"Yes, sir. It was dark," the witness admitted, "And I was about a half block away."

"But in spite of the darkness and that great distance you recognized and can identify my client as the one who rushed out of the store and crossed the street?" the defense attorney pushed his point. "You must have mighty fine eyes."

"Yes, sir, it was him," the witness said confidently.

"That's asking the jury to believe a lot, young man. Just how far do you think you can see at night?" the defense lawyer cross examined with a sarcastic sneer on his face.

The young witness was quiet a minute or two and squirmed in his seat. He didn't know just how to tell the lawyer how far he could see. Then his face lit up and he had the right answer.

"I don't know how far I can see. How far is it to the moon?" asked the witness.

The jury found the defendant guilty.

Dad liked to tell about the truck driver who was transporting a whole load of new cars on one of the big carriers that deliver eight or nine cars at once. It seems that the carrier was headed down a long stretch of Highway 74 between

Hamlet and Lumberton when the headlights went out. He couldn't drive at night without lights, but he managed to get the big truck off the hard surface and out of the road. The driver sat in the truck a few minutes wondering how he could do anything but sit there the rest of the night waiting for daylight. But then he had an idea. He could climb up on the truck and switch the headlights on the new car that was over his cab and facing forward. That would get him enough light so he could at least get to the next town and find a place to sleep. He cut the lights on on the car above him and slowly moved on down the highway.

He had driven only a couple of miles when he saw a car in the distance that was approaching. But when the car got to within a couple of hundred yards, it swerved sharply to the right, jumped across a side ditch and stalled in a corn field well off the highway.

Thinking the man must have gone to sleep or passed out or something, the auto carrier driver stopped, ran to where the car was stuck in the field to see if he could be any help. He found the driver under the wheel and perfectly alright but scared.

"What happened? Why did you leave the road?" the carrier driver inquired.

"Well I saw you coming toward me and I didn't know what to do. I knew that if you were as wide as you were tall, I better get the hell off this highway," said the car driver.

I never had but one car wreck while I was at home and driving Dad's car. That was in 1940 when I was home for a few days from school and had a date with a nice little lady in Charlotte. Dad loaned me his 1937 Plymouth and O.K.'ed my trip but cautioned me that Charlotte was a big town and for me to be careful. "Don't wreck my car," he said.

Chad Efird, a neighbor, was with me and we got to Charlotte, picked up the girls and everything was fine until we drove down the four lane Tryon Street about 9:00 that evening in the slow traffic right lane. Out of nowhere, a car flashed across the median at breakneck speed and despite my turning sharply and going all the way up on the curb, the wild car hit us on the rear left fender. It then veered across the street and wrapped around a telephone post.

I was about as mad as you could get. I jumped out of the car and ran to where the culprit who hit me had been stopped by the phone post. The car was empty. The driver had fled. Moments later, a policeman arrived and shortly after that, a gentleman drove up with a friend and said the car around the post was his. Someone had stolen it while he was getting a Coke a few blocks down the street.

Our car would run after we fixed the tire and pulled the fender up a bit. We had to go to the police station to file a report. It was way past midnight when we finished. Our dates with the young ladies had been ruined and we worried about what their parents would say when we got them home so late. But we carried them home and returned to Endy. We never saw the girls again.

I don't believe there ever was anything that I had to do that I dreaded like telling Dad I had done just what he said not do -- wreck his car. Sometimes you have to accept punishment when you really are not guilty of anything.

Dad's Thoughts About Fat People

He was overweight himself when he reached fifty or thereabouts but prior to that, he was a trim 145 pound muscular man. He had his own thoughts about the people who were overweight.

"I know what makes people overweight. It's eating cottage cheese. I know that must be what makes them overweight because every heavy person I know is eating cottage cheese," Dad said.

We walked down the main street of Albemarle and a giant of a woman, who must have weighed nearly 300 pounds, came across the street and wobbled along in front of us. Dad looked at me and grinned.

"She looks just like a bale of cotton that has the middle band busted," he said. And indeed that was a pretty good description of what the big lady looked like.

How Dad Treated His Cuts

Today people rush to doctors for tetanus shots following even the most insignificant cut or scratch. You take this precaution because you don't want to come down with lockjaw. Oh how things have changed!

We went barefooted around our house every summer from the day it was warm enough until we returned to school in the fall. Sometimes we went to school shoeless too. It was only natural that we kept our feet skinned and bruised throughout the summer, stone bruises often causing a lot of soreness and pain. Those bad bruises had to be split to let the deep infection out. Dad did that with a razor blade while we yelled and cried. But after the lancing, the trouble quickly got better.

The most dangerous injuries we suffered that had a threat of tetanus, were caused by stepping on rusty nails in boards. These nails would go right into the foot, and a few times I have seen them go all the way through, penetrating the top of the foot. It was this kind of piercing injury that we were told caused lockjaw and probably that is right. But suffice it to say, I'm sure I had well over a dozen nails in my foot in those days and never a tetanus shot. Maybe I was just lucky, Mitchell and Betty too.

As a mechanic, Dad was always getting his fingers, elbows and hands bruised and cut. Somehow he would come in every few weeks with a deep, mean looking cut on his hands or arms, some severe enough that in our routine of today, they would have required stitches and medicine; costly doctor bills.

Dad's treatment was unique. While most people would pour merthiolate or iodine that burned like fire into the cuts. Dad would hunt up a can of automobile motor oil and pour it all over the open wound. He said it helped kill all the germs in the cut and it would get well quicker. He seldom even put a bandage or bandaid on the open wound, firmly convinced that the motor oil and air would heal it quickly without complications. It worked well for him. It was certainly unhygenic but I never knew a wound of his to linger. Maybe he was just too tough for the cut to beat him down.

Another popular treatment for stings and cuts was tobacco. Dad just opened up a tailor made cigarette when he smoked those, or got a pinch of tobacco out of a Prince Albert can when he rolled his own, wet it and stuck it on the injured part. It might have been purely psychological, but stings subsided and cuts healed. The pain always seemed to go away quicker when the tobacco mess was applied.

What Grade Did Dad Reach?

I once asked Dad what grade he reached in school in that it was obvious that he worked from early childhood until he left home at 21. It seemed that school was not available to him even though his older brothers and sisters had a chance to get a little education.

"I don't know what grade I got to in school. I got to whatever grade you can get to in three months because that's all I ever got to go," he said. He had said it often before.

Taking that for the truth, it was amazing that in that short period he learned to read and always glanced at the newspaper enough that you knew he could read a little. He could add and subtract and was great at multiplying figures in his head. He could sign his name "W.R. Carter" although it was a laborious chore for him that he accomplished slowly. Today we have college graduates who can't read. What would they have learned in three months?

Once when I was in the Navy in World War II, I got a letter from him. I suppose it was the only one he wrote to anybody in his lifetime. It wasn't any great in-depth message, simply a how are you and we are doing fine. Hope you will be back home soon, etc. But I don't think I ever appreciated a letter from anyone as much as I did that one. I knew it took a great deal of pain-taking effort to write those few sentences and he wouldn't have done it had he not missed me, loved me and wished for me God speed in returning back home.

I wish I had kept that letter.

Rice Eating Contest And The Miller's Meal

Dad was raised in an area of Carolina where people did not eat much rice. A few residents of the Piedmont section ate rice like it was a cereal with sugar on it, and at times it was on the dinner table with chicken or beef gravy. But North Carolinians in Stanly County didn't eat rice three times a day and the year 'round like it was consumed in the coastal areas where families bought rice in 100 lb. bags and served it for breakfast, lunch and supper. Many families in the East bought 500 lbs. of rice at one time each fall. In Stanly, rice was most often bought in two or five pound lots.

Poking fun at the rice eaters was one of Dad's regular maneuvers when we visited in the East. He said a 100 lb. bag of cooked rice would expand and cover a whole county like snow.

"Eating rice is like not eating at all. I remember a time when a rice eater and another man decided to hold a contest to determine just how good rice was as a food. They agreed that the man eating the rice could eat all he wanted every day while the non-rice consumer would go out each night, lie on his back, open his mouth and let the moonlight shine down his throat. The contest lasted a couple of weeks until the rice eater starved," Dad said.

When he was growing up in the Palestine section of the county, a rocky, poor farm land area not far off the Pee Dee River, the family looked forward each fall to cornbread made from the new crop of white corn that they grew. As soon as a few ears were ripe and dried sufficiently, a member of the family would carry a sack of corn to the water-powered mill a few miles away where a miller ground it into meal, taking a few pounds of toll for his work.

One brisk September morning, Dad's father told him to take a sack of corn to the mill and get it ground. He put a halter on an old mule, fitted the sack of corn across the animal's back, mounted the mule and rode off to the mill on the lazy, plodding old work animal.

"The miller put my corn in the hopper and started the water wheel turning. Slowly a little stream of meal began pouring out from the stones that were grinding it. It was such a slow stream and so tiny that I got a little impatient and told the miller that I could eat the meal as fast as he was turning it out," Dad remembers.

"Yeah, you might eat it as fast as it is grinding your corn but for how long?" the miller asked.

"Well, if it doesn't get any faster than it is now, until I starved to death," he remarked.

The miller had no rebuttal.

He Was Leaving The Country

Dad said he had a neighbor when he was growing up in the rural Stanly County community of Palestine, who never left his farm except to go into town a couple of times a year to get some staple groceries like coffee, sugar, flour, salt and pepper. He was happy just working, eating and sleeping and was not envious of those who traveled the country.

One fall morning, a neighbor stopped by his house and invited the recluse to ride with him to Troy, county seat of Montgomery on the east side of the Pee Dee River. Surprisingly, the old loner accepted and jumped in the car for the ride. He had no car and made his infrequent jaunts into Albemarle with an old wagon pulled by a team of plow mules.

The old T-model putt-putted down the road to the narrow river bridge at what was then called the "Swift Island" bridge. The car chugged along over the bridge and the old recluse looked back at the wooded hills and Stanly County behind him. It was a novel experience for him. He had to say something to show his enthusiasm that was bubbling.

"Goodbye, old United States," he said, as he sat back down and looked into Montgomery county for the very first time.

Dad Cured The Hogs Of Worms

We always had a few hogs on our little twelve acre farm where we moved when I was three years old. They provided most of the meat that we ate in the winter time, although occasionally we killed a young heifer. We had milk cows all the time and when there was an extra calf around, Dad and Mom had it slaughtered and we ate beef. There were no deepfreezers. The beef had to be canned in glass jars and Mom worked long and hard to preserve it. The pork was cured with salt and hung in an outbuilding. That was easier but every now and then immediately after a hog was butchered, the weather would turn warm. That was a disaster. The pork would often spoil and I remember several times when we had to take big hams way off in the woods and throw them away. They were ruined. The buzzards had a feast. Losing a hog or two that you had fed for months was a big loss in our family.

One fall, Dad was disturbed because the three hogs we had were not growing. They were eating but not putting on any weight, and he knew it would be hog killing time in a few more weeks.

One afternoon late when he got home from mechanicing in Albemarle, he had a box of a powdery poison in his hand. He went to the hog pen and sprinkled a cup or two of the poison on the "slop" that the hogs ate from the dinner table. They gulped it all down and Dad came on in the house.

"I put a little poison in the hog feed. I understand from talking with Sam Potter, who raises hogs, that it would kill the worms and the hogs would grow faster," Dad said as he sat down to supper.

Early the next morning I heard Mama sobbing. She had gone out to feed the pigs and found all three of them dead and stiff.

"It worked like a charm. The hogs had no more worms, Sam really knows how to kill worms," Dad said.

We had kind of tough luck with animals. Once when Mom had saved pennies for years, she got enough to buy a registered Jersey cow. Heretofore, we had raised mongrel cows, mixed breeds, and thoroughbred Jerseys cost much more money and supposedly gave more and better milk.

But this new full-blooded Jersey had always roamed free in a pasture. She was not used to being chained out to graze where there were good growths of tender grass that helped make milk and fatten the cow. We began tying out this $200 cow and she seemed to adapt to the chain around her horns after a few weeks. Then one day I came in from school and she was lying on her head in the yard, the chain tight from the stake where it was looped. The Jersey had somehow fallen and broken her neck. It took Mama a long time to get over that loss.

The best cow we ever had was an old brownish mixed breed named Daisy. She lived for at least 16 years, and I must have milked her twice a day for half those years. She gave a lot of milk and was as gentle as a lamb. About the most trouble she ever was happened when she was trying to avoid some fly bites at milking time and set her foot right in the milk bucket. It happened many times and kind of caused a milk shortage that day. It happened with Mitchell and Betty too. It never happened to Dad. He said he didn't know how to milk.

Milk was something we always had available. For a long time we had no refrigerator and had to keep the milk cool so it would not sour. We kept it in a spring run near the house for years. Later we had an ice box that was lined with tin and held a 300 lb. cake of ice. Guarded carefully, a cake of ice that cost about 90 cents then, would last out the week. When the new delivery was made on Friday, we looked forward to a special event. If we had enough ice left, we made homemade ice cream. That was a special occasion. We had the milk and only had to buy sugar for ice cream. I got addicted to ice cream then and it still remains a choice food today.

But milk was also necessary when eating cornbread. Then and now I love to eat baked cornbread with sweet milk or buttermilk. It may not be proper etiquette, but I like it crumbled in the milk and eaten with a spoon. Soul food, I suppose, but still a favorite of mine. I still contend that my favorite winter day meal is cornbread, buttermilk, pinto beans, and raw onions. You can work a sawmill on food like that.

Prank Almost Got Me Whipped

Dad gave me a few whippings as punishment for breaking some of the rules when I was growing up but generally this was Mama's duty. I can't remember what the whippings were for, but I'm sure I probably deserved the floggings. I do remember that the worst thing about these whippings was having to go and cut my own switch from the hedge bushes that grew along the fringe of the backyard. That was like having to choose between the electric chair and the hangman's rope. If I came back with a puny little switch, Dad or Mom would send me back for a better one and that made them madder. If I got a really strong and limber limb, I knew it was going to sting something fierce when they struck me around the buttocks and lower legs. I learned to compromise with one of medium size and length that wouldn't hurt too much that they accepted.

But what I remember perhaps most about those whippings was the time when I narrowly escaped the lashes after playing a rather bizarre practical joke on Dad and the rest of the family.

Often in the evenings Dad would get us in the car and we would visit some of the neighbors in the community. It was the custom then and one or two nights each week we went to someone's house for an hour or so to chat, maybe pop popcorn over an open fire with a screen wire popper that you jiggled with a long handle over the wood coals. That was fun. Then when the first radios came into the community, we often got together to listen to Amos and Andy, Lum and Abner or some such program that was a real novelty in the early 1930's. Folks in the rural community of Endy enjoyed these social events, and often on a Saturday night, several families got together and had a feast. Usually the women made chicken stew from a big, fat hen that was cooked and then mixed with milk and butter in a black pot. It was eaten with soda crackers like soup. It was a gourmet meal for most of us that made Saturday night something special.

The men and older folks more often in winter made oyster stew, much like the chicken stew except they used oysters from the coast that were put into the milk and butter.

When I was in my early teens and wanted to join the men at the oyster stew table, I found I was allergic to this mixture. I liked the taste but every time I ate it, I ended up nauseated a couple of hours later. Oddly enough, I kept right on trying and by the time I left home in the late 1930's, my system had adapted and I could eat all the oysters I wanted without getting sick. Today it is one of my favorite meals.

The chicken stew that we ate at those neighborhood dinners remains a favorite of mine today, but when I moved to Eastern North Carolina in 1946, the populace there had never heard of such a dish. In the East, they cook the same big fat hen until the meat falls off the bones and then cook a couple of cups of rice in with the broth. That's chicken bog and a long time delicacy in Tabor City and over much of coastal Tar Heelia. I like that too.

At dusk one Saturday evening as we prepared to drive to the J.B. Poplin home a couple of miles away for the chicken stew-oyster stew feast, I saw a five foot piece of black velvet about an inch wide lying in the trash pile. Noting the length and width that resembled a chicken snake in the dark, I picked up the velvet and as the rest of the family got in the car, I coiled it rather expertly near the back door so it looked for the world like a snake. We rode on off to the Poplin's for dinner and didn't return home until about 10:00. It was a half moon night and when Mama walked near the door, she let out a scream and hollered "Snake!"

Now Dad was not as scared of these reptiles as Mom was but he rushed to the rescue. The only weapon to kill this viper that he could get his hands on was a twelve foot 2 x 4 pine timber that was stacked nearby. He picked it up and proceeded to beat the life out of the "black snake" that seemed to take all the punishment without the least bit of hostility. Finally, and after Dad had bruised his hand with the timber, he smelled a rat. He reached down and picked up the black velvet scrap and ominously asked:

"Who did this?"

I stammered a few seconds and then admitted that I had

made the "snake" just for fun. I didn't know he would get hurt trying to kill it. I fully expected another good whipping but presumably a full stomach and an enjoyable evening had Dad in a better frame of mind. Eventually, he smothered a little laugh, put down the timber and we all walked into the house. It was the closest I ever came to getting a whipping and didn't.

Snakes were rather plentiful in the community in that era and some were copperheads that were dangerous. Mostly the snakes were harmless kings, rat, chicken and garter snakes but since Adam and Eve, the majority of people have feared snakes regardless of how innocent the reptiles were. Mama was no exception and I'll never forget the morning she was cutting cabbage with a long-bladed butcher knife in the garden. I heard her scream and ran to see what was the problem. Amazingly, she had cut off a cabbage head and flushed a big chicken snake from under it. The snake was much more scared that his disturber. But Mama was so frightened that she simply threw down her knife and ran for the gate. Daniel Boone could not have done better. That knife went right through the snake's midsection and pinned him to the ground. He wriggled back and fourth for several minutes trying to escape, but by then Mama was back with a hoe and chopped off the snake's head. It would have made a circus act.

Many outdoorsmen today do not kill snakes, even the poisonous ones. They are becoming scarce and many hunters and fishermen feel that what few of the reptiles are left should be protected for other generations. But in that era, a snake was looked upon as a real hazard and every one was killed instantly.

- - - - - -

Once Dad and a friend, Leslie Turner, were on the way to the sandhill section to buy peaches for canning. They passed some children with holes in the seats of their pants and Turner asked, "Why do you suppose the kids have holes in the seat of their pants?"

"To keep the gnats out of their faces," Dad said without so much as a grin.

The Moonshiner Turned Evangelist

Dad often told the story about a Georgia moonshiner who saw the light, stopped his lawless liquor making and turned to preaching the gospel.

As the story goes, this old reprobate had a still in the swamp that was a long way from the nearest road and federal alcohol and tobacco tax officers heard about the liquor making operation from an informant who wanted the bootlegger caught. They had to try to catch the moonshiner after the report had been filed and their abilities challenged.

One hot August day they drove to the community and trudged miles through the dense undergrowth looking for the still. They found it right on the edge of a desolate farm field where the informant said it was. It had taken hours of hard work to fight their way through the water, mud, undergrowth and mosquitoes to get to the still. But there was no one there. The still was not in operation. A lot of mash was ripening in the vats, but it would be another day or two before it was ready for boiling and distilling. The officers decided not to cut the still down but to leave it exactly as they found it and try to catch the moonshiner red-handed so they could send him off to the Atlanta Pen for a year and a day, the normal sentence for bootlegging the first half of this century. They calculated he would be back there operating his still in two days. They fought their way back out of the swamp to their car and were wet with sweat when they got there.

Two days later on even a hotter day than the first one, they drove back to the swamp. The officers really dreaded the thought of again fighting their way through all that jungle.

"Why don't we just drive to the other side of the swamp and try to slip into the still through that little cotton field that was near the operation? It would be a lot easier, and I don't feel like trudging through all this swamp again," one officer said.

"That's O.K. with me but we will certainly have to be careful and not let the bootlegger see us. If he does and we botch this raid, we might get fired. The informant gave us good information as to the exact location and the boss knows it. If we get caught in that field and the bootlegger smells a rat, abandons the still and never comes back, we'll have to cut it down, but we'll never be able to make an arrest," one officer pointed out the problem.

"Yeah, you're right. The informant is a real activist in the community who says we are in cahoots with the distillers anyway. He told the boss if we screwed up this raid, he was going to Washington and charge us with conspiracy with the bootleggers. He doesn't think we ever try to catch them," the first revenuer recalled.

After a little more discussion, they decided they would slip through the field and get to the still undetected and save a lot of energy. They drove around the swamp, parked in a desolate sawmill path and walked a short distance to the cotton patch. They got down on all fours and started crawling across the cotton rows toward the swamp clearing. But luck had played a cruel trick. Old John, the bootlegger, had decided to plow out the crab grass in his cotton that morning. About the time the officers got to the middle of the patch, they heard a rattle of a harness and a mule. Glancing above the knee high cotton, they saw John at one end of the field and he started cultivating the middles. He would pass within a few rows of where they were crouched.

"It's too late to worry now. We are caught. John will see us and know why we are here. He'll never go back to that still and we won't have any jobs long," the leader of the raiding officers said with disgust on his face. "We never should have tried this easy way. We have really screwed up."

"Well, if we are going to be seen anyway, we might as well have a little fun," one officer said as they snuggled down as low as they could and tried to be inconspicious in the growing green cotton. John approached a few rows away and the officer used his most mystical voice to say, "Go ye and preach the gospel."

John glanced around, looked at his mule and then at the sky. He slowed a moment but didn't stop as the officers' positions weren't discovered. He went on down the row and the officers scrambled a few rows further away from him while his

back was to them. Soon John was on the way back and the officers again hid close to the ground.
"Go ye and preach the gospel," the officer said again in a kind of ghoulish tone when John was only a dozen steps away.
John looked every direction, but miraculously didn't see the officers. He stopped the mule in the middle of the row, unhitched him from the cultivator, climbed on his back and rode away toward his house a mile away.
Puzzled at the action, the officers lay low for half an hour, then crawled on to the still wondering what had made John quit cultivating. The still and mash were intact. It hadn't been touched since they were there two days previous.
"Well, maybe he hasn't smelled a rat. Maybe the mash needs a little more time to ferment. Let's go home and come back tomorrow afternoon. Maybe John will have this thing in operation then," the leader suggested. And they walked back to the car and went home.
Early the next day, they drove to the cotton patch and carefully crawled over the rocky rows to the swamp clearing. They looked around with disbelief. Some one had chopped that still to bits. All the mash had been poured out, the big wooden vats were chopped full of holes and even the copper still smashed to pieces. It looked like a better job of destroying a still than any the officers had ever accomplished, and they had cut down many.
"We have surely played hell now. He must have seen us yesterday and just played like he didn't. He decided that we were aware of his still and would be back. He tore it up just to make us look silly," the officer said.
"You're probably right but you know there's a path here that leads towards John's house. We might follow it and if it does go to his house, we might be able to make a case against him with that evidence. Let's walk it out and see where it leads. We can at least scare him," the leader divulged his idea.
They walked the path toward John's place and, sure enough, it went right to his backyard. They went to the door and knocked. A middle aged, forlorn lady came to the door wiping her hands on a dirty apron.
"We are looking for John. Is he around?" they asked.
"No, I'm his wife and he ain't here. I don't know where he is. Yesterday morning he went over to the cotton patch to

cultivate and came right back in a few minutes. He looked strange and talked crazy. He said the Lord had called him to preach. He had heard His voice clearly. He picked up his axe and went over there where his still was and came back. He said he cut it all to pieces. Early this morning he got his Bible and told me he was going to Atlanta to see if he could enroll in some Bible school. He was going to obey the Lord and spread the gospel the rest of his life and he would be back for me," the troubled wife told the astonished officers. They thanked her and walked away.

That is not the end of the story. It really happened that way. John did get some schooling in the Bible and for years preached all over Georgia and elsewhere. Even today you can see some of his humble signs hanging on trees along roadways that carry a variety of scriptural messages like "Jesus Saves," "Christ Loves You," "Repent Today And Be Saved," and a myriad of others that he personally painted and erected. That bootlegger took the prank of a careless ATTU officer seriously and he made a complete change in his life. He never again was in the liquor business.

The Lord does indeed move in strange ways.

The Misunderstanding

Once Dad came down to Tabor City and we went to Myrtle Beach for supper. We couldn't eat all the food that was served and when we were ready to leave, Dad asked the young waiter for a doggie bag.

"We have two 'coons at home that would like to have these leftovers. Would you bring me a bag to put them in?" he asked.

The waiter looked straight at Dad and said, "Mister, that's a racist remark."

Dad was a little shocked. The two old raccoons that frequently came to the door at night and begged for handouts certainly wouldn't think Dad was racist.

He just took the doggie bag and grinned.

The Bootlegger Hid The Whiskey Jars

Dad had to work on a lot of stubborn Fordson and International tractors back in those early days when mechanized farming was just beginning in Stanly County. The tractors were not very well engineered to begin with and most farmers were totally inexperienced at starting and operating them. So it was a regular experience for Dad to have to go deep into the rural areas to hand crank and adjust these tractor engines. Originally farm tractors did not have batteries for cranking engines. The Ford agency that he worked for in Albemarle assigned these jobs to him and he always managed to get the machines running again. He even suffered a broken arm when an engine kicked back, yanked the crank out of his hand and snapped his arm at the wrist.

One cold winter morning he was told to go to the Ridgecrest Community in northwestern Stanly to get a tractor going for a farmer there who was preparing his land for small grain. He knew the farmer and was aware that he reputedly was one of the leading moonshiners in the area. Making liquor that could be sold without the costly tax stamps was profitable if you didn't get caught. You could sell the stump hole booze cheaper than the "bottling bond" whiskey that few people in our area had ever seen. We only knew that the tax paid whiskey was called "bottling bond" liquor. It had not been voted in at that time in Stanly County and most of the drinkers got their supply from bootleggers who had little stills hidden in the deep woods and bays. Law enforcement officers from both the county and the federal government caught the bootleggers from time to time and they usually got a year and a day in the Atlanta penitentiary. But the punishment didn't stop many of them for more than the length of their sentences. It was easy money, selling the white lightning, and some families were in it for life. Some were really adroit at hiding their stills and their finished product.

When Dad got to the farm where the broken down tractor was that morning, he was surprised to find the house was under surveillance. Federal officers were hiding in the bushes along the roadside and they stopped Dad before he got to the house.

"You'll have to wait right here, mister" a big tough looking officer commanded. "We know Sam is going to come in from the woods pretty soon with some of his non-tax paid whiskey and we are going to catch him. He has avoided arrests for years but we got a tip that he was running the still somewhere last night and would probably bring some of his liquor to the house this morning."

The bootleggers always ran their stills at night. You had to have fire to make whiskey and in the day time the trail of smoke would reveal the still's hiding place. Moonshiners usually fired up right after good dark, worked until an hour or so before good daylight, then put the fire out, bottled their product, and came home to get some sleep in the daytime. During farming seasons they slept very little as plowing, cultivating and harvesting took up the daylight hours.

Dad had no choice but to wait until this raid was completed.

A few minutes later, Sam came down a sawmill road from behind the house, walked to the back door and went inside to the kitchen. He was carrying a half gallon Mason jar of whiskey in each hand.

"Let's go now before he has a chance to hide the stuff!" the officer in charge of the raid yelled. And within seconds they were knocking on the door of the moonshiner. Sam's big feet could be heard moving across the kitchen toward the door, and soon he came out on the screen porch and greeted the officers.

"What you fellows want?" he asked.

"Sam, we saw you come in with some whiskey. We got a search warrant here. We are going to find that stuff and you'll go to court this time," the almost jubilant, confident ATU officer promised.

"I ain't got no whiskey. You fellows are just imagining things, but if you want to search the house, come in and make

103

yourself at home," Sam extended what seemed to be a sincere invitation. "I'm not in the moonshine business."

The officers knew Sam had not had time to pour the jars of whiskey out. They had to be in the house. He had had only a minute or so to hide the stuff. It should be easy to locate. But it wasn't.

The three officers worked for hours. They searched every room meticulously. They looked in closets, under rugs, even the pile of stove wood. They looked for hidden compartments in the floor, in the walls, in the attic, everywhere. But no moonshine could be found. Exhausted and exasperated, the leader of the raiding party finally gave up about midmorning.

"Sam, I don't know what you did with it. We can't find it and without that liquor we have no evidence. You'd swear it was water in the jars if we took you to court based on just what we saw. But, we'll get you one of these days. You can't get the best of us forever," the officer said sternly as he left the house with his associates and shuffled off toward their car a half mile down the road. The officer was confused and disgusted.

Dad greeted Sam about the time the search started and Sam told him to go ahead and fix the tractor. He did and had come back to the house at about the time the officers were leaving.

"I got the tractor running. I think it will be O.K. for awhile," Dad told a grinning Sam.

"Raleigh, you know what those fellows were trying to do?" Sam asked, as they disappeared down the road.

"Yeah, they made me wait with them in the bushes so they could catch you with your whiskey when you came in. I saw you with the jars when you went in the back door. Did they arrest you?" Dad asked.

"Naw, they couldn't find the stuff. But they sure did tear up the house looking for it," Sam said.

Years later Sam gave up his moonshining and went to full time farming. He was never caught in the illegal liquor business despite numerous raids. One fall morning when he was walking down the hill of Main Street in Albemarle, he bumped into the ATU officer that had tried so hard to find those jars that memorable morning. They recognized each other.

"Sam, I know you are out of moonshining now and you are clean. But I sure would appreciate it if you would tell me where you hid those two jars that we saw you take in the house that morning. I've lost a lot of sleep and scratched out many a hair from my head trying to figure out just what you did with them," the officer was truly interested.

Sam had no reason to keep his secret. He, too, had got some good laughs after the episode of the disappearing whiskey jars.

"I tell you it was a stroke of luck. You know I'm in the hog business and we feed the pigs a lot of slop from the table. We throw the scraps in a big five gallon bucket, pour the dishwater over it and about once a day I take the bucket out to the pigs. That morning that you almost caught me, I saw someone hiding in the bushes before I went in the house. I kind of guessed it was you revenuers and just as soon as I stepped into the kitchen from the back door, I saw that big bucket two thirds full of slop beside the old wood stove. I just slipped both jars down in the mess and the water covered them instantly. I didn't believe you would ever look in that slop bucket for the whiskey and you didn't," Sam laughed as he revealed his secret. What a hiding place!

The revenuer just shook his head and smiled. At least he had finally unraveled the secret.

"Thanks, Sam, I sure appreciate your telling me," the officer said as he shuffled on down the hill. Now he could sleep better.

Dad said one winter morning when someone talked him into go rabbit hunting, they drove out to a remote, rural section of the county that was notorious for its bootleggers. They found a farm that looked like good rabbit hunting land and went up to the farm house door and asked for permission to hunt.

"You got the wrong house. They sell it over there at the next place," the lady told them, evidently confusing the hunting request as the password for a place to buy white lightning.

On another occasion he said he was in this same bootlegging area to work on a farmer's Fordson tractor. The man wasn't home and the lady of the house refused to tell him how to find her husband, who was evidently at work at a still in the desolate woodlands.

"But I need to find him and let him know I'm here to work on his tractor," Dad pleaded.

"I'm sorry, I can't tell you where he is," the lady apologized. A little boy was playing in the yard.

"I'll tell you where he is and go with you to find him, if you'll give me a dollar," the kid said.

"O.K., I'll do it. Let's get going," Dad implored.

"Well, give me the dollar," the kid solicited.

"I'll give you the dollar when we get back," Dad said impatiently.

"Mister, where I'm taking you, you won't be coming back," the youngster logically explained his request for advance compensation.

One cold morning Dad was told to go to a farm house well out in the backwoods of the county to crank a tractor that was giving trouble. He arrived at the place shortly after daylight and knocked on the door. There was no light and no one answered the knock even after repeated banging. Eventually he went back to his car and was about to drive off when he saw a narrow crack open in the front door.

"What you want, mister?" said a faint female voice.

"I'm from the Ford agency and I came up here to crank Sam's tractor that is giving him trouble," Dad replied.

"Well he ain't here. He is up in the woods behind the barn at his sawmill. You can walk up the old road and find him," the voice said as the door closed.

Dad walked up the road and into the woods and shortly began to smell wood smoke and the stench of boiling corn mesh. Then he came right up on Sam at a liquor still. Sam greeted Dad and told him the tractor was on up the road a couple of hundred yards. Dan thanked him, looked the still over and walked on to the tractor.

With the machine cranked and humming, Dad walked on back to the house and was about ready to get in his car when the crack came in the front door again and the same small voice asked, "Did you find him, mister?"

"Yeah, I found him. He has just starting sawing but had about half a gallon sawed when I left him," Dad answered, got in his car and drove away.

The Joke Was On Mama

Immediately after Dad and Mom were married, they lived in a little two bedroom house on the Efird Mill hill in West Albemarle. They lived there until I was three years old when they moved to the Endy Community, bought twelve acres of land and built the house that still stands today and is occupied by my sister Betty and her husband, J.A. Herlocker. Dad and Mom lived there until their deaths. I remember Dad telling about the move years later when he revealed that he bought the land and built the house for $1,200. My how things have changed!

But while the newlyweds were living in that rented house on the textile mill hill, Dad had a job for a few months with a maintenance crew that kept up the company houses by repairing the plumbing, painting and generally keeping the little bungalows in living condition.

One day Mama looked out from her work in the kitchen and saw the crew coming up the street, and she thought she saw her man among the workmen. Knowing he wouldn't pass right in front of the house without at least coming in to see his petite new wife, she rushed to a closet and pulled the door shut, hiding and romantically hoping to get him to looking for her when he came in and she wasn't right there in plain view as she usually was.

The closet door latch snapped shut but she wasn't worried. She waited, waited and waited. No one came to the door. And no one came until after 5:00 p.m. that afternoon. During all of that day Mom had been locked in that closet with no way to open the door. Dad was not part of that maintenance crew. He hadn't been anywhere near their house all that day. That was another crew.

That probably cured Mama from hiding in a closet. She had

spent many miserable hours waiting for footsteps that came only when the day's work was done.

Dad and Mom lived a reasonably happy life with a few arguments every now and then like all couples have, even those who say they have never had a cross word passed between them. Most of those people have never learned the meaning of truth. Living a lifetime together is going to be spotted with some disagreements, some arguments and few, if any, married couples can escape that certainty. I don't believe any live without some rain mixed with the sunshine.

Dad never repeated a sentence that he said. No matter if you didn't understand what he said and asked, "What?" he ignored you and didn't answer. That brought on a few arguments with Dad generally remarking that Mom couldn't hear very well. In truth, he couldn't hear well at all and never did from the time he ruined an ear drum working in the boilers of the battleship Maryland. But he thought it was others who didn't hear well. He could hear fine, or so he always said, and he wouldn't repeat his remarks.

As he grew older and watched people become softer and more sophisticated, he had an observation that brought grins then and now:

"People today can't even climb a ladder and we used to have to climb trees," he philosophized.

Lightning Rod Salesmen

A little over half a century ago there were a myriad of salesmen going house to house in the rural areas of the Carolinas peddling lightning rods that were designed to keep houses from being damaged by bolts of fire from the heavens. You never see any lightning rods on new homes today so presumably they were not functional. But the salesmen of that era made a good pitch to the gullible in our area and installed the lightning protection devices on hundreds of homes and out buildings.

One unusually glib salesman called on us about dusk one summer evening and proceeded to give Dad a real sales spiel. Now Dad didn't have much faith in the new-fangled home saver to begin with but he kept smoking on his cigarette and listening. The salesman knew he had Dad's attention and he smiled, certain a sale was in the making.

"These lightning rods will draw lightning for several hundred yards right to these metal poles that we will install at both ends of your house and in the middle," the talkative peddler expounded.

That really got Dad's attention. "You mean these lightning rods will actually attract the lightning and draw it to them?" Dad asked with enthusiasm.

"Sure, it will attract all the bolts of lightning that strike anywhere in the immediate area," he confirmed.

"Well, I sure as hell don't want them on my house. If I bought any, I would want you to install them in the top of some of the pine trees in the woods back behind the barn. I don't want anything that brings the lightning to us," Dad said.

The salesman's feathers dropped. He had talked too much and lost a sale. It did no good to point out the lightning was supposed to hit the metal rods and then run harmlessly into the ground. That was how they reportedly operated. But Dad's mind was made up. He wanted something that would repel the firey bolts, not draw them to the house.

There was a great deal more fear of lightning in our home then than there is now. Anytime that a black cloud gathered, particularly in the hot months, Mama called us inside. We sat on the beds, not touching the floor with our feet or any walls with our hands. It was supposed to be the safest place we could get until the thunderstorm abated.

We had to be quiet too. It was a reverent time with no hollering, laughing or playing around. Some said God was moving his furniture and we should be quiet until all the rumbling ceased. In that respect it was like our Sundays. Mama wouldn't put up with noise and rowdiness of any kind on the Sabbath. Dad wasn't that concerned with our Sunday activity but he acquiesced, never stepping in to disagree when Mama told us to be quiet and properly observe the Lord's Day.

Stove Wood And The Moon

We had a big old wood burning cook stove in the kitchen with a warming oven over the top, a reservoir for heating water next to the fire chamber, and a two-tier oven on the right where Mama baked biscuits from scratch three times a day.

To cook on the old "Majestic" stove, you put some kindling wood in the firebox, sprinkled a little kerosene over it, then filled the rest of the chamber with split pine wood before touching it with a country stick match.

Dad always said kerosene wouldn't burn much better than spring water and indeed it didn't explode when you put a match to it unless there were some lingering hot coals from the previous meal's fire. It would light with a bark when a white smoke curled up through the wood from some heat underneath, and at times blow the six metal eyes on the top of the stove right out of their holes.

The secret to getting a hot fire quick in such a cooking machine was the stove wood, as we called it. Stove wood was always from pines. It was sawed into logs with a crosscut saw, a man pulling on each end of a straight six foot, coarse tooth blade. It was hard work pulling a crosscut saw and it took hours for two grown men to fell a pine and saw it into sixteen inch blocks. Often, the tree would be cut into ten or twelve foot logs, snaked to the backyard by a mule, and then sawed into stove box length at a later date when some neighbor with a "wood saw" would call on each house and saw the logs with a circle saw either pulled by a belt to the wheel of an old T-model Ford or, on occasions, powered by a gasoline engine mounted on the "wood saw." It was a real time saver when compared with the old crosscut that pinched and stuck and brought a lot of profanity out of sawyers.

Stove wood couldn't be cut just any time you needed it. If

you cut it in some summer months, the bugs would get in the stumps and limbs of the downed trees, spread to the standing timber, and often destroy a whole forest of pines. You had to pick a fall season for cutting your winter's supply.

You couldn't do that just anytime during the month either. Mama insisted that the wood must be cut on light nights. It didn't mean you had to cut the trees in the night, but it had to be during the three or four days of the full moon. Her observations over the years convinced her that anytime wood was cut on dark phases of the moon, it would not dry out light and clean. It would turn blue and moldy and would hardly burn hot enough to bake bread. Whether Mom's idea had a valid scientific basis, I do not know. I do know that we did cut it and split it with an axe and stacked it in neat cords between backyard trees or posts -- and we felled the trees on the light nights. After all, Mama did the cooking and we didn't want to hear any excuses if the bread didn't rise.

In that era, flour mills for the first time began adding baking powder and other additives to the ground wheat to make it rise. Prior to that, all flour was "straight," nothing but flour, and you had to add the ingredients that made it rise. There was considerable controversy about the bad health effects of baking powder and some families wouldn't dare eat any baked products from "self-rising" flour. I suppose at today's point in time, we would have a lot of ink in the newspapers and words on the air about "self-rising flour believed to be a cause of cancer." Just about everything else is suspected today and something as novel as "self-rising flour" would have called for study and evaluation.

Hotdogs Were A Favorite

When we children were growing up at Endy, five miles west of Albemarle, we only went to town as a family two or three times a year. And we didn't speak of going "up" town or "down" town. We said going "to" town. I suppose the up and down were for people who already were in town.

Each fall before school opened, we went to town to get a pair of high back overalls and a denim shirt and maybe a pair of brogan, high top shoes, for Mitchell and me. Mom usually found a good washable dress for Betty. Overalls from J.C. Penney's cost about $3.95 and shoes were priced in the same bracket, and we got them from the G.C. Morton store. Betty's school dress was about the same price.

We didn't change clothes every school day, usually wearing the same overalls and shirt Sunday afternoon through Saturday. We wore our one and only Sunday pants on the church-going day and put on clean overalls Sunday afternoon that we wore until the next Sunday morning. We probably smelled all week but everyone else did too. We were no different from all the other kids. We never heard of deodorant.

I suppose we were poor but no one told us we were, and we had as much as most of the neighbors. It's funny how you can have only the bare necessities and be poor but not recognize your plight because the government didn't point us out as being in need. No government agency was around to label us poor and the neighbors didn't say we were, so we made the most of our poverty and enjoyed every day that we lived. I'm glad we didn't know any better.

The other times the family made it to town were just before Christmas and on Halloween night. Those were special occasions.

The first thing we did when we got to town, was run into the Goody Shop, a greasy spoon cafe that served the best hotdogs we ever tasted. We got six hotdogs for a quarter, two apiece for us kids and we couldn't have been better pampered if Dad had carried us to New York's Waldorf Astoria. It was a treat to remember.

Occasionally, we traveled to the Rowan Mills village in Salisbury where Mama's folks lived. Hotdogs made those visits something special too. Charles 5 & 10¢ store sold seven hotdogs for a dollar and piled a lot of slaw, chili and onions on them too. The family had a regular feast for a quarter.

All soft drinks then were a nickel and often we split these when we were eating hotdogs. But the meals were memorable. You never know how to appreciate an abundance of food. That appreciation comes when it is scarce and available infrequently. It has to be different from the usual daily fare. Then, even if it's just hotdogs, you savor every bite and remember the esctasy of the moment a generation later.

Dad's Goody Shop Friend

During the more than thirty years that Dad held a public job in Albemarle, he always left home on the five mile ride to town at least an hour before work time. His day was almost always the same. He parked in front of the Goody Shop, a hot dog - hamburger cafe, and drank coffee. He seldom ate breakfast. The main street eatery was long and narrow with only stools for seats along the counter.

The proprietor was Henry Morris, a legendary figure whose hotdogs and burgers were generally considered the best you could find anywhere. But Henry had another trait that made him the topic of many conversations and the brunt of jokes -- he was as scared of a mouse as the myths say elephants are.

Henry was short and fat and must have weighed at least 250 pounds but a tiny mouse, nevertheless, was his nemesis, a threat that he had feared from childhood.

One morning as Dad sat down on the bar stool for his coffee, Henry came running out of the kichen holding a handful of his pants just below the beltline and yelling.

"Raleigh, cut it off! cut it off"! he nodded toward the handhold he was squeezing so hard his knuckles were white.

"What you want to ruin your pants for"? Dad logically questioned.

"Cut it! Cut it! I've got a mouse. He ran up my britches leg!" Henry was begging in hysterical yells.

Dad took out his pocket knife and cut the chunk of pants Henry held. Henry opened his hand. A bloody little glob of fur dropped to the floor. White with shock, Henry looked at the six inch hole in his pants.

"I've got to go home," Henry said, as he left without even taking off his white apron. He didn't come back to the cafe for three days. He was so nervous from his encounter with the mouse that a doctor prescribed tranquilizers, and he never forgot that terrifying experience.

Dad kept on stopping for his morning coffee until about 1955. Henry decided to increase the price of coffee from five cents to ten cents. Dad never stopped there for coffee again. The price was too high, even though you got seconds and thirds for nothing.

Dad had predetermined ideas about what things were worth. When the pricing exceeded his expectation, he didn't buy it.

The Day Dad Lost His Job

It was the height of the Depression. Jobs were scarce and those that were available paid wages so low that it was hard for a family to keep body and soul together. Dad was a mechanic at the Albemarle Ford car agency and had been in the repair business for years. Employers and employees were on edge in that period as work was not plentiful for the mechanics and dealerships were closing all over the country because they couldn't make enough sales to show a profit.

Dad came home gloomy one Friday afternoon in the summer and we were sitting around in the shade of an old chinaberry tree in the backyard, waiting for him to come so we could eat supper. We always waited for that evening meal until the whole family was present.

"I guess I have something to tell all of you. Today was my last one at Auten-Wolfe Motor Company. I quit this afternoon. I just couldn't take all the abuse they kept pouring on me. I know we need the money but it isn't worth it when you are being yelled at all the time," Dad said with more than normal chagrin.

"Anyhow, there may be some of their buddies that will keep on working but I can't. You have to be a Democrat, Presbyterian and a son-of-a-birth to work for them and I'm not either one of those," he said, and you knew his sense of humor had not vanished.

He found another auto mechanic job at a smaller garage nearby and continued to keep food on the table.

My Working Mother...
Made Me Learn To Cook

When I was about thirteen years old, Mama went to work on the night shift in an Albemarle textile mill. She had worked there as a child but not since she married. She wanted us children to have more clothes and things than Dad was able to provide even when he worked hard to support us. I'm sure he never really wanted her to work but he realized the need for more income in the family. I suppose we were poor but strangely, we didn't know it.

The thing that is amazing today about Mama working is that she continued to do all the hard work of the household, then put in eight hours at night from 4:00 in the afternoon until midnight. Every summer of her life when we were growing up she canned from 400 to 700 quarts of string beans, beets, cukes, corn, tomatoes, kraut, pumpkins, among many other crops that she grew in the garden and worked with a hoe. In addition to all that cooking, she quilted in the winter months, looked after the chickens, hogs, cows, etc. No woman anywhere ever worked harder than she did when her family was growing up. While doing all these things to provide food, remember she still had beds to make, floors to scrub, clothes to wash and meals to cook. She never had any maid service. What little help she got was from her three offspring and I'm afraid we didn't do as much as we should have.

When she went to work, I had to learn a little bit about cooking, being the oldest child. She would often leave food cooked that needed only to be warmed when Dad came in from work and we ate supper. And it was supper. We had dinner at noon, and I didn't know the word lunch until I was grown. Just about every night I cooked the staple vegetables. That meant warming jars of beans, peeling and boiling potatoes, or maybe warming up kraut, corn or canned tomatoes for soup. I knew how to dress rabbits, squirrels and quail and often I cooked these in a skillet or made a kind of stew out of them that we ate with saltine crackers, butter and milk. I could also bake cornbread and in a pinch, made biscuits. They were made from scratch. There were no canned biscuits.

On rare occasions, I even boiled an old hen and made dumplings, still one of my favorite meals. I could, of course, fry fish. I had never heard of a filleted fish nor had anyone else at Endy. The fish we caught were about the size of three fingers and anyone who would have tried to separate that meat from the bone with a knife was crazy. All our fish were fried whole after scaling, deheading and gutting. Nothing has ever tasted better.

Maybe I didn't mind learning to cook, even though men and boys looked upon that chore as women's work, because Dad often cooked on Sunday morning. It was something he looked forward to and so did the rest of us. He often fried king mackerel steaks for breakfast or sometimes salt mullet that had been soaked overnight to get some of the salt out. Then there were times when we had country fried steak for Sunday breakfast or ground beef patties and fried chicken too. Ground beef was ten cents a pound or less. We grew our own chickens.

I think maybe Dad's work in the kitchen on Sunday morning resulted from his feeling sorry for Mama having to work in the mill and still do so many things around the house. And it was always a struggle to get dressed for church. It was a tiny bit of relief for her. And she needed it. I never knew anyone then or since who worked harder than she did. Nor have I ever known anyone who was any better Christian mother. If she ever did anything wrong, I don't know what it was. The Scriptures say that there are none of us who are good. But I believe she was, certainly relative to the rest of us in the world. I now appreciate her more than ever and what she taught me about cooking has been a blessing.

Dad liked to joke with kids that visited him and often talked about toasting ice cream. That always raised an eyebrow or two and with a look of seriousness, he often said, "Yeah, ice cream is sure good when you toast it up real brown on both -sides."

'Possum Hunting and Dogs

Dad was never much of a hunter but from growing up in the country with an older brother who hunted, he learned to climb trees like a lumberjack. After he was married and had moved to the Endy Community in Stanly County, some of the neighbors learned that he was a good tree climber. It was in an era when no country people had spiked climbing equipment like telephone and electric company pole climbers use to scale the poles that hold their lines. Tree climbers had to make it up the trunks of trees by clamping their knees and feet tightly around the trunk and then using their hands to pull upward. Good climbers could shinny up limbless trees almost like monkeys.

When you hunted opposums, you used dogs at night to tree or bay the animal. Dogs usually picked up the trails around persimmon trees in the fall. Persimmons are a delicacy that 'possums love, and a dog or two close on the track of one of these slow, ugly creatures soon chased the scavenger up a tree. That's when a lonely bark lets the hunter know the 'possum is "treed."

Once you have the 'possum in a tree and the eyes sparkle diamonds back at your flashlight, some one has to climb the tree, shake the critter off a limb and the hunter on the ground grabs him by the tail, stuffs him in a tow sack, and you then sling the creature over your shoulder until you return home at the end of the hunt.

People ate opossums in that era but not before penning the animal up for a couple of weeks to get the carrion out of its system. Opossums will eat almost anything dead or alive that they can get their teeth into and down their throats. Most hunters didn't want to put a 'possum on the dinner table until he had been in a trap and fed wholesome cooked sweet potatoes and milk for a week or two. This supposedly made the 'possums clean and healthy. It was always more white fat than lean meat but it was before the time of cholesterol and no one abstained from eating 'possum for health reasons.

Some just didn't like it but most Carolina outdoorsmen were ready to eat 'possum whenever it was served.

There was a great deal of pride in 'possum dogs in those days. Just about every hunter thought he had the best dog in the neighborhood and was quick to tell of his dog's experience on the 'possum trails whenever there was a bull session at any of the country stores, known far and wide as "liar's corners."

The Endy hunter who perhaps had the best opinion of his dog of any that Dad ever talked about said his beagle was such a good 'possum tracker that he had to put a bandaid over one side of his nostrils before going into the woods because if he didn't, the beagle would trail two 'possums at the same time. That was some tracker!

'Possum hunting in the deep woods at night when there was no moon was a good way to get lost. Dad often laughed at an experience one fall evening when he was hunting with the next door neighbor, Cephus Blalock. Dad did the climbing and Blalock caught the 'possums when Dad shook the limb and they hit the ground. He caught them with his hands and the help of several snarling hounds.

One night they had been talking and catching 'possums for several hours when they decided to head back home. But alas! They couldn't determine which way home was. They walked awhile, in circles, and finally came out in a clearing where there was a crop of unharvested corn. Blalock looked at the corn and at Dad.

"I don't know where we are. I thought this would be my field but my corn rows run the other direction," Blalock said.

Dad grinned. It was Blalock's field but when you are lost, the rows do run the wrong direction, as does every landmark.

One of the thrills of 'possum hunting is treeing and catching a really big one, not a kitten 'possum as the young ones are called. And perhaps the uncertainty of what size creature you have up the tree when the dogs stop trailing and start baying is what makes it thrilling. You are anxious to see what you have in the flashlight beam. It might even be a house cat the dogs put up a tree by mistake. The uncertainty of what you have cornered and caught is what makes it thrilling. And that may be a lesson of life. We strive for goals and have hopes of success. When we have the end in sight, the thrill comes from the unknown and only when everything is revealed in its entirety are we certain of success or failure. Like fishing, the thrill begins when the cork goes down. We experience the full adventure when the line tightens, the fish breaks the surface, and we know what species we have hooked and how large it is. If we knew exactly what size and what species took the cork under, much of the enjoyment would be lost. The unknown that eventually is revealed gives meaning to our experience and to life itself.

Like the 'possum hunters, many people have a hard time finding their way. They appear lost all their lives. It doesn't make any difference what road you are on if you don't care where you are going.

A Smoker --
Dad Resented Advisors

All of his adult life, Dad smoked cigarettes and he resented anyone trying to convince him it was detrimental to his health. He must have smoked several million during his life and while he coughed and wheezed for years, he died quickly in an automobile wreck. Cigarettes didn't kill him.

He was not sure that nicotine from cigarettes ever killed anyone and he often told the story about the one man that he was sure died from cigarettes.

"A man was visiting in Durham, N.C. when he stepped out on the street and a big cigarette truck ran over him. He was smashed in the asphalt. That's the only man that I know for sure was definitely killed because of cigarettes," Dad said.

Mom made a point of telling Dad how expensive it was to smoke cigarettes even though in his time they cost only ten and fifteen cents a pack. He was a Camel smoker and they cost fifteen cents during most of Dad's life. Other brands like Avalon, Twenty Grand, Wings, among others, were only a dime.

When Mom got to passing out statistics on how much money Dad wasted buying cigarettes, he rebuked that economy lecture by telling the story about two men who were walking along Times Square in New York. One was a chain smoker and the other had quit smoking some years back. Those who have smoked and who have quit are the great proponents of non-smoking, they always want to convert others.

The two men walked briskly down the street and the smoker was puffing away on his fag. The teetotaller looked at him and said: "John, how many cigarettes do you smoke a day?

"I smoke about three packs," was the answer.

"How much do they cost a pack?" was another question.

"About fifteen cents a pack," he replied.

"And how many years have you smoked three packs a day?" the non-smoker asked.

"About forty years, I think," he answered.

"John, do you realize that if you had saved all the money you have spent for cigarettes and put it in the bank with compounded interest, you could own one of those buildings you see over there?" the non-smoker made his point.

John looked at his companion. He took another puff and succinctly made his point.

"Which one of those buildings do you own?"

Dad was not an alcohol drinker. I never saw him drinking in my life but Mama remembers an occasion when he did drink something. It was when I was a tiny baby. Dad came home one night and sat down in the middle of the den floor to take off his shoes. He was having trouble getting them off. Mama knew something was wrong and she reprimanded him sharply for his condition. As far as I know, he never drank any liquor again. He was a good father and husband, a good provider who worked hard and loved us all.

But he did make some home brew during the Depression and bottled it. He placed the bottles in the pantry and a few nights later he awoke thinking the place was being attacked. The home brew hadn't finished fermenting and when it did in the bottle, it blew off the tops all over the place and sounded like a string of firecrackers had been ignited. Dad helped clean up the mess and didn't try his hand at distilling any more booze.

The Curse of Seasickness

One fall weekend Dad and Mom took off from Endy and came to visit with us in Tabor City. He had talked about wanting to go deep sea fishing, so we scheduled a trip on a charter boat out of Little River. It was a big 60 foot boat and there must have been nearly 100 people aboard, all excited and anxious to start hauling in the black bass off the bottom when the boat idled and baits were dropped over the side some 20 miles out in the Atlantic.

No sooner had the first swell rocked the boat than Dad felt the terrible nausea of seasickness. He didn't bother to let his hook down the first time. He just went below deck and crawled into one of the bunk beds that were stacked three high just to accomodate those with this affliction. He got sicker and sicker and a weak voice from the bunk above him meekly said, "Sir, you better be careful. I'm awful sick and I might vomit on you."

Dad half heartedly glanced above and saw a lady with her head leaning over the side of the bunk and it was obvious whatever she had inside her stomach was coming out soon.

"Don't make no difference, lady. You just go right ahead and throw up. I'm not going to live to make it back in anyway," Dad said, with the kind of attitude you almost always have after being seasick for a few hours.

Later that day when he no longer had anything in his stomach, Dad decided to come back on deck and maybe have some fun with the rest of the fishermen who were pulling in a lot of fish.

"I think I'll drink one of them Nehi orange drinks," he said, and I handed him one that was dripping cold water when I pulled it out of the open barrel that had several crates of soft drinks iced down for the passengers. Dad took a long swallow on the orange pop and almost like it was automatic, he vomited again spewing it right over the railing.

"My God," he said, "it didn't even change colors."

We had some fine neighbors in the Endy community and among them were Glenn and Lee Efird, brothers who lived within sight of our house. These Efird brothers were good farmers and provided for their families well by working hard almost all of their lives. They hunted some in the winter and fished a little in the local rivers, but, like Dad, they had heard a lot about the good fishing in the ocean and wanted to try it. It was a good 150 miles to the coast and with cars and roads what they were back in the 1930's, you didn't make the long trip many times. But they decided upon a date one fall and scheduled a bottom fishing adventure with a charter boat out of Little River, S.C.

They left home about midnight and were at the Little River dock at dawn and ready to go. Dozens and dozens of other people began arriving, and by the time the boat was ready to leave at 8:00 a.m. there was a deck full of laughing, talking fishermen anxious to start pulling in the black bass from the Atlantic's bottom.

The captain collected his $5.00 fee from each of the would-be anglers, cranked his old gasoline engine and the boat headed through the inlet and out into the ocean. It was less than a mile from the shore when Lee suddenly turned almost purple and rushed to the rail. The up and down motion of the boat in the swell was making him deathly sick. With a handkerchief over his mouth, he staggered to the captain at the helm and said:

"Captain, turn this boat around and carry me back to the dock. I've been looking forward to this trip a long time but I can't make it," Lee pleaded.

"Sorry, fellow, I can't do that. All these good people have paid me to come out here and fish just like you did. If I carried you back, we might miss the high tide and I wouldn't be able to get past the sand bar and out to sea again. We won't be going back in until the tide changes about 4:00 this afternoon," the captain responded.

"I can't stand it out here that long. I'll pay you for the trip. Just carry me back now," Lee really pleaded now.

"I'm sorry, Mr. Efird, but it is impossible. You'll have to stay on out here until we complete the day's fishing and head back in," the captain tried to be sympathetic.

"Lee's seasickness grew worse than ever. He was now visualizing how sick he was going to be for the next seven or eight hours out here and he was desperate. He wasn't a cussing man but he just couldn't stay out here all day.

"Listen, captain, dammit, I have got to go in right now. I have a few hundred dollars here that I'll give you but if that isn't enough, I'll give you my whole farm, house, car and everything I own. Just get me back to the shore," Lee made a desperate offer to the captain that makes sense for all of us who ever suffered acute seasickness and couldn't do anything about it.

The captain just laughed and shook his head. Lee finally made it through the day flat of his back in a bunk bed. He didn't catch the first fish after all those months of planning, hoping, and anticipation. It was an experience that he didn't want to remember, but he had lived through it without giving his good farm and home away. But when you really have the seasickness bad, nothing seems quite as important at the moment as getting off the boat with your feet on the good earth and feeling like you might live again, something that seemed doubtful while you were bouncing around in the swells.

I suffered from seasickness week after week while I was in the Navy during World War II and our ship was in the North Atlantic where storm winds often blew waves completely over the 400 foot assault craft (AKA) where I served as assistant navigator. Cooking was often impossible and we lived many days on cheese and apples. Despite the diet, seasickness gnawed at my insides day after day. It made me remember the plight of Lee Efird on that fishing trip. I, too, would have given everything I owned to be off that ship and back on the dry land of Endy again.

Dad liked to eat oysters, stewed, fried or any other way but for some reason he didn't think shrimp was a gourmet food, at least not for him.

"I never ate those little crawfish but one time and that was a mistake. I was on that boat deep sea fishing and before I got sick the captain came around with a big platter of pretty brown French fried potatoes. At least, that's what it looked like and I ate a few of them before someone told me it was fried shrimp," Dad told later. "I didn't eat any more."

123

It's strange how some foods are frowned upon by people who declare their dislike for them until they eat some by mistake. Most of the time after that, they admit the food is O.K. But that is not always the case. Once we had the Virgil Treece family at our house for homemade ice cream. We all enjoyed that delicacy and after the feast was over, Mrs. Treece was bragging on it being the best ice cream she had ever eaten. She asked Mama for the recipe for mixing this homemade delight. Mama proceeded to tell her she put six quarts of milk, three cups of sugar, a couple of tablespoons of vanilla flavor and three eggs.

Mrs. Treece was writing it all down until she heard about the eggs. She stopped and said they had to go home. Later we found that they didn't eat eggs and after learning of that ingredient in the ice cream, they were nauseated and really sick on their stomachs.

"I don't think they would have gotten sick if Waulena hadn't mentioned the eggs," Dad said many times when telling the story.

A lot of ailments are in people's minds.

Hog Killing Time

Each winter we killed one or more hogs that provided ham, sausage, lard and other protein during the cold months. It was a kind of festive occasion for all but the hogs that were the featured attraction.

Pigs about six weeks old were bought in early summer and fed table scraps and dish water, called "slop," along with what corn we had available and sometimes slop from an Albemarle cafe that Dad brought home. By the time Christmas came around, the pigs had grown to hogs and usually weighed in excess of 200 pounds. You had to kill and dress this meat when the temperature dropped to around freezing and stayed that way for several days after the slaughter. The fresh meat was always covered with salt but even that would not preserve the pork if the weather turned warm and wet. We lost our pork supply several winters when the weather was inclement. That was a real tragedy.

There were no commercial slaughterhouses in the area we lived in and hog killing day was a community affair. Dad would ask a neighbor or two to help and they would show up about daylight after we had a roaring fire under a couple of old cast iron washpots in the yard. Mama used these pots to heat water for washing clothes but they served a dual purpose on hog killing day. Once the water was really boiling, the men went to the hog pen with a .22 rifle, long bladed butcher knife and often an axe. These were the tools necessary for killing the big animals.

In that this portion of the event occurred before the school bell rang, I asked Dad one winter if I could shoot one of the hogs. He knew that I could hit a squirrel's head in the top of a seventy foot tree nine out of ten times, and he saw no reason why I couldn't put a long rifle bullet in the brain of a hog at four or five feet. He gave me the little rifle and I nervously aimed at a spot on the hog's head just above his eyes. The hog usually was given an ear of corn or something so he would be still while the marksman did his job.

I pulled the trigger at the same instant the hog decided to look up. The bullet missed the brain by inches and tore into the animal's nose and on into its throat. Needless to report, the hog began squealing and running around and around. It was very much alive and so much so that even the men couldn't get the hog stopped long enough to put a bullet in the fatal area. This went on for several minutes, and I was getting sick on the stomach. I had caused this unnecessary chaos and it was not a good feeling for a thirteen year old. Eventually, the hog paused long enough for another shot to blast into its brain. Dad jumped into the pig lot with the knife and stuck the hog in the throat deep enough that the blade ripped the animal's heart. It kicked its life out and the blood spurted all over the place as it was being pumped out. I was relieved that the animal was dead.

While I had made a blunder that caused this disaster, it happened often with the most professional of the neighborhood hog shooters. Sometimes an old hog would have a bony noggin so thick that the rifle bullet only made the porker grunt a time or two and it would keep right on eating, even after four or five shots. When this happened, the axe came into play. A strong man would pound the hog over the head a time or two, stunning the hog long enough for one of the men to stick the butcher knife into the animal's heart. It was a messy business but so is an abattoir today where animals are knocked unconscious with a mechanical hammer and killed by a sticking that lets them bleed to death. It's survival of the fittest and the domestic hog is not one of the fittest. They are destined for short lives.

Once the hog was killed and had stopped kicking, the slaughter crew cut slits behind the big tendon in each of the back feet that made it easy to slip a strong metal hook through that was attached to a one horse singletree. This gave the men something to take hold of and drag the dead porker near the boiling wash pots. Sometimes they used a mule to drag the hog to the pots.

Gallons of hot water went into a fifty-five gallon steel drum, the animal was hoisted off the ground with a block and tackle attached to a tree limb, and then lowered into the steaming water. The carcass stayed submerged a few minutes until the most astute of the slaughtering crew commanded that the hog be raised so he could test the hair to see if it was ready to be scraped off easily. Ususally, it took two or three dousings and then all able bodied men began scraping the hair off the hog with sharp knives. You can't skin a hog like you would a cow, deer, rabbit or squirrel. You have to get the hair off the hide and leave the skin on the animal, as you do an opposum. Sometimes they shoveled a few gallons of wood ashes into the hot water when the hair didn't want to come off easily. This reportedly helped loosen the hair for the scrapers.

When the hog is free of all hair and hangs white and wet from the tree, he is ripped open and the intestines removed. But these are not all waste. Mama picked out several of the long, slimy small intestines, squeezed the still undigested food from them, turned them wrongside out, and then after a lot of scraping, washing and cleaning, she used these skins for storing the pork sausage that was ground from small pieces of meat trimmed from the hams, shoulders, middlings, etc.

Other portions of the hog were made into liver pudding, souse meat and lard. The lard was rendered by cooking the scraps in the already hot wash pots. The meat would eventually dry up, leaving only the cracklins that were dried and cooked with cornbread. Some of the unedible fat was cooked with Red Devil lye to make homemade soap for clothes washing. It was as hard as a baseball and smelled like a barnyard, but when portions were scraped off into boiling water, it made suds and was often the only soap Mama had for cleaning our dirty overalls and shirts. I don't believe you could have washed your face with it and maintained a desirable complexion. The lye might have eaten right through the skin. I know in later years, we used this lye in a bottle with a few spoonfuls of water to make a gas that would make balloons rise out of sight. We just stretched the balloon over the top of the bottle with the bubbling air and gas would fill it quickly. It was a country boy's helium.

One of the attractions of hog killing day was the dinner and supper that followed. Always we had tenderloin, fried a golden brown after being sliced about a quarter of an inch thick. While it is a fact that this tenderloin is the same meat that you eat in pork chops, I never ate a pork chop that was as tasty as a piece of hot tenderloin that was free of all bones and fat and half burned. This delicacy grows along each side of the hog's backbone and is stripped out by the cutter. It can be nearly two feet long and as big around as your upper arm. Sliced and fried, I have never tasted a better piece of meat. Often at supper time or just before bedtime, we would put a few slices of tenderloin on some red coals in the fireplace and let it simmer a few minutes. That was a mouthful to remember and not even scarce candy approached this tidbit for real eating pleasure.

Neighbors who helped on hog killing day seldom asked for pay, but Mama always filled up a bag with the new sausage that smelled like sage, tenderloin slices and maybe a few inches of the side meat that commercial slaughterhouses made into bacon. I never heard the word "bacon" until I was grown. We cut the middlings into fatback and fried it with eggs for breakfast on occasions, but generally Mama used it for seasoning beans, collards, cabbage and other garden vegetables.

Today we would hear a lot about cholesterol if we ate all this pork and by-products. And perhaps people died from the grease of those hogs. You had to die from something and it was better to eat, live and die from clogged arteries than to starve for food. In that era, no one ever heard of cholesterol. And while what you don't know may hurt you, the options seemed mighty clear.

A neighbor by the name of Torrence Almond was a big hog raiser at Endy and his son Keith was my very best friend from the first grade through high school. We were two of the four boys in our 1939 graduating class. Cronies that we were, we visited each other frequently and one day when I was helping him and his father feed a pen of hogs, Mr. Almond picked up a runty little Poland China black pig that had been abandoned by an old sow and trampled on by other bigger pigs in the lot.

"Horace, you want this little pig?" he asked. "It's going to die if it doesn't get some special attention."

"Sure, I'd like to have it and I'll take care of it," I said.

He handed me the feeble little pig, and I headed for home in a brisk trot. I burst through the back door and showed my pig to Mama.

"It looks mighty sick to me. Probably die in a few days but if you want to nurse it, give it a try," Mama agreed.

I started feeding that helpless little pig with a medicine dropper. It would go crazy over the cow's milk that I trickled into its mouth, and I was pleased a few days later when I put it on the scales to see it had grown four ounces from the one pound and twelve ounces it weighed when I brought it home. In a week or two, it was lapping up milk by itself from a saucer on the ground and it began following me around like a puppy, squealing every breath for more milk. It had learned quickly that a few squeals gets its reward. It was like a squeaking wheel that gets the grease while the quiet one goes unattended. It took no rooting and hunting for this little critter to get something to eat. He had a welfare dinner free that required no work and because of the compassion for the pig, I seldom let him squeal long before I went after food to keep him quiet.

It wasn't long before the pig was too large to let run loose. He would root up Mama's flowers and break into the garden for some meals meant for the human family. I tried to build a pen that would hold him, but as Dad often said, "Anyone who can build a hog pen that will hold a pig, is a talented carpenter. That ought to be a test for carpenters applying for jobs. They should be told to build a pen that will hold a hog and if they succeed, hire them. They know their business."

The pig ate and grew all through the winter and because he was my personal pet, he was allowed to survive through the summer and on into his second cold weather. One day in January Dad gently asked me what I wanted to do with the hog. He pointed out that I couldn't just feed him forever and the animal had already lived many months beyond the life expectancy of hogs. He was ready for hog killing day. Tearfully, I consented and hurried off to school the next morning when the wash pots were rolling with white foamy, boiling water. I didn't come home until after 3:00 in the afternoon. The tenderloin was still on the stove. Sausage hung from racks in the smokehouse and huge hams and shoulders were covered with salt on an old homemade table.

"Horace, make you a tenderloin biscuit with the meat that's on the stove. I know you must be hungry," Mama beckoned as I walked around looking over the results of the day's slaughter.

I wasn't hungry and never wanted any pork until there was a new hog killing day the next year. Somehow I had lost my taste for tenderloin and all pork. I wasn't even thrilled at my hog raising success when Mama told me the hog was a giant that weighed 512 pounds. It all started with tender, loving care and a medicine dropper filled with milk that was relished by a sickly piglet that was bruised and battered and weighed less than two pounds.

It's remarkable how life sometimes is so cruel and survival appears hopeless only to be overcome and eventually reaches heights far above those blessed with opportunity and easy living. Struggle makes us grow stronger and better. Nothing worthwhile is ever free. You pay one way or another for advancement but once within your grasp, you have the capacity for appreciation. While it may be truthfully recounted that man seeks throughout his lifetime for an untenable something called happiness that is always just beyond his grasp, and he never quite catches up with it, you come closest to happiness when you struggle for every gain and recognize success when you have defeated adversity. As a high wire tight rope walker has so aptly said, "the only time that really counts is that you spend on the wire."

Dad's Tire Order To Spiegel

Few people had any money and unemployment swept the country in 1930. Herbert Hoover was president and took the brunt of the jokes and criticism about the "Great Depression" that was world wide. He still does! It was in this critical time period that Dad needed tires for his car. He had to drive about a dozen miles a day to work and tires were crucial to our survival. But he had no money, and the white thread of tire fabric showed along the bald face of all four of his tires on the Model A Ford. He knew he ran a risk of blowing out a tire any day when they were bald headed, tires then not made to endure nearly as many miles on the road as they are now.

Despite the Depression, a mail order house in Chicago, Spiegel's, continued to promote easy credit with a catalog so thick that it would last for months in our outhouse toilet where it was not considered reading material. The thin, easy to wrinkle yet tough book paper was a good subsitute for the rolls that were hard to buy when groceries were scarce. All the out of date seasonal books had a place in the outhouse. The Spiegel catalog was not as long-lasting as the Sears, Roebuck, but it held second place in the outhouse, first place in our living room wishing place.

Dad became more and more concerned about his slick tires as they wore thinner and thinner. With hot weather coming, he knew tires must be bought soon. But he couldn't do anything about the predicament. He didn't have the $16.00 needed to purchase four new A-Model tires. Then while visiting the outhouse one Sunday morning, he discovered the easy credit terms of Spiegel. Right on the front page it said "no money down, easy monthly payments, shipment made in seven days and all tires fully guaranteed." That was just what he needed and he came back to the house ready to place his order.

It took some tedious labor for him to fill out the order form in the back of the catalog. After all, three months of school in a one room building with 60 other students of various ages and skills, wasn't the best way to learn how to read and write and get an education. It particularly was not conducive to learning when you were barefooted, cold, and never had the money to buy books, walked miles both directions to get to school, and had a teacher who never studied past the seventh grade. That applied to Dad's education. After hours of printing with a lead pencil that he wet in his mouth after every few words, Dad signed his W.R. Carter at the bottom of the sheet, put it in a pre-addressed, stamped envelope and carried it to the rural mail box so it would be picked up around noon on Monday. He was in better spirits that afternoon as it appeared a serious problem had been solved. Alas! There were complications. Maybe Spiegel's credit was not just what the doctor ordered after all.

It was ten days after he mailed the tire order when he got a reply from Spiegel, not the four tires. The credit department needed a few questions answered, the form letter read. Would he be kind enough to answer a few simple questions and return the questionnaire so his tires could be shipped promptly?

Dad's difficulty in writing at all made his first impulse after opening the big manila clasp envelope to throw it away and give up on the easy terms for tires advertisement. But he hadn't been able to make any deal in town and Spiegel might be his last resort. He could be grounded any day now if a tire blew out.

"I decided to look at the questions and see if I could fill in the answers. I could appreciate the fact that they needed to know a few things before shipping, and when I saw the first line wanted to know my name and the second one my address, I conceded that those were answers they obviously needed. I filled in my name and the Rt. 4, Albemarle, North Carolina address. It was before the time of zip codes.

"I didn't see any sense at all in the third question. It was 'Are you married?' Senseless or not, I didn't want to skip any questions and I wrote 'Yes, I'm married but my wife doesn't even have a license. She can't drive a car or fix a tire. The tires are for me,' " Dad wrote.

"The next question was even less appropriate than the one about being married. It wanted to know if I had any children. Well, maybe they had some reason for asking it, so I wrote,

'Yes, I have three children but they wear shoes. They don't need any tires.'

"Then came the silliest question I ever saw. 'Do you have any money in the bank?' Of course, I didn't have any money in the bank. If I did, I wouldn't be buying tires on a credit, I told them.

"But strange questions continued on a long sheet of paper that was printed on both sides. It wanted to know if I had a refrigerator. I told them as simply as I could that we did have a refrigerator on order that we would get as soon as the light company ran the electricity to our house, but I didn't want the tires if they had to be taken off and stored in a refrigerator. I wanted tires to go on my car.

"Then it asked if I had a job and how far did I have to drive to get to the job. Of course, I had a job, that's why I needed the tires. And the distance to town and back I drove each day was the next question. How could they have any need for that question, I wondered. But I wrote 'Yes, I have a job. Been working since I was seven years old. I drive to it about five miles each way every day. It's too far to walk. If your tires won't stand that much driving, I don't want them anyway.' " he penciled in the spaces.

"It was getting sillier all the time. Did I have a telephone, they asked. I told them the truth again. No, I didn't have a telephone. I ordered the tires by mail and not by phone and there was no reason why they should have to call me. I placed the order in good faith and filled out all the spaces in that catalog order blank. They didn't have to call me now or ever.

"Then they left a whole lot of spaces with the next questions where they asked if I could give them some references. Sure, I could give them some references. I referred them to the Yadkin Hospital that I owed a lot of money from my wife's kidney surgery and the loss of our baby. I told them about the Gulf Service Station that I owed a couple of month's gas bill that I couldn't pay. Other than that, I gave them the name of my preacher, but he didn't know a thing about ordering tires. Then I thought about giving them the names of my neighbors but I didn't particularly want them to know that I was buying Speigel tires on a credit. I just skipped that question and looked on. There were dozens of other questions with big spaces for my answers. I couldn't go on with this mess. I just wrote in the space 'I'm tired of answering questions. Just send the tires or go to hell,' " Dad said.

A week and a day later, in came the tires by parcel post. There was a first class letter attached to the packing slip. It read: "Thank you, Mr. Carter, for answering our questionnaire. Our whole office force got a lot of belly laughs from your unique answers. We appreciate your effort. We have shipped the tires and henceforth you are listed among our very best customers. Thank you and order as often as you like," the letter read.

The questionnaire answers were typical of Dad's keen sense of humor. Today I can't help but wonder what he would have to say if he got as many pieces of mail as I do that jump out with big bold type, "Mr. Carter, you have just won $10,000,000. Just open this envelope and see what you must do next." Dad would have searched the envelope for the check and, it not being inside, he would probably have written the sender and told him his check must have fallen out of the mail before it reached his box. Please send it in the next mail.

How Long Has Man Lived On The Earth?

Dad was often irritated with the scientists of the world who released their research studies indicating that man had lived on the earth for tens of thousands of years. He thought he could read into the Biblical record that God created man only about 6,000 years ago. He believed that there was a 2,000 year span after Adam and Eve were created before the days of Moses and that there was then another 2,000 years from Moses' time until the birth of Christ. Then the last 2,000 years of man's existence was from Christ's birth until today, a total of 6,000.

"That just adds up to about 6,000 years and that's all the time people have lived in the world," Dad often argued.

He would have really shaken his head with a recent announcement by scientists that they had located bones and manmade arrow heads that were at least 92,000 years old.

My argument with him about this 6,000 year belief was that these students of anthropology must be right. Science can calculate accurately when a sun and moon eclipse will occur hundreds of years in advance and they always hit it right on the minute. They predict comet sightings that occur only once or twice in a century that are millions of light years away and they appear right on time. Any scholars who are that smart must also be knowledgeable enough to analyze bones and objects and determine how long they have existed. But Dad never went for that rationale.

He didn't have much belief in evolution either although it seems to have been accepted by the majority of scholars everywhere during Dad's life. He did often question where Adam and Eve found spouses and when some one said, "from the land of Nod" then he wanted to know how people got there if Adam and Eve were the first to be created. Like a lot of the Bible, there are some dead ends for which there is no documented answer.

A few times after the advent of television, he was influenced toward a belief in evolution when he spotted some huge athletes with slanted foreheads, flat noses, and protruding teeth and lips that honestly did make them look like apes with clothes on.

"That fellow is sure a good argument for the evolution believers," he often said in all seriousness. But he never really accepted that theory as fact and had a lot to say about it when it was first taught in the schools. He thought that was absolutely asinine.

Then when the atheists got the courts to declare it illegal to say a prayer in a public school, he just threw up his hands. He couldn't believe it.

"That's the end of democracy. The whole country was started by Pilgrim people who believed in God and now the schools that taxpayers finance can't even let children say the Lord's prayer! He couldn't believe that the country's ideals had reached such a low level during his generation.

―――――

We lived in the outdoors so much that we wanted to move the outdoors indoors.

Jennings Blalock's Dare Devilry

Jennings Blalock was a couple of years older than I and his family was our nearest neighbors. A robust physical specimen who was not very good academically, Jennings had as much determination as anyone you will ever know. If you dared him to throw a rock 300 yards, he would throw until his arm ached and almost fell limp at his side before giving up. When he played centerfield on the local sand lot baseball team, he would strain every muscle trying to get the ball to home plate on a fly when the distance was obviously prohibitive.

Once when the temperature was way below freezing and there was six inches of snow on the ground, a hunting companion dared him to jump in a fish pond that was coated with ice and swim across it with his clothes on. The dare grew bigger when Jennings was offered a dollar to swim the pond. With no further ado, he put down his shotgun, jumped in head first and swam across the pond, collecting his dollar and then building a fire to dry his clothes on the pond bank.

Jennings was a sadist who apparently enjoyed seeing animals suffer. I watched him squeeze the life out of tiny hoot owls that strayed away from the nests. And he killed baby birds just for the hell of it. He had no qualms about destroying unwanted kittens and puppies, while most of us shied away from killing the little critters even when they were useless and surplus. Even mules and cows provoked his anger quickly, and he often retaliated when he was mad with some vicious licks. In that respect, he was much like Dad who had little or no patience with ornery farm animals that didn't obey.

The one thing that Jennings was scared of was a snake, any snake, big, little, poisonous or non-poisonous. He just didn't want to have anything to do with them. Like many people then and now. There was fear of snakes that dates back to Adam and Eve.

One summer day, he and a Whitley boy were grabbling for catfish in the holes along the bank of Little Bear Creek. They would pull catfish and turtles out of those hiding places and carry them home for the dinner table. Every now and then a snake would flush from the bushes and grass along the shoreline and Jennings would scramble out of its way. Whitley was not afraid of the snakes nor the devil himself for that matter. And he knew how frightened Jennings was of these reptiles. Whitley also knew that Jennings just wouldn't turn down any dare. He considered a challenge as paramount to his masculinity and it made him a sissy if he refused to accept.

"Jennings, I'll bite off the next snake's head that I see with him alive if you will," Whitley said.

That was a pretty hard dare to consider. Jennings had that deathly fear of snakes.

"Naw, I don't believe I'll do that," Jennings said a little sheepishly, an attitude totally out of character.

"You're just yellow. I dare you to bite one's head off after I do," Whitley cajoled his fishing companion.

Jennings couldn't stand that kind of challenge.

"O.K. I'll do it, but you have to catch one and bite his head off first," Jennings said and he hoped Whitley would back down and stop this reckless adventure. But Whitley was serious. Minutes later he caught a little banded water snake, popped its head in his mouth and quickly bit off the head, tossing the remains of the squirming critter on the creek bank.

"It's your turn now, Jennings," Whitley laughed an evil kind of sound.

"Yeah, yeah, I'll do it," Jennings said but his heart wasn't in it. For half an hour he kept feeling along the bank for catfish and was happy no snake had appeared.

"Here's a snake, Jennings," Whitley said, as he grabbed another non-poisonous, wriggling snake off an over-hanging bush. "Take it and bite its head off."

"I don't believe I'll do it. That thing looks mean and I'm just not going to do it," Jennings said, backing away from Whitley and the squirming snake.

"The hell you're not! You already said you would if I would

and I've bit one's head off. Here take it," Whitley insisted and his face was turning livid with anger.

Jennings continued to stammer and back away.

"If you don't take this snake and bite its head off, I'm going to beat you to a pulp right here in this creek. Now get to it before I really get mad," he commanded.

Frightened and cautious, Jennings finally took the snake in his hand, gripped it a few inches behind its head and then almost like a machine, he jammed the snake's head in his mouth, then twisted the head off with his teeth. It was done and so was Jennings. He was shaking like the proverbial leaf in a summer gale. He crawled out on the bank, put his clothes on and headed for home. He was unusually quiet. That was the last time any one ever saw him socializing with Whitley. Their friendship ended that morning.

Dad had several run-ins with Jennings, the worst one over a dog fight. The Blalock's big dog had crossed over the meadow to our house and seriously wounded one of the dogs that ran loose at our house. Dad felt that the Blalock dog was far too big and strong to be attacking our smaller species, and he argued with Jennings about the fight that Jennings had apparently promoted. Jennings liked a dog or cat fight. They never were very good friends after that.

Despite Jennings' streak of meanness, I spent many an hour with him hunting, climbing trees, playing ball, flying kites, etc. One of our favorite treats was cooking a big fat hen in an old black pot over a wood fire in some remote corner of the farm on Saturday night. We added milk, butter, salt and pepper to the pot after the meat started dropping off the bone and ate this chicken stew with soda crackers. It was a cheap meal. We had the milk, butter and the chickens. Crackers were only ten cents a pound when you bought them loose from a big barrel in a country store and carried them home in a paper sack after they were weighed.

One night we were cooking out when Jennings' Dad decided to try to scare us by playing ghost. It was near Halloween and a good season for playing ghost games. He put a white sheet over his head, then started crawling down an old road toward our fire on all fours, groaning and moaning. Jennings looked up and saw the strange sight coming toward us. Without a minute of hesitation, he reached down, picked up an arm-size oak limb that was blazing in the fire. He threw that missile with uncanny accuracy and it slid right under the sheet that was covering Mr. Blalock. He came out of that four point stance instantly and narrowly escaped getting burned. The joke had turned and Jennings came out a winner. Many other times he didn't, and his Dad never spared the rod to try to break him of bad habits.

Despite our association and friendship over many years, Jennings still got some kind of sadistic pleasure out of trickery that often brought pain. He was more a man of the world than I was and being older, I pretty well took what he said as the fact. And when he told me to do something, I generally complied.

One day we were playing around the school yard that was in sight of both of our homes, when Jennings pulled out a .22 caliber rifle shell and stuck it in a tiny hole in a pine board that was rotting near the old school bus shed. He looked around and found a broken cast iron leg from one of the old classroom desks that had been abandoned. Now I had been shooting a rifle at squirrels and rabbits for several years and should have known better, but when he handed the iron desk leg to me and said "hit that cartridge with this piece of iron" I didn't act like I knew it could be dangerous. I smacked the cap of the shell with the desk leg and, of course, it exploded just as it would if the hammer on a rifle punctured it.

The next thing I knew, my right thumb felt like it was on fire. Blood was spurting everywhere. The copper shell casing had torn right into the thumb and cut it to the bone. The bullet went into the wood and did no damage. But the shell cut like a butcher knife. If it had hit me in the eyes, I'd be blind today. I grabbed my hand and ran home to Mama. But on the way I was thinking. If I tell her how I got this thumb hurt, she'll whip me for sure. Parents then, and perhaps now, whipped children for accidents almost without thinking. But I surmised that if I told her I fell and cut it on a nail, I wouldn't be as likely to get whipped as if I told her about hitting the rifle bullet. I held on to the bleeding hand and told her a tale about falling on a nail. She believed it. She took some tobacco from one of Dad's cigarettes, wet it and placed it on the cut for a few minutes. It quit bleeding and she tied it up with a piece of an old bed sheet. In time it got well, and she never knew about the real cause of the cut.

On another occasion, Jennings and I were daring each other to jump a three strand barbed wire pasture fence. He could do it better than I could. On one of my dashes to the fence for the jump, my feet went out from under me and I slid right into the sharpest barbs around. One tore through my overalls, cut into my thigh and left a seven inch cut that was nearly half an inch deep. I didn't dare tell Mama. That tear in my overalls and gash in my leg from such stupidity as trying to jump a fence would certainly warrant punishment. I managed to conceal the overall tear for several days and by the time I had to take a Saturday night bath in an old No. 2 tin tub with warm water from the kitchen stove reservoir, the cut had scabbed over and was on the way to healing. Mama gasped at the sight of that long cut, but it had happened so many days earlier that she waved the punishment and sewed up the overall tear. No one then bothered to get stitches or tetanus shots. It was too inconvenient and cost too much.

Jennings went off to war as I did early in the 1940's and he never returned. The word that came back to his family was that he drowned on an island in the South Pacific. It brought back memories of his swimming the fish pond on that cold day and I have often wondered if some cronies didn't dare him to swim one of those jungle lakes. But then with the grit that he had, who knows? He might have been going after a Japanese sniper on the other side who was shooting his American buddies. Either way, Jennings was a free spirit with a lot of courage, even though often it was misdirected.

Despite his faults, I liked him. His passing brought a few tears to my eyes.

Dad was not as afraid of snakes as a lot of people are and Mitchell and I often picked up the non-poisonous snakes and played with them for awhile before releasing them. Dad had an experience with a black runner that he often joked about, although it wasn't funny to the victim or the snake.

He was walking through a field and saw this six foot black snake easing along in the grass behind his companion. He picked the snake up by the tail and gave it a whiplash jerk much like you would a whip that people once used in buggies and wagons to sting horses into moving faster. The lower jaw of a snake is hinged so that it will release and allow snakes to swallow rats, birds, and fish many times larger than their mouths. The buggy whip jerk Dad put on that snake ripped the lower jaw from the snake's head and it hit his companion right beside the ear. The man went berserk. He had turned just in time to see Dad flip the jaw off and when it hit him, he thought surely he was snake bit. It wouldn't have been damaging even if it had been a rattlesnake, but the deathly fear many people have of snakes made the incident traumatic.

Fear is a terrible malady that millions of people suffer when an incident involving a snake occurs. One of Dad's friends who had a deathly fear of snakes, often said that when he saw a snake his impulse was to kill it but when he found a pole long enough to smash the snake, it was always so heavy that he couldn't lift it. He didn't want to get too close to the reptile with a short weapon.

Dr. John N. Hamlet, the great naturalist who captured the monkeys used to experiment with and perfect the polio vaccine, tells the story of a farmer who was walking through some high weeds in a pasture when he heard a noise like a rattlesnake and at the same time felt a prick in the calf of his leg. Hysterical from fright, he rushed home and yelled that he was snake bit and they rushed him to the hospital where he stayed for a week. But he hadn't been bit at all. A weed that grew in the pasture had a pod of seeds that when it dries out it rattles like a snake when it is disturbed. The farmer's leg brushed against the pod and it rattled just as the hard, sharp end of the pod slightly scratched his calf. He connected the prick with the rattle and surmised he was snake bit. Certainly, it proves that things are not always what they seem. Dr. Hamlet told me this story that I wrote in my first book, **"Land That I Love."**

Along that line I am reminded of the cotton farming experiences Dad had with his Grandfather Mason in Texas. He said in that era there was no water fit to drink in Terrell, Texas and what they did drink was caught in barrels when it ran off the house and barn during the infrequent rains. "And it had all kinds of little animals in it after it stayed in those barrels for a month or two," Dad recalled.

"One day I was plowing some long rows near a thicket and I heard water running. That stopped me and I started looking. It was unbelieveable but there was a tiny spring where the beautifully clear water bubbled up and trickled down a shallow ditch. That's what I had been wanting to find ever since I got to Texas. I plopped down on my belly and took a big swallow. It came out quickly and I had to spit and spit to get the taste out of my mouth. It tasted like pure sulphur or something worse and was terrible. I wished I had never found it," Dad remembers. Certainly, that was not what it had at first seemed to be.

While Jennings was older and bigger than I was, he often left our house after playing with Mitchell and me and went home crying, telling his Mama that we had hit him with a rock or otherwise mistreated him. I never understood that because he was stronger than either of us and could beat us up almost any time he wanted to. But I suspect that Mitchell and I came to the rescue of each other when one was being man handled. We often fought each other but were very protective when a third party was in the fight.

Dad got tired of hearing from Jennings' parents about how we were mistreating their son and one day when he was in our yard playing, his mother giving him two hours of leisure time before he had to return home, something our Mom always did with us when we went somewhere to play, Dad called him to the door before we started cowboys and Indians or whatever game we conjured up.

"Jennings, I'm going to be here while you are playing today. If any rock falls on your head, I'm going to see where it came from," Dad said and nothing happened to Jennings while Dad was around.

A cousin of Jennings', Eugene Morris, came to visit him a few days almost every summer when we were out of school and we played in our barn loft much of the time on rainy days. We rigged up what we called rubber guns that would shoot bands cut from tire innertubes. The trigger released the bands from clothes pins and that's how we played cops and robbers and other games where we shot each other with those makeshift and near harmless guns. A band in the eye wasn't exactly harmless but didn't hurt much unless we were shot at close range.

Eugene was trying to get away from one of us and running at full speed across the barn loft floor. A two by three foot hole was in the center of the barn where we forked down hay for the cows in the stables on the ground level. Eugene failed to see the hole and he went tumbling through it and head first into an old ice box that was in the feed room where cotton seed meal was stored for the milk cows. It could well have killed the city boy but it only broke his right arm in two places. He went screaming home to the Blalocks who carried him home to Albemarle. He never played rubber gun cops and robbers with us again.

Dad Made His Mark In Court

He never had any opportunity but Dad always said if he had been given a chance to go to school, he would have liked to be a lawyer. And he said the country needed some finished lawyers and doctors because all of them were simply "practicing" their profession. Some needed to be through practicing and get to work. Some had "practiced" for years.

Once when he was a mechanic, he was called to court as a witness when the car's owner sued an insurance company for damages he received when he was burned in the face by a car radiator that spurted hot water on him when it was cranked by some one else inside.

The defense attorney was pointing out to the jury that the man was not entitled to damages. Damages were granted only if he had been injured from an explosion. Then the prosecution put Dad on the stand and started asking him questions.

"How did this burn happen? How did the water suddenly boil over and spray hot water in this driver's face?" the lawyer asked.

"When the motor was not running, the hot water just boiled in the radiator and in the cooling chambers of the head on the motor. But when it was cranked, the cylinders exploded the gas in the block and it put pressure on the water system. That pressure from the explosion of the pistons in the block caused the water to gush out of the open radator and burn the plaintiff," Dad testified.

Needless to say, the burned man won his case. And Dad was so proud that he had had a part in establishing the cause.

Old John Had A Fit

Mules are hybrids and can not reproduce but the old mule that we had seemed to have ideas about sex and reproduction because he almost always walked about the pasture with his foot long manusculinity hanging out. That foolishness created a real circus one Sunday afternoon that Dad laughed about as long as he thought about it.

We were sitting around under a shade tree in the yard and John was strolling among some high weeds and bushes in the pasture around the old spring run in front of the house. There was a water hole there that the cows and John drank water from and it had grown up around the shoreline. John walked into those bushes and was almost out of sight for a few moments and then he burst out into the open at a full gallop and as Dad said, "He was blowing his horn with his tail lifted high and a lot of gas was filling the air behind him. He ran about a hundred yards, stopped suddenly, lay down and rolled over and over several times. Then up he jumped and headed back for the waist deep watering hole. He dived right in the water and it came up over his belly. He stood there blowing for several minutes and then dragged himself out of the pond like he was really relieved. Indeed he was. What we found out later when we went down to the spring run and looked around was that John had picked a terrible place to use the bathroom. There was a giant wasp nest there covered with mad, wet red wasps that had taken their anger out on John when he carelessly let his kidneys act right over their hat-size nest hanging in a gallberry bush.

Any need for sex was quickly erased and John didn't display his tool for days. He was afraid to, and with good reason.

The Tadpole Stew

Dad and several of the neighbors went seining one fall afternoon for catfish in Rocky River as they did occasionally, coming out late in the day, cooking up a big stew and having a feast before going home. Even with a long fifty foot drag seine, the crew was having difficulty catching enough catfish for the stew but they finally did. They cooked the cats, added the potatoes, tomatoes, corn, beans, onions, etc. and enjoyed the meal. There was about a half gallon of the stew left over and Torrence Almond carried it home with him. Near his house at Little Bear Creek was a country store operated by Tom Kelly and his wife Lisa Jane. Torrence stopped at the store and when Lisa Jane asked him about the day, he told about the catfishing trip and how much he enjoyed eating the catfish stew.

"By the way, we had some left over. It's in the car. Would you and Tom like to have it for supper?" Almond asked like any good neighbor would have in that era.

"Yes, if you don't need it. We would like to have it," Lis Jane said and Torrence went to the car and brought back that half gallon jar of catfish stew.

The following afternoon Dad stopped by the Kelly store as he came home from work. Lisa Jane was sitting at the counter and they passed greetings.

"We had a strange shindig yesterday." Dad began. "We went seining and couldn't catch any catfish. All we could catch was them great old big potbellied tadpoles about five inches long. We had worked so hard and were so hungry that we just put all them tadpoles in the stew and cooked it up. It ate pretty good too. It was the first tadpole stew I had ever eat," Dad said without so much as a grin.

Lisa Jane's mouth popped open and even the quiet Tom looked a little bewildered.

Was Torrence Almond at that cook out?" Lisa Jane inquired with some panic in her voice.

"Yea, he helped seine and make the stew. He thought it was pretty good and carried what we had left home with him. He had about a half gallon for today.

Lisa Jane had heard enough. She was nauseated. The stew had tasted a bit strange, come to think about it, but they had downed every spoonfull of it.

Dad got a loaf of bread and left. He never let on that Torrence had told him he had given the left over catfish stew to the Kellys when he ran into him in Albemarle earlier in the day.

Lisa Jane was sick on her stomach for a week.

Crazy Like A Fox

Game wardens early in this century were more or less disliked by the general public. The country was made up mostly of small landowners, family size farm operators, and it took awhile for many to understand that wildlife and fish were the responsibility of the State and the Federal government, not the property owner who often felt like the creatures on his land were his.

It always reminded Dad of the uneducated friend who lived off the land and the water along a river bank where he had built a squatter's shack and lived there all his life. He had no education, couldn't read or write and made his own rules. He was an expert fisherman and hunter. While he was void of any formal education, he was Phi Beta Kappa in the woods.

Game wardens were aware of this woodsman and while it was distasteful, they were determined to enforce the game laws on him and others alike. The man would simply have to buy a license if he was going to hunt and fish. But despite their best effort, the old codger could never be caught hunting and fishing. He seemed to always know where they were.

One fall afternoon the warden watched the man go into the woods with a gun on his shoulder and at last he figured he had him nailed. He followed at a safe distance and before long he heard a shot. He raced toward the noise and found the hermit standing over a nice buck that was kicking its last life out.

"Well I have finally caught you hunting. You been getting away with this hunting without a license for a long time but this is it," the warden said confidently at last.

"Pick up that big deer and bring it back to my truck. I'll need it for evidence," the warden commanded.

"You take the deer. It's mighty hot to be lugging a big buck a half mile through these bushes. I'm not going to help you get me lawed and take my money," the old codger reasoned.

It was a long hard pull but the warden needed the deer for evidence and he swung the dead animal across his shoulders and headed for the fire lane where he had left his truck. The poacher followed a few steps behind, chagrin all over his face.

Tired and wet with sweat, the warden put the deer on the pickup's tailgate, wiped his brown and went to the cab to get his citation book.

"This deer you killed without a license is going to really cost you. You been hunting a long time and getting away without a license but I have finally nailed you," the game warden grinned.

The old hunter was fumbling through his billfold. He slowly unfolded a small piece of paper.

"You know I can't read. But I have this little old piece of paper that I got the other day at the courthouse when my sister came by and said I needed to get things straightened out. Is it any good?" the hunter asked sheepishly.

The warden dropped his pad. He looked at the crumpled paper. He couldn't believe it. This was a legal, up-to-date license.

"Oh, hell" he said in disgust, as the hunter smiled and picked up the deer, shouldered it and walked away.

It was a true story that Dad never got tired of telling. For some reason, stories that got the game wardens goats were enjoyed by almost everyone.

A Try At Eating A Hawk

Today almost all of us who love the outdoors like to see the red shouldered hawks and other raptors protected. They almost disappeared a couple of decades ago and with good reason. Farmers who had chickens that ran loose in the barnyard often saw the biddies swooped down upon by the hawks and the screeching chicks carried off to a nest where the predators made a meal out of the catch. Mad with the hawks for stealing the baby chicks, it was a common practice for all of us to run for the shotgun and shoot at every raptor that sailed within shooting distance. Hawks were the enemy. Many were killed by rural residents protecting their chickens, ducks and turkey flocks.

Not only were the hawks shot when they attempted to invade the farm yards, hunters believed it was proper, even a duty, to shoot every hawk they saw sunning in a tree along the roadside or in the deep woods during rabbit, squirrel and quail season. Mitchell and I shot many with a rifle when we slipped close enough to shoot them sitting on a limb and we killed many others that sailed over us at tree top level when we were hunting small game as we did from an early age until we left home at eighteen.

A hawk will not eat carrion. They are predators and live by capturing live food, primarily snakes, mice, rabbits, chipmunks, and gray squirrels in Stanly County. In that they eat cleaner food than the barnyard chicken, I decided that we should try to eat the next one that we killed. A few days later, I shot one and broke its wing. It came tumbling down and I jumped on it. Somehow I kept its claws out of my hands and arms, locked it in the garage and kept it alive for several weeks. Then I decided to shoot the hawk, dress it like a chicken and eat it.

I got the feathers off, the insides out and washed it clean. It looked like a real meal. Mom cut it up and we put it in a pot to boil. We boiled it and boiled it and boiled it. It never got tender. Finally, we tried to eat it but every bite was like a mouthful of rubber and the more you chewed it, the bigger it got. I never did get any meat chewed up enough to swallow it. After a lot of chewing, I had to spit it out. We certainly proved that a red-shouldered hawk is not made for gourmet eating.

Crows have always been plentiful just about everywhere and we shot a lot of those. There was a time when the county paid a 25 cent bounty for crow's heads and people shot them by the dozens and collected the bounty. Hawks, for a time, had a $1.00 county bounty and that wasn't revoked until late in the 1930's. Crow kills were promoted because the old black critters would pull up newly-sprouted corn and cause the farmer considerable loss at harvest time. It was not until many years later when wildlife agencies recommended that corn planters simply put out a few quarts of corn along the edge of the fields after they were finished planting so the crows could eat all they wanted from the dumped seed corn and not have to bother the row crops. It saved a lot of crows from being killed. Today most crows live off the dead animals killed on the highways.

I never knew anyone who tried to eat a crow. Its meat is as black as the dark side of the moon, like a guinea and people then didn't have much use for any meat that was dark. They looked for white or flesh-colored meat. The meat of a hawk is very much like that of a chicken, but in that hawks have to make a living by out-maneuvering another wild creature, it is muscular and the meat is tough as leather.

There were no wild guineas but even the barnyard variety can fly like a goose and they can outrun the best athlete when you try to catch one for the dinner table. While the meat is dark, guineas make pretty good stew and we often had several at home that ran wild. Once Mom told me to kill one for dinner. I chased an old male all over the place for hours without getting a hand on him. He eventually flew to the top of a tall pine and looked down at me with a smirk on his face as if to say "now see if you can get up here, you jerk." I couldn't get up the pine and I could not dislodge the guinea by throwing rocks at him. I went in the house and got Dad's old single, barrel, hammer shotgun. I put a shell in it, walked directly under the guinea, and pulled the trigger. The next few moments are hazy. I only remember that the guinea came tumbling down flapping, bleeding and dying. I too was bleeding profusely. Blood was all over my face, in my eyes, my hair and everywhere. I had carelessly set the gun stock on my shoulder and hadn't held it tight when I pulled the trigger. The kick or recoil jolted the gun off my shoulder and the hammer struck me just above my right eye. It cut an inch long gash right to the bone and I never saw such a wound bleed so much. I could have lost on eye from the silly mistake.

I picked up the dead guinea in one hand, left the gun on the ground and went to the house with my other hand clutching my bleeding forehead. Mom screamed when I opened the door. She was sure I had shot myself. In a way I had. It wasn't the shot in the shell that got me. It was the other end of that old gun. It was a lesson. I'd always hold that gun firmly against my shoulder when I shot it again. Mom pulled the cut shut with a strip of adhesive tape and it healed quickly. We never got any stitches even for deep cuts.

The old guinea didn't taste real good even though Mom made dumplings and cooked them with the high flying fowl, one of my favorite dishes. I kept thinking about that cut over my eye when I forked up another mouthful of the pastry. I had some sinful thoughts for that old reprobate guinea that had brought on such an embarrassing day for me.

The Christmas Scooters

Regardless of how scarce money was, Dad and Mama never wanted us to go through Christmas without getting something. The first thing that was bought was a variety of fruits, nuts and candies. These were a treat every year because we didn't have these goodies just any day of the year like folks have today. To have a supply of such delights around for a week or so made Christmas something special if we didn't find anything else under the tree on Christmas morning. Appreciation of things comes from not having them. Plenty breeds boredom, dissatisfaction and even selfishness.

In addition to the foods of Christmas, they managed to have Santa Claus bring us a toy or two. I can remember well the year when I told them I knew there was no Santa Claus. He didn't come down the chimney and indeed didn't exist at all.

"You have just spoiled your Christmas. It will never again mean as much to you as it has until now," Mama pointed out a reality. The fantasy made Christmas special. It was another year or so after that before Mitchell and Betty discovered the tragedy of Santa Claus' passing. I wish I never had learned the truth.

One year Mitchell and I got scooters. Folks today probably wouldn't want a scooter because its only power comes from the foot and leg you use to propel it. Many of today's toys have motors and propulsion that require little energy. But we loved those scooters and rode them for years. We thought it was fun because no one told us it was work.

There was one occasion in particular that I recall. Mama had us hauling leaves out of the yard to a pile some distance away near the woods where she burned them. To make play out of work, that always makes effort more fun, we set the tub full of leaves on the scooter and pushed it to the dump. Unloading the leaves, I put the tub back on the scooter, put one foot in and started legging it back to the house for another load. But halfway to the yard, there was a ditch and I dared to push that scooter into the little ravine while trying to keep my balance with the foot in the tub. I didn't balance very well. My peddling foot got tangled up and I couldn't get my other one out of the tub. The next thing I remember, Mama was standing over me with a cold wet rag in my face. I had toppled over, hit my head against the ground and was out for several minutes. It just goes to show that sometimes it's better to perform these chores the hard way and forget about making fun out of drudgery. The easy way isn't always easy.

Rich or poor, Christmas was a wonderful time at our house. We laughed in front of a blazing open fire. We ate our fruit and nuts for a whole week until they ran out. Played with a toy or two and filled our stomachs with chicken and dumplings or something equally as appetizing that Mama cooked special for Christmas. Perhaps the greatest fun of all was seeing the smiles and hearing the laughs from Mama and Dad who loved their children enough to make sacrifices so that they could feel the blessing of giving on the birthday of the Man we worshipped. Christmas is the greatest of American holidays.

Pony Bill and Our First Bicycle

When I was about twelve and Mitchell ten, we had a fit for a pony. We had the barn and pasture space but no money for such a luxury, but having heard Dad talk about his experience in Texas where he traveled everywhere on horseback, we were obsessed with the idea that we must have one of these little animals.

In desperation, Dad cashed in a small life insurance policy he had been paying on me almost since my birth. I think the policy had a death benefit of $250.00 and its cash value was $50.00 at the time. He cashed in the policy and bought us a heavier than normal Shetland pony from Jack Little, a horse and mule dealer who lived at what was then called Locust-Level, a crossroads town east of Charlotte. I believe he paid the full $50.00 for the pony named Bill but that included an old saddle and a one-pony wagon.

Jennings Blalock knew how to hitch up a pony and he went with us to Locust to get old Bill and drive the wagon back down Hwy. 27 some twenty miles or more to Endy. The ride was a joy except a hame string broke about half way home and the hames dropped back on the pony's back. Jennings had the foresight to retie the hames that fit into the collar around the pony's neck. I believe he took out a leather shoestring from a pair of brogans to patch up the hame string. Anyhow, we got home just before night and Mitchell, Betty and I were happy over the new member of the family. We didn't imagine the future problems this critter would cause.

We didn't realize then what a real pain in the neck a big pony can be for youngsters our ages. First, we were responsible for seeing that he was fed regularly. Often in the summer this meant tying him out with a rope to a stake and letting Bill graze on the plentiful wild grass and weeds. That might have been easy for some ponies, but Bill was as stubborn as a proverbial mule. You had trouble pulling him to a spot where you wanted to stake him out and a rope around a 900 pound pony with a 90 pound boy on the other end doesn't always win such a tug of war. Often Bill broke away and played cat and mouse with us for hours as we tried to regain control over him.

Once when I just happened to walk within his tethered range, and completely innocent of any harassment of Bill, he suddenly laid his ears back, gave me that mean look and dashed upon me. His teeth cut a three inch slash along my forehead at the hair line that bled profusely. Bill then went back to eating as if nothing happened. I ran to the house, held a rag to the wound for half an hour, then taped it shut with some bandaids. We never went to a doctor to get a cut sewed up. That was too costly and very little better than pulling the cut shut with tape anyway. I still carry that scar on my head where Bill attacked me.

On another occasion, I was riding this mean devil a couple of miles up the Canton Church road to take a piano lesson. Just before I got to the Helms residence where I was going to tie him out for an hour while I tried to learn some music, Bill decided it was time to run. He galloped off at break neck speed right down a steep hill and I was bouncing forward with every jump. I couldn't hang on any more and fell on my face over his head in the dirt road. Bill immediately stepped right on my chest and for days I had a perfect imprint of Bill's hoof bruised in my chest. After acting a fool like that, Bill simply ran off a few yards and seemed to laugh at his prank. Usually, he wasn't too hard to catch and mount again.

But that pony dearly liked to get out of the pasture on moonlight nights. We would discover he was loose and knowing he would damage some of the local farmers' corn crops, we would put on some overalls and try to find him. Sometimes he would run at full speed up and down the highway, always taking off when we got to within a few yards of catching him. He just teased us hour after miserable hour.

Exasperated one night after chasing the playful pony for hours, Dad went in the house and came back with a shotgun. He put a load of No. 8 birdshot in the gun and when he got to within a 100 feet of the mischievous pony, he poured that load into Bill's fanny. Bill didn't know what had happened but he blew a hard puff of breath out his nose, jumped straight up a time or two and took off for the pasture. He was not known as a fence jumper, but that three strand barbed wire fence didn't bother him at all. He ran right through it getting back to where he was supposed to be. That time he stayed in the pasture for more than a month before breaking out again. He didn't like that lead in his tail. The punishment kept the bad out for awhile.

Bill was the only pony or other farm animal I ever knew that liked to eat live meat. We grew our own chickens by setting a couple of dozen eggs under an old hen for three weeks in the spring and summer. When the eggs hatched, the old mother hen would leave the nest and scratch for her brood for weeks until they reached a size that they could scratch wild food for themselves. We fed them a little grain but generally they earned their living by working. There was no welfare program for lazy chickens. But when a flock of these tiny biddies worked their way along the ground in the pasture, Bill thought this was a delightful change of diet. He would walk along and pick the biddies up in his mouth one by one until he either ate them all or the squalling mother hen succeeded in distracting him from his predation on her family. Sometimes the old hen was left with just one offspring and she would still take care of it, hovering over it to keep it warm at night, and scratching up worms and seeds in the daytime. She provided food and shelter, humble though it might be. The rooster that fathered the family never played any part in assisting the chicks and the old hen in making a living. The chicks were strictly a one parent family and depended entirely on their mother, as do many mothers of children today. Sometimes seeing an old hen laboring trying to scratch up food for a single surviving biddie, you felt a little sorry for her. She had to work for her loved ones. Yet, it is a mighty poor mother who can't scratch out a living for just one biddie.

Bill was often used in the summer pulling a cultivator or one horse plow in the garden. I tried to plow him many times when I was a young teenager and sometimes he was agreeable and cooperative. At other times, he insisted upon turning around in the middle of the row and tearing up the vegetables. I would holler and fuss at him but he wasn't afraid of me. Yet when Dad was around, you never saw a more disciplined work pony. Once when I was trying to plow the grass out of the middle of some rows, Bill was acting like he owned me and was tearing up the potato patch. Dad saw what Bill was doing from his store-garage a couple of hundred yards away. He picked up a four foot piece of timber, put it behind him and walked close to where I was trying to plow. Bill saw Dad about the time he stepped in the potato patch and as if by magic, Bill was the acme of good manners. He became an excellent work animal. He pulled the plow easily and quickly up and down the rows and didn't rebel at any "get up" or "whoa" command. He kept eyeing that timber Dad held behind him. Just for good measure and to teach him a lesson, Dad slapped Bill across the buttocks with the board a time or two before going back to work. Bill got the message. He didn't cause any more trouble pulling the plow for weeks. When he was tempted, he glanced toward the garage and decided against any more rebellion. Spare the rod and spoil the child certainly applied to our pony Bill. You always had to let him know who was the boss. He respected authority with a board in his hand.

Dad was the proudest man you ever saw when he hustled up the money to buy the pony for us. A wagon and harness came with the deal and that July 4th, we had the pony and wagon all decorated for the occasion and entered it in the big parade at Oakboro.

He was always happy that he could buy us gifts, like the pony or on Christmas. He couldn't ever remember receiving any kind of Christmas present from his parents and said he never had a toy in his life. That was sad but it made him that much happier when he could give us something on Christmas Day.

At about the same time we were learning to ride old Bill, we had a hankering for a bicycle. Neither of us had ever had one of these two wheel riding machines and some other children had them. Dad and Mom always wanted us to have as much as other children and while we were definitely poor, no one ever told us about it. As long as you don't know you are poor, you are happy. It's when you find out that you are poor that causes dissatisfaction and the family becomes a social community problem. Today's federal government continues to tell millions that they are poor, deserve assistance and should be unhappy. They are, and the welfare rolls grow and grow as they learn how desperate their situation is. You can't make it without charity once you learn how unhappy and desperately you are impoverished.

Virgil Treece was a neighbor who lived a couple of miles away down a dirt road toward Bear Creek. He was a kind of fixer of things and had rebuilt a lot of old worn out bikes. We heard he had some for sale. We went to see him late one afternoon and before the visit ended, Dad had given Virgil $5.00 for an old 28 inch wheel, boy's style bicycle. Neither Mitchell nor I had learned to ride a bike, but we practiced all the way back home in the dark. The thing I remember best happened in sight of our house when I was rolling downhill along the asphalt road and gaining speed every second. I didn't know how to use the brakes and when the bike got so fast that I feared for my life, I headed it straight into a six foot deep side ditch. The bike dropped in the hole, I made a swan dive into the bushes and by the time Dad and Mitchell caught up with me, I was scratched and bleeding from a dozen wounds. In time we learned to ride that old bike and Mitchell was one of the best trick bike riders in the Endy community.

But that first adventure could have been a fatal experience. I could have run right into an oncoming car but you have to remember that in those middle 1930's, even on a main highway like 27 between Albemarle and Charlotte, sometimes a car passed at night only once an hour or even less. They putt-putted along slowly with their four cylinder engines and deaths on the highway were infrequent. There was almost no speeding. Vehicles were not then designed for speed.

But motorcycles were faster and speedcops began appearing on the highways to monitor the traffic a few years later. Dad liked to tell about a situation with a speedcop who was trying to make a name for himself by passing out citations to speeding motorists. One of Dad's friends was a bachelor in Albemarle who was quite wealthy, named T.C. Rivers. The old reprobate started to Salisbury in the adjoining county of Rowan one summer afternoon and was moving up Highway 52 at a clip of about 35 miles per hour. A speedcop saw him and considered his speed dangerous. He revved up his motorcycle and pulled Rivers over.

"I'll have to give you a ticket. That will cost you $5.00 for speeding," the cop said as he wrote out a citation.

Rivers paid the officer, cranked his car and started on

towards Salisbury. Two miles up the road the same cop pulled him over again for speeding. Again Rivers paid him $5.00 but now he was a little riled, angry in fact.

"Officer, how far is it from here to Salisbury?" he asked.

"I guess it is about twenty miles," the motorcycle cop replied.

"Well, you figure out how many times you are going to catch me between here and Salisbury and let me pay it all at one time. I'm in a hurry and I expect to drive the rest of the way just like I have driven so far," Rivers said. I never did learn from Dad what the speedcop's reaction to that proposal was.

Dad Took Me To The Dentist

The first time I ever went to a dentist I must have been about twelve years old. A jaw tooth had decayed and had been hurting me at night, disrupting the household, and Dad carried me to a Dr. Polk in Albemarle. Dad had to do these kinds of chores because Mom didn't drive to begin with and we also never had two cars. Dad drove to work in the only one we had. Mom did eventually try to learn to drive, and I remember on her frist trip to town she backed into a chinaberry tree limb and knocked out a glass rear window at our Aunt Net's. That kept her out from under the wheel a long time. Matter of fact, I'm not sure she ever drove again.

Anyhow Dad carried me to the dentist to get the hurting tooth extracted. Pulling a tooth in that era cost $1.00 and because of that "high" price, most teeth I had lost up to that time were pulled with a pair of pliers at home or else with a string tied around the tooth, then to a door knob and the door slammed. Both methods worked pretty good but I remember well the night that Dad had a tooth bothering him and he went to the bathroom with the pliers to yank out his own aching molar like he had ours. He pulled the tooth and came back to bed only to discover he had pulled the wrong one. He went back and pulled the second one, took a swallow of rubbing alcohol and went back to bed.

But the afternoon that Dad carried me to Dr. Polk, I was as nervous as a pregnant fox in a forest fire. I had never been to a dentist before. I was scared of the unknown. I did remember that the worst whipping I ever got in my life was when I was a little tot and Dad carried me to a barber shop to get a hair cut. I had a fit and wouldn't sit in the barber chair. The clippers and scissors looked like weapons to me, and I was half scared to death of that barber and the tools he used. Dad beat the tar out of me and Mom was the maddest she ever was. She thought I shouldn't have been whipped for being scared. I whimpered and sobbed for hours after I went through the hair cutting ordeal and got back home. I must have been two or three years old at the time.

I sat down in the chair and Dr. Polk put a shot or two in my gums and began pulling on the tooth. It shattered and his pliers slipped off. My whole mouth hurt like crazy. He picked up a bright and shiny little crowbar and began prying the pieces of tooth out of my jaw. It took what seemed like hours, and he finally got all the tooth out. It had broken into nine pieces. I was hurting all over, scared and almost in shock when we left that office. Dad was mad, really mad.

"That guy's not even a good horse doctor," he said half to himself and half to me. He was really sympathizing with all the pain I went through that afternoon and he held me with one arm and drove the car with the other. The experience was traumatic and the fear of dentists stayed with me a long time. I did appreciate the sympathy Dad had for me that long afternoon.

One of the more prominent dentists we had in Albemarle was Dr. Fitzgerald. He was looked upon as being on the rough side with his patients, but he had a lot of business because of his rates. He charged 50 cents to pull a tooth and $1.00 to fill one. He filled several for me. His drill was operated with a foot pedal that he worked like a treadle sewing machine Mom had. It took a long time to drill out the decay and put in the filling. It was slow, noisy and the vibration was painful. Today's electronic miracle drills rout out the decay in a few seconds but it took the good Dr. Fitzgerald half an hour or more to get even a small cavity ready for filling. He saved a lot of teeth for a lot of people with his humble equipment and expertise.

The only other dentist I ever went to in Albemarle was Dr. Senter. I remember I liked him because he didn't hurt me at all when he pulled a baby tooth in front of my mouth. But he might have had trouble with the old rotten molar that Dr. Polk smashed and dug out with that little crowbar. That's what Dad called the instrument.

Dad's Duck Hunter Tale

This sounds like an ethnic joke but that's not the way Dad often told the story that he said he heard while working in the Newport News, Virginia, shipyard during World War I.

"There were these two helpers in my department where we were making the boilers for the battleship **Maryland** who had heard about the fantastic duck hunting on the Eastern Shore of Maryland. Neither of the fellows had ever been duck hunting and indeed were city boys totally unversed about any kind of wildlife sports.

"One summer Sunday afternoon they were talking and decided to drive over to a duck hunting inlet and make reservations for a morning adventure when the season opened. They saw a sign on the coastal road that indicated a duck hunting guide lived in an old weather beaten house close by and he provided blinds, the sign said. They went to the door and knocked. A gnarled old man came to the door, and they told him they wanted to go duck hunting when the season opened. They asked if he would schedule them for one of his blinds early that winter. The old man wrote down their reservation dates and the city dude shipyard workers drove back to Newport News.

"They talked about their trip frequently for several weeks and then on the morning the hunt was scheduled, they left home in the wee hours of the morning and drove to the duck outfitter's home. The old man came to the door and he was smiling. 'You fellows have picked a great day. It's cold as blazes. The wind is puffing at 30 miles an hour and it's raining. Those ducks will be coming in mighty low and you can sure get some today. Where's your dog?' he asked," Dad recounts the events.

"We ain't got no dog," one answered.

"You'll have to have a duck dog retriever when the birds are coming in fast and low like they will be this morning. I'll loan you my dog but you take good care of her," the duck hunter said. "She's old but a fine duck dog." Soon he had placed the two novice hunters in a tiny blind a few feet from the brackish water, bade them good luck and returned to his house just before daylight.

An hour passed, then two, and the guide didn't hear a shot although from his front porch vantage point he could see ducks flying all over the area where he had stationed his customers. He began to worry that perhaps in the cold they were in trouble. He bundled up and hurried off to the blind. Yards away from the stand, he was open mouthed with surprise. Both men had their coats off and were wet with sweat despite the freezing temperature. His old duck retriever was panting on the ground and resisting one of the dude's attempts to pick her up.

"What's the matter with you fellows? The ducks are flying in here all over the place and low. You ought to have a limit and you haven't got a single duck," he said glancing at their shotguns leaning against the outside of the blind.

"I'll tell you, mister," one of the dudes blurted, "You ain't got much of a duck retriever. We have thrown that dog up at them ducks everytime they have come over the blind and he ain't caught a one yet. I'm throwing him up one more time and if he fails again, we're going home. I'm give out."

At least, that's the way Dad often told the story.

Dad once was traveling with us to Florida for a few days of fishing. He began laughing when we stopped at a light in Starke, Fl.

"What's so funny?" I asked him.

"That sign over there," he said.

The sign read: THE BEST PLACE ON EARTH TO TAKE A LEAK---STARKE RADIATOR REPAIR.

No Holding Hands In Public

One Saturday night Dad drove us to town to do some shopping for school clothes. Mama and we three kids got back to the car in an hour or so and sat around waiting for Dad to return. There was a steady flow of people walking up and down the street.

A boy and girl about twenty came by, smiling and holding hands.

Mom looked at me on the back seat.

"Horace, you just look at that! I don't want to ever see you in public holding some girl's hand. I think that is just awful. It's disgusting," she said with conviction.

I have often wondered what she would think of the rock concerts, half dressed men and women at the beach and the pornography on television and the movies. For sure, she would have never consented for her offspring to take part in any such "awful" behavior. Times have surely changed!

Dad was always loaning a few dollars to the Negroes who worked in the garage in Albemarle with him. They were always broke on Monday after having been paid on Friday afternoon and they needed a little money to get through the week.

Dad couldn't understand why they were always out of money but he had compassion on everyone and while he had little to loan, he often let them have a few bucks.

"Why are you always broke on Monday?" Dad asked one of the blacks looking for a loan.

"Mr. Carter," the borrower started, then stopped and began scratching his kinky hair, "If you were ever a nigger on Saturday night, you'd never want to be white again."

Dad just grinned at that and let him have the money. Indeed, often the poorest people with practically no economic or social opportunity, seem to enjoy life the most. Unburdened with ambition and responsibility, their nonchalance breeds free spirit and a contentment often missed by the more sophisicated.

A Truly Intelligent Machine

Dad laughed at a story he often told about the short man who went to a drug store and put a quarter in a vending machine that was supposed to diagnose ailments by electronics when a sample of urine was placed in the machine. The man put the vial of urine in place and dropped his coin in the slot. Quickly the machine recording said, you are damaging your arthritis by stretching so high to put the money in this machine.

The man was a little astounded at the machine's observation. He wanted to test it the next day he came in with a Coke crate. He stood on the box, put the urine in the correct spot and slipped the quarter in the slot.

Again the machine analyzed the urine and a voice said, "You are still making your arthritis worse by stretching to put the money in this machine."

The man was upset. He concluded that this was the only message the vending machine relayed to its customers. He hit upon a plan to test its intelligence. That night he collected a sample of urine from his mare, another sample from his wife and a third one was his own like the previous two. He mixed all these in the same vial.

Early the next day he went to the drug store, put the mixed up urine into place and slipped his quarter in the slot. The machine whirred buzzed a few moments and then said, "Your mare has diabetes, your wife is pregnant and you are still stretching so that it is hurting your arthritis when you put the money in the slot."

Some Of The Pills We Take Better Go Down Whole, Not Melted In Your Mouth

The last few years of my father's life, he had considerable difficulty breathing. He probably had a bad allergy like I have, plus emphysema from a near lifetime of smoking, something I quit 21 years ago.

Anyhow, some doctor prescribed a tiny pill for him to take every day, and while he almost never knew just what any medicine was, he knew it sure did help his bronchial problem.

"But it is the worst pill I ever tasted. When I let it melt just a little bit in my mouth, it makes me think of a chicken house. That's why I call them my 'hen house pills,' " Dad said on many occasions.

Now I have gathered the hen eggs in chicken houses many times and I know the smell he is talking about. The nitrogen-filled black manure from chickens has an unbelievably bad odor and I don't want to be swallowing any medicine that tastes anywhere close to that smell.

But now I know what he was talking about. It must have been prednisone, that little five milligram tablet that helps you fight asthma and other breathing problems. It is taken in small quantities, about 5 mgs. a day, by all organ transplant patients. I have been taking it in large and small quantities for three or four years when my allergy gets so bad that breathing is difficult and coughing chronic. Several times I have been slow in swallowing one or two after taking a mouth full of water, and indeed it does have the taste of a dirty chicken house where the droppings have stacked up for several months. Dad was right in referring to them as his "hen house pills."

Dad was not one who had a great amount of faith in doctors and medicines and he was almost never known to take whatever prescription he had filled in the manner dictated by the physician and the drug store label.

I remember one summer afternoon when he came in from his mechanic's job in town and flopped down on the bed in great pain. He was subject to kidney stone formations and the resultant kidney colic that inflicts suffering of which there are few equals. Having endured this pain myself several times in later years, I can now respect his doubling up and groaning as great drops of sweat popped up on his face and ran down his forehead.

He pulled out a little box of white pills from his pocket. He had seen a doctor before coming home who had authorized these morphine tablets to relieve the pain and suggested he not take one until after he had parked his car. He shouldn't drive with the drug in his system. Now desperately hurting and safely in the house, and I'm still surprised that he didn't take one before he got home as he often would do in rebellion against any doctor's advice, he poured out the dozen or so pills in his hand and gulped them all down at once with a half glass of water.

I looked at the label. It plainly said to take one pill every four hours for pain as needed. But it was too late. The pills were in his stomach and within an hour he went to sleep. You could hear his deep breathing and snoring all over the house. He didn't wake up until the following afternoon, 24 hours later. We had worried throughout the day and night that he might never awake. We had no phone and he was the only driver in the family. We had called no doctor. But he did awake and the pain was gone. Apparently the stone had moved on down to the bladder and the cutting, terrifying pain was gone. He looked around with his rare smile.

Mom was quick to reprimand him for taking such a mammoth dose of a strong pain killer. "Raleigh Carter, you should be ashamed for scaring us to death," Mom cajoled him.

"The way I figured it, Waulena," he addressed her as he pulled on his pants and was ready to go back to work, "If one of those little pinhead size pills would do some good, a lot of them ought to do much more good." In that case it worked but that's not a recommendation for today's kidney stone victims. It was Dad's way.

Stones harassed him many times and some of the experiences he had in those early days when urologists apparently cared little for the patients' suffering, are classic tales of nonchalant procedure. I remember well a story he told when he returned from a series of cystoscopic kidney operations in Charlotte. In that era, urologists wouldn't put the patient to sleep for cystoscopic procedures. They performed the cutless surgery with the patient awake and often in great agony much of the time.

"Always they wanted me to be still. How in the hell can you stay still when someone is probing around a foot up your penis with a metal rod? The surgeon would say he had to keep me awake for fear he would do damage to my urethra or something up there if I was asleep and didn't flinch. I flinched all right and they cussed and fussed because I wouldn't be still.

"Then the final touch was their pure lack of compassion when they had finally got the stone in the basket, and I was dripping wet with perspiration from the hour I had endured the worst pain I had ever felt," Dad said, and he was not one with a low threshold of pain. He could stand it in most cases when most folks would have cried for relief.

"They picked up a leather punch and recklessly poked a hole in the skin of my penis, ran a hay baling wire through it and attached it to a plastic hose that they left in for a drain," Dad recounted. That was the most inhumane post surgery story I ever heard him tell and he capped it off by telling them, "You fellows ought to join some veterinary group. You work like a bunch of horse doctors."

Albemarle had a general practitioner in that era who was widely considered rather rough with his minor surgery and handling of patients. Dad knew him well but wanted no part of his doctoring. One day when he was in need of a doctor, he came home to sweat out his ailment.

"Did you go see a doctor?" Mama asked and hoped.

"I couldn't find one. All I could find was Dunlap so I just forgot about it," he said. "I wanted a doctor."

On one of his kidney stone experiences, Dad knew that the object causing so much pain had left his kidney and bladder and was actually hung inside his penis. He took the wire from a shipping tag in the garage where he worked, wrapped it around and around a few times, then proceeded to fish the stone out with the wire loop. Miraculously he got the stone and had no infection from it. Such a crude maneuver today by a physician would certainly bring on a malpractice suit quickly.

When Dad returned home from his cystoscopic operations for kidney stones in Charlotte, he was glad to be rid of the pain but critical of his doctors.

"They shot me so full of holes with the needles that they had to put bandaids over the punctures to keep the medicine from running out another hole," he said.

He was often full of humor when being critical of doctors. I recall a story he told about a man who went to the doctor because of acute constipation. The doctor sympathized and gave him a handful of suppository capsules.

"I think this will take care of the situation quickly," the doctor told the patient.

A week later the suffering patient was back in the doctor's office.

"Doc, I took everyone of those damn capsules and they didn't do me a bit more good than if I had stuck them up my hind end," the confused sufferer said.

He liked the story about the man who went to see a doctor and he prescribed croton oil for the man's lazy bowels. The patient took a couple of swallows of the stuff and walked out of the drug store confident but unaware of the fast action of the cathartic medicine. No sooner had he left the building when he felt a pain in his bowels. He grabbed his rear end and hung on all the time trying to hold his breath.

"What are you doing?" a passer-by asked.

"I'm just hanging on here for a few minutes. I'm afraid I'm going to sneeze," he said fearfully.

Once he had an old seed wart on his elbow that often got banged up and bled when he was working underneath a car or fixing a tractor's mechanical problem. He knocked the top off it one day and it was stinging and bleeding. He wiped his hands off a bit and walked a couple of blocks to the old Stanly General Hospital in the middle of Albemarle. He knew the doctors because my mother had been sick and required considerable medical attention time after time.

165

"I want to see Dr. Brunson," he told the receptionist. Brunson was a partner with Dr. Tally and was a surgeon.

Brunson soon came out and asked, "What can I do for you, Raleigh?"

"Doc, I want this wart taken off of my elbow. It's always getting hit and bleeding and stopping me from doing my work," and that's something Dad couldn't stand. He worked like a mule all his life and had no patience with anyone who didn't work.

"O.K., come on in the office," Brunson invited.

The surgeon picked up a knife from his arsenal, reached back for a sharp pin-like instrument, stuck the pin in the wart, pulled it up about half an inch and sawed the wart off with the dull knife. Blood spurted everywhere and Brunson picked up a bottle of some clear liquid, poured it on the cut and the blue smoke rose to the ceiling as it seared the freshly cut wound.

By this time, Dad was fuming mad and hurting.

"How much do I owe you, Doc?" Dad asked in his most controlled tone.

"I guess about $5.00," Brunson said.

Dad pulled out the five dollar bill and put it in Doc's hand as he turned to walk away, holding his arm with a little patch of gauze covering the wound. It was really stinging.

"Thank you, Doc. I'll not bother you with taking off any more warts. The next one I have, I'll do it myself. I'll just pull it up a mile with my pliers, saw it off with my hacksaw, and then turn my blow torch on the cut. That's about how you took this one off," Dad said as he left the smiling surgeon who knew how to take Dad's maligning.

Yet with all of his painful experiences with doctors, they eventually were responsible for a turning point in his life. It was in 1932 and Mom had been hospitalized with her fourth pregnancy while at the same time her kidneys were blocked with stones and infection. After a solid month in the hospital in Albemarle, the baby was born dead and Mom was critically ill. The doctors sent her home to die.

It was a tearful time at our house. Dad was trying to work to keep our bodies and souls together and the bills paid. Mom could barely turn over in the bed and we three children could do little more than milk the cows, bring in the stove wood, open some of the home canned vegetables at meal time and look around frightened at the dark shadows we were promised for the future.

Dad was losing weight and desperate. While he had been a church goer as long as I could remember in my 11 years, he had not been a member nor had he shown any desire to be. In the middle of a week he hunted up the pastor of the Canton Baptist Church that we attended in the rural community.

"Pastor, I want to be baptized. I want to join the church and be a better man. I'm taking my wife to Charlotte to the hospital tomorrow to see if they can help her. I want you to pray for her and for me. But right now I want to join the church. I'll feel better about her chances if I can tell her I am now a Christian. That's something she has been begging of me since she had a turn for the worse," Dad tearfully told the pastor and tears were not something that came often to his cold dark eyes. He was raised tough and remained tough all his life.

The pastor granted his wish, baptized him immediately and the following Sunday he was accepted into membership. He had packed Mom up in an old A-model Ford car by removing the seat on the passenger side and folding some quilts on the floor so she could lie down. He drove her 40 miles to Charlotte on Friday. By the time he became a full-fledged church member Sunday, Mom had been treated, the kidney blockage removed and the infection was subsiding. Five days later she was home and lived about four more decades, going back to public work for at least half that time to help make the financial ends meet.

Dad's conversion had resulted from her desperate condition and near fatal experience. Perhaps this was no divine healing. Who is to know? Suffice it to say that between making Mom happy with his sudden decision to join the church, and putting her weakened body in the hands of better physicians and more sophisticated facilities, a miraculous recovery resulted almost overnight. It had a lasting impact on our family.

It served another purpose too. I never heard Dad express much criticism of the medical profession after that. At least in that one instance, he saw some tangible results and some pain relieved that kept our family together for almost another generation.

Sneezing, Athlete's Foot And Eye Glasses

Dad was a sneezer all his life. He didn't just sneeze once or twice and wipe his nose and eyes. He often sneezed eight or ten times in quick succession when he started. Much of the year he had what people called a "summer cold" but in reality was an allergy, a word few people ever heard of early in the 20th century. He never stifled a sneeze, but let it all out, a house-shaking explosion.

Sneezing so many times irritated him, and he often fretted and fumed about his sneezing saying he had never sneezed less than fifteen times when he started. Most observers thought it was funny but he didn't and he kept right on until his death. Once when his nose was itching and he was on the eve of sneezing, Mama asked if he wanted to sneeze.

"I have never wanted to sneeze," he said.

He never went to a doctor with his allergy, accepting it as just one of the crosses he had to bear. Allergies are seldom cured by medicines or doctors anyway but Dad didn't give the medics any chance to practice on him.

"Doctors and lawyers sure use the right word when they say they 'are practicing medicine or practicing law.' That's just what they are doing. They practice on every client and patient that comes in but they charge you for practicing," he said. "Mechanics don't get paid for practicing."

Another of Dad's ailments was athlete's foot. He had it for years and while it never really got out of control, it itched and the way he handled the problem was amusing, often down right funny.

At night when his toes started itching a little, he said he would let it itch for awhile and then decide maybe he would scratch it just one little tiny bit. That's a mistake. He would scratch the itching place a time or two and suddenly he knew it had to be scratched some more, a whole lot more. He would end up with the bed sheet sawing it between his toes for awhile until he had the skin about worn off. You can't scratch athlete's foot just a little bit. He finally got to pouring Clorox on his toes and that relieved the itching.

"I don't want to ever get rid of my athlete's foot. When it itches and you start scratching it, that's the best feeling I ever have," he said. As one who has been inflicted with this same foot problem since a Navy tour of duty, he is right about it feeling good to scratch but I have no desire to keep it forever. Too much of even a good thing is too much.

Dad never went to an optometrist in his life, but he began wearing eyeglasses when he was about forty years old. He always bought his specs from Rose's 5 and 10 store in Albemarle. There the store had a whole counter filled with glasses of every size, lens power and color you can imagine. Dad just went to the counter and began trying on glasses until he finally picked up a pair that he could see through well enough to read. The glasses at one time sold for 25 cents. Later they went to a dollar and Dad felt that he was getting what he could see though at a bargain price. And he was.

"Why not get them at Rose's by trying on pair after pair? That's all an eye doctor does. He just keeps letting you look through one lens after another until you tell him which one you see through best. I can do that at Rose's for myself and it costs a lot less money," Dad reasoned and you had to admit he was not entirely wrong. It worked for him.

Once he came in grinning with a new pair of glasses. He said he looked through several dozen pairs and finally put some on that seemed to be better than any others. He was about ready to pay for them when he discovered there was no glass in them. He had just the frames. He put them back on the counter and kept looking until he came up with some that he could see through well enough to read a newspaper. He saved a lot of money over the years and could still see well enough to read when he was killed in an auto wreck when he was seventy-six.

While Dad bought his eye glasses at the 5 & 10 for a quarter, I had to have an examination and glasses when I was twelve. I had spent so much of my time reading Wild West Weeklies in poor light that I had strained my eyes. I couldn't refrain

169

from batting them constantly. A Dr. Forbes fitted me with my first glasses in Salisbury and the price for the exam and glasses was $18.00. The last pair I bought in 1987 cost me $250.00. Things have certainly changed.

My first glasses were rimless with screws holding the ear pieces in real glass. They broke easily and often.

I remember once when Chad Efird and I were working on the flooring of the old Boy Scout cabin, we were driving a nail together. He would hit a lick and I would hit a lick. We had the rhythm going pretty good but got out of kilter and both struck at the same time. The hammers collided and mine bounced off my face, breaking my glasses. That was always a sad time. I knew it would cost Dad a day or two of work to get them repaired.

T-Model Was Scrambled

When Henry Ford first designed the T-Model and it went on the market in a big way after World War I, there were few repair body shops for the rough old cars. While not many ran into each other, some did hit trees, turned over, and in various ways were damaged. Ford knew car owners had this trouble and Dad said the manufacturer advised dealerships that damaged cars could be shipped back to Detroit and the company would make the body repairs. Costs were minimal as the new vehicles sold for less than $500 and didn't increase much when the style changed to A-Model.

"One day this Model-T owner was driving through a community that had been struck by a tornado. The storm had lifted off the galvanized metal roof from a tobacco barn and rolled it up like an accordian. He had an idea. He shipped the mutilated roofing back to the Ford Motor Company and said it was his car that had been slightly damaged in a storm. Would they please repair it?

"About a month later he got a Ford back on the train with the message 'This was the worst wrecked car our company has ever tackled, but we have made the necessary repairs. Thank you for buying a Ford'."

At least that's the way Dad told the story.

Learning To Swim

We had no chemically treated, clean swimming pools to jump into and dog paddle our way to the other side. If we learned to swim, we had to do it in Little Bear Creek and most of the summer it was barely deep enough for even a kid to swim. Your arms touched the bottom when you paddled and only when you reached a deeper hole and your arms didn't reach the bottom, were you sure you had really learned to stay afloat. I learned that in the Old Cook Lake, downstream from Highway 27 a mile or two. The recent rains had brought the creek up a few inches and when we went swimming and flattened out to paddle, we found we could stay on top a few yards by kicking and paddling for all we were worth. It was years later when I learned you didn't have to work that hard. You could relax, get your shoulders, neck and more of your face in the water and you would be buoyed up more, could stay afloat easier. We didn't have bathing suits to show off. Our creek swimming was always in the nude. Women didn't go to the creek.

The men of the community made a deep hole in the creek on the Lee Efird property and rigged a rope swing from a limb. The innovation brought a lot of thrills to those who grasped the rope, swung out over the creek and dropped into the cool water from ten feet in the air. With the right kind of start, you could swing out over the thirty foot wide creek and come back to the bank without going swimming. Only when a well-dressed bystander tried it with his clothes on and found himself yelling for help over the deepest part of the creek, did it occur to him that it took a little expertise to get back to the hill. That gentleman had to let go and scrambled back ashore as wet as the proverbial drowned rat.

Most of the men of the community considered swimming easy and had little patience with the unskilled who couldn't stay afloat. When there were youngsters hanging around the Efird Lake who couldn't swim, the men would grab them, throw them out into the deep water and yell, "Now sink or swim." It was their theory that anybody could swim if he had to. It taught a few non-swimmers to kick and paddle back to safety but many times the men had to jump in and rescue their frightened victims who would have drowned had not help arrived.

Dad did not go to this swimming hole often. Sunday was a day of rest for him and he wasn't inclined to spend that day working, and swimming was work. Sunday was the day when most of the fun took place at the creek. The men there were generally farmers of the area looking for a little break from the field work.

But one Sunday Dad did go with us and he was paddling about in the creek. He could swim pretty well. I paddled over near him, gasping for breath as I had swum maybe a hundred feet or more. I stood up panting and looked at him. "Boy, I'm out of breath," I said.

"Out of breath? When I do a lot of work like that, I'm never out of breath. I have too much breath. I can't get it out fast enough," Dad said with a grin. I had never thought of that. But it does seem like the proper expression. You breathe fast and seem to have more than you can get rid of. It is kind of like dressing fish. When my four year old grandson Wesley Carter watched me dressing some bream and asked me what I was doing, I said I was dressing the fish.

"It looks to me more like you are undressing them," Wes said. And he was right.

The Case of the Bursting Gall Bladder

In the Palestine Community Dad grew up with a tall, gangling boy about his same age by the name of Leroy Ledbetter. Roy was a mischievous fellow who was always in trouble either with his family, the law, a neighbor's daughter or someone, and while I didn't learn much about what trouble Dad got in with him, he probably had his share of problems from that association. At least he said many times that he didn't believe today's teenagers were any meaner than they were during his adolescence, the newspaper just wrote about it more and the record keeping and statistics were better than in the previous generation.

One fall day they were picking cotton in the community and taking a rest for lunch in the shade of an old maple tree at one end of the cottonpatch. Roy put a sack of cotton under his head and went to sleep. Dad saw an opportunity to play a trick on his cohort that Roy would have enjoyed doing to someone else.

Roy's mouth was wide open as he sawed a lot of logs lying there on his back. Dad reached in his pocket and found a quinine capsule, a medicine used widely then to fight malaria. Quietly he sprinkled the quinine in Roy's wide open mouth and for several minutes the snoozing teenager didn't wake up. Then he turned over and with his eyes flashing he sat straight up, frightened and unsure.

"What's the matter, Roy?" Dad asked innocently from his seat on a log a couple of yards away.

"I don't know for sure but I believe my gall bladder has busted," Roy sputtered as he tried all kinds of spitting motions to get that horrible bitter taste out of his mouth. Dad was amused but conquered his impulse to burst out laughing. Roy never knew the truth about his gall bladder erupting.

On another occasion Dad, Roy and another teenager were resting under the same maple tree at the cotton patch during the lunch break when Roy conceived a devilish prank to play on the other youngster who was fast asleep, getting some rest from a tired back that really suffers when you hand pick cotton as they did in those days.

The sleeping youngster was wearing only overalls and Roy cautiously unbuttoned the fly on the front (it was before the day of zippers) and slipped the dead-to-the-world, tired cotton picker's penis out. He looped a piece of tobacco twine over the penis and tied the other end of the string to a rock a couple of yards away. He carefully stuffed the penis back inside the overalls.

After a few minutes to make sure the youngster was sound asleep, Leroy yelled "Fire! Fire!" and jumped up as if he was putting out a fire in the broomstraw that surrounded the tree on three sides.

The sleeper was instantly awake and on his feet, only to be cruelly yanked down with the crude lasso that connected him with the rock. Needless to say, he grabbed his crotch and anger flushed right to his hairline. Roy was laughing like a hyena and had a one hundred yard running start to the woods. The victim of the painful prank was more concerned with his pain and wounded penis than with revenge. That would come later. He headed home for some merthiolate and a bandage and neither he nor Leroy picked any more cotton that afternoon. Leroy later was beaten to a pulp by the youth whose dignity and penis suffered that day.

There was no permanent damage but the bruised and skinned penis was sore for a week. And the wounded cotton picker never forgot it.

"That fellow was really hurting. His ears were always bigger than most people's but after he got that horrible yank from the rock, they stood out so that they looked like a T-Model Ford with the back doors open," Dad said when he told of the incident many years later.

Wade Tucker -- A Comic Of Dad's Equal

A few country miles west of Endy where we lived, the Wade Tucker family farmed. Wade was never lost for words and Dad really liked him because both of them had a sense of humor that they displayed daily almost all of their lives.

After Franklin D. Roosevelt was elected President and was trying to pull the nation out of the depths of depression, some folks in our neck of the woods were so destitute that they went to grocery stores, picked up sacks of flour and carried them home without paying. They didn't have anything to pay with and they would steal rather than let their families go hungry.

As we did one or two nights every summer week, after supper we visited various neighbors of the community if they didn't visit us first. Phones came later. It was the first one that arrived stayed and we had no schedule that meant we had to visit somewhere and repay a visit. We just went because it was the neighborly thing to do and in that it was way before television and in the early pioneering radio era, visiting and conversation was the recreation we enjoyed. We just listened to each others' experiences and tales and had pleasant evenings, a lost art today.

One of those late afternoons, we went to the Tucker residence and Wade was sitting in the yard in an old homemade swing rocking back and forth under a white oak tree.

"Hi, Raleigh," he said as Dad got out of the car and the rest of us piled out behind him, anxious to play with the Tucker children, several of whom were our age.

"How's things going?" Dad asked Wade.

"Not so good, Raleigh," Wade said slowly. "We are having a hard time getting enough to eat here but I wrote the President about it and I got his reply today. Maybe it will help feed these children."

Dad grinned, suspecting he was going to have his leg pulled, something which Tucker was adept at. "Well, what did Roosevelt say?" Dad asked in his most serious tone.

"He said he respected the plight that small farmers were in and my problem specifically but there was an answer. He said the season was fast approaching when the blackberries would be ripe and we could eat those for a few weeks and then the muscadines in the woods would be coming in. I could take the kids in the woods and be able to live off the wild grapes another couple of weeks. Then, the President said the mollypops would be ripe in the corn fields and that would get us through until winter. Maybe by then he would have solved the country's economic problem," Wade related his imagined letter with all the seriousness of Santa Claus.

Dad just laughed and told us about the conversation after we got back home.

"Wade said every dollar he gets look as big as a wagon wheel but the President hoped to cut down the size to that of wheelbarrow wheels once he got a handle on what was causing the Depression," Dad recalled the final sentence of the Tucker revelations.

Tucker was always humorous about everything. I remember once when we were visiting at his house on a cold winter night when we were popping corn over an open fire and sitting around the room eating it by the handfuls. Popcorn was a treat.

"Raleigh, you hear about that fellow up the road who froze to death a couple of weeks ago?" Wade asked.

"No, I don't believe I did," Dad answered.

"Well he was walking past our back door the other night and looked down on the ground where I had dumped a popper full of corn that we didn't eat. He saw all that white stuff and thought it was snow. He froze to death right there on the spot," Wade said without any semblance of a grin.

That was typical Wade Tucker in the 1930's.

The Pocketbook Prank

When Dad was running the country store and garage in the fork of the road that went to Canton Church from Highway 27, some of the neighborhood kids hung around the place when we were not in school. We looked for something to do, and having heard of someone else kidding the travelers on the highway with the old lost pocketbook trick, we decided to have some fun doing it ourselves.

Someone brought a big ladies' pocketbook to the store and we tied a strong string to it, opened it a little and let some green play money extend out of it. Then we placed it carefully on the pavement just a foot from the grass shoulder of the road. We took the string down the road bank, and into a concrete culvert that ran under the road a hundred yards or so from Dad's store. It was about five feet high and kids had plenty of head room.

Holding the string in hand after we carefully placed the pocketbook, we listened for on-coming cars. Few motorists could resist the temptation to get something for nothing. They would see the half-open pocketbook on the side of the road and presumably visualize finding money that someone had unfortunately lost. Brakes would squeal and often we could hear the fast plopping of feet on the asphalt as someone ran from the car to the phony fortune in the road. We would be peeking out from the other side of the culvert, and when the excited motorist got to within a hundred feet or so of the pocketbook, we jerked the string, picked up the pocketbook under the culvert and high-tailed it for parts unknown through the dense honeysuckle jungle down the branch from the opposite end of the culvert.

We were called a lot of bad names and some motorists even threatened to get the sheriff and come back after us. Mostly they were embarrassed at having been hoodwinked by a couple of country pranksters.

I don't know why, but that was fun. I guess we got a kick out of seeing someone expecting to get a passel of dollars for nothing disappointed when he found he was the victim of his own greed.

Cottontail Hunting Yesteryear

In the 1920's in Piedmont North Carolina, there was very little wildlife management. It was a land of small landowners who had some quail, rabbits, and squirrels on their farms and they generally hunted them when they had the time and the need for meat. There were specified legal seasons for harvesting the wildlife but there was little law enforcement and most land owners considered it was the season to hunt any time he had the time.

Dad was fixing Fordson tractors all over the county in that era and he overtook a friendly farmer several miles out in the country on his way home one fall afternoon. The farmer was holding two cottontail rabbits in his hands and had his old single barrel shotgun across his shoulder. A car stopped alongside the hunter and the driver called the man with the rabbits to the window while Dad observed.

"John," the man greeted the hunter whom he obviously knew, "Where did you get those rabbits?"

"I got them up yonder in my new ground. They been setting around them brushpiles and I needed a couple for supper. I went up there with Old Boss, my redboned hound, and we shot us a couple," the hunter-farmer answered.

"But, John you can't do that. The rabbit season is closed now. Rabbits are still breeding and will for a couple of more months. I'm the game warden in this precinct and I'll have to give you a citation for shooting rabbits out of season," the warden said as he pulled a ticket book from his pocket.

"Now hold on there, Mr. Game Warden. I'm hunting on my own land," John said.

"That has nothing to do with it. You shot them out of season and that's against the law."

"That don't make no sense. I bought this land and paid for it. I own it. I pay the taxes to the county every year. I bought this gun and these shells and my old dog. They belong to me and the rabbits belong to me," John was getting a bit riled.

"Hold it! Hold it! Yeah, you own the land, you pay the taxes, that's your gun and those are your shells and your dog. But them rabbits belong to the State," the game warden pointed out a little known fact to the farmer. He was trying to be kind.

John was stymied for a moment and then he came up with the classic statement. "O.K. if them damn rabbits belong to the State, you get them off my land," John said and turned and walked away from the officer.

Dad witnessed the conversation and couldn't help but laugh. Just how was the State going to get those rabbits out from under all those brushpiles, off those hedge rows, creek banks, gallberry bush, woodland undergrowth and from the broom straw fields that covered acre after dense acre of John's land.

"I never did find out whether that game warden gave John a ticket or not. If he did, he had to catch him at home. He didn't give him any paper out there on the road," Dad recalled. "Maybe he just forgot about the citation while he mused over the problem of getting those trespassing rabbits off those farm lands."

A Seining Experience At Little Bear Creek

Dad taught us at an early age how to make a minnow seine out of old fertilizer tow bags or from the harder to get but larger mesh onion sacks. You rip the bag open, wire or thread a six foot limb from a popashe bush to each end, and you have a seine, even though no lead line bottom or bobber line on top made it differ from the more sophisticated, conventional drag seines used by the men of the community for carp and catfish.

We used the homemade seine to catch small edible sunperch (redbreast), suckers, stonetoters and other native species that were abundant in the nearby Little Bear Creek. Sometimes we caught a few sunperch as big as three fingers wide. That was a nice one. More often we caught tiny little fellows about two fingers wide. In either case, we carried them home, scraped off the scales, cut off the head, removed the inside and fried these little fish in a hot skillet, often on an open fire in the yard. I can tell you even after half a century has rushed by, that no seafood meal anywhere has ever been as tasty as those few bites we got from an assortment of minnow - size fish that we trapped from that clear, rocky creek, and it was those stretches of slick rocks that the water trickled over for years that brought catastrophe one hot summer day.

Chad Efird, a boyhood close friend and school vacation time daily companion, Mitchell and I had made a pretty good sack seine and were pulling it through some of the knee-deep eddy places in the creek near the Hawn farm, about a mile from our house. You get an idea of what size fish we were catching when I note that Mitchell was carrying a half gallon fruit jar. It was half full of water and we stashed our keeper minnows and sunfish in the glass jar. I'll never know why we were not using a metal bucket for our catch. Children often do not see danger until after disaster strikes. They may act prudently and make good decisions from obeying commands and suggestions from parents or other advisors but without direction, they make their own mistakes and gain from the experience. That's general. Some youngsters never learn and disaster follows them all the days of their lives.

But Chad, Mitchell and I learned that memorable day that a glass jar is a poor container for holding your fish when you are seining a rocky creek.

We had just dipped up a five or six ounce sunperch from under an over-hanging red maple bush. That was a whopper and we were jubilant as we poked it through the jar mouth. Three stark naked kids were all smiles as we admired our catch and then decided to make another dip under that same bush. The whopper perch might have some relatives hiding there. We plopped the seine back to the bottom and moved toward the shoreline bush. Alas! Mitchell moved toward us, clutching the jar with our catch success. His foot slipped on the greasy-slick, wet slate stones half submerged in the two feet of water. He fell on his face, the jar shattering under his midsection. He was on his feet instantly as Chad and I scrambled to catch the fluttering, flouncing fish that had escaped from the jagged half gallon broken jar. The fish were loose and lost. But it was moments after that when we looked up at the ashen face of Mitchell. He was scared and with reason. Blood was pouring down his right side and making the creek water red. An inch-long gash was spurting blood from his belly area. The first thing he thought of was the safety of home. Half crying, he scrambled up the creek bank, ignored his clothes lying on a log, and headed for the house at a gallop. He didn't stop even for breath when he ran through the Efird's yard with the red blood flowing, still naked but on a beeline to our house.

He was scared, out of breath, crying and hysterical when he dashed through the back door. The blood frightened Mom too, but she had the good judgement to lay Mitchell on the concrete porch floor, swab off the blood with a wet towel and press it to the wound long enough to halt the blood flow. A few minutes later, she took a look at the glass jar cut. A sharp jagged point had made a sizeable incision in Mitchell's side at about the same place an appendectomy operation would have. Fortunately, there was no detectable glass left in the wound and it had stopped short of his intestinal cavity. A couple of strips of Johnson's adhesive tape sealed the gash and a day or two later, Mitchell was ready to seine again. Once over his fright, he was back playing again and needed no medical attention or bed rest.

Chad and I had rolled up our humble seine, pulled on our overalls, picked up Mitchell's clothes and arrived home about the time Mama had stopped the bleeding. We listened to some stern advice about our seining operation and the use of glass containers but that was the end of the punishment. She wanted to know why we didn't stop Mitchell's cross country run in his birthday suit. No one could have caught him. When you are scared, your feet are light and you can outrun even the most fleet-afoot tracksters. Mitchell might have been close to the four minute mile up the pasture lane, by the Efird's barn and house and on across the woods to home. We might have run faster than he did normally but that day he was the champion. No clothes hampered his movement and he was hell-bent for Mom's loving care.

The Seven Year Itch

Residents of the Endy Community a half century ago and more did not consider it a disgrace to have the Seven Year Itch but it was a disgrace if you kept it. This irritating rash, caused by unhygenic care of the body, afflicted many school children in an era when there were few bathrooms and minimal facilities for proper bathing in the cold of winter. It was contagious and if one student had it, it often spread throughout the class and beyond to others, who made contact with the disease on buses, on the playground or the gymnasium. It was considered difficult to cure and thus its name "Seven Year Itch."

I remember one January morning when Mama told Dad to stop by a drug store before he came home from work and buy a half pound of sulphur. At the time, I had no idea what she wanted sulphur for. I found out that Friday night. Mama stripped us bare and pasted a coat of smelly sulphur and water all over us from foot to hair. It smelled awful and was uncomfortable, but we had to go to bed with the stuff on us and not take if off until the next afternoon. We followed the instructions.

At the time I didn't know we were afflicted with this despicable itch. I did know that I surely itched and only years later when I contracted athlete's foot in the Navy did I have something to compare with that childhood rash. Seven Year Itch doesn't just get between your toes, it is on your hands, legs, face, feet, chest, belly and everywhere else. It takes a lot of scratching to keep up with the itching.

It's easy to see how we came down with this itch. We had no inside bathroom. Even the toilet was a hundred yards from the house in the pine grove. Mama tried to keep us as clean as possible by making us take a bath whether we needed it or not each Saturday night. That was an ordeal. We had to squeeze into a No. 2 galvanized tin tub that she used outside for washing clothes by hand. In the cold weather, we got in this tub and she scrubbed us good with strong soap in front of an open fire. It was hard to heat enough water on the old wood stove for all of us to take a bath and Mama liked to change the water when each of us was washed. When the temperature dipped into the teens and snow was often on the ground, it was like punishment to take a bath at all. This lack of facilities probably led to our infestation with the itch bug, something that many other students suffered with in those ancient times. You could get rid of it, but those families who didn't bother to fight the itch until spring, passed it along to many others and thus the adage that it was a disgrace to keep it, not to catch it.

I can remember when we got that sulphur treatment that Mama and Dad insisted that we stay in the house until all trace of the plaster was washed away. They were embarrassed that we had the disease and they wanted it as hush-hush as possible. We weren't anxious to broadcast our dilemma either. But I don't see how we could have hidden it very well from the playmates we had because you had to be scratching somewhere virtually all the time.

By the time Sunday morning came and we had the sulphur washed off, we looked and smelled better and made it to Sunday School on time. We hadn't disgraced the family by "keeping" the Seven Year Itch.

My Sister Betty -- A Letter Writer

The member of our family in recent years who does the most to keep up with relations scattered about is my sister Betty. She and her husband, J.A. Herlocker, live at the old Endy home place. J.A. is retired from **The Charlotte Observer** but both he and Betty worked with **The Tribune** in Tabor City for years before they returned to Endy to stay with Mama after Dad was killed in a car wreck.

I do not believe there has ever been a human being with more compassion for others than Betty. For years she has spent the greater portion of every day doing some good turn for a sick person, needy individual or someone otherwise in need of attention. It's wonderful to have such a humanitarian sister, and if there is any reward for doing good in this world, Betty should win first prize.

Before Mama died, Betty wrote letters to various relatives for her and among those was J. William (Bill) Mason, a cousin of Dad's and a member of the family in Texas where Dad cotton farmed for a year. He was about the same age as Dad, and they socialized together the year he was in Texas. Mason later became a minister and pastored various Baptist churches in the southwest for years.

Each year Betty got a letter from the preacher around Christmas time. Written in poetic verses, it kind of rehashed the past year and wished better things for the coming months. The 1979 letter that Betty dug out of the chest of drawers follows. It has the sad commentary as a P.S. on the outside of the envelope that his wife Lillian died after he wrote the letter and before he mailed it. It said "A sad P.S.--Lillian went home to be with her Lord Sunday evening after a very brief illness." That letter was from Plainview, Texas.

CHRISTMAS 1979

CHRISTMAS time is approaching - that happy time of the year;
Soon we will be readying for company whom we expect to be here.

CHRISTMAS is the gladsome day - a time we anxiously await -
It is a time when hearts are gay - when CHRIST's coming we celebrate!

We want to forget the mundane things, and think of God's great gift;
We want to make our hearts to sing as praises to the Lord we lift!

Make this CHRISTMAS what it ought to be - a time we'll not soon forget -
A time when all are able to see many smiles and not so much of fret!

This year has been a busy one, and no money has been made,
Not much substutite teaching has come - our deposits really fade!

But what's the use of earning money when one can't keep it long?
We know it's not so very funny how short a time to us it can belong!

We both enjoy what health we have - our aches and pains are not so bad,
But Lillian's family is decreasing, and for this we are so very sad!

We've traveled to Batesville, La Pryor, and Utah - gone miles by car and plane,
Funerals for Lillian's Brother, Sister and Sister-in-law - lucky there was no rain!

A trip was made to the East Coast, we visited with loved ones and friends,
And relating all about the good times, we fear would never, never end!

Nacogdoches was something special, a great niece of Lillian's was wed on
    a rainy day!
Bill performed the ceremony - the wet weather - a great occasion we would say!

Another wedding closer home: Granddaughter Elizabeth and Rick Devereaux
    took their vows.
Granddad Bill performed the wedding rites - all were happier than the law allows!

Bill has had one funeral and three weddings - has occupied a pulpit once or twice,
But he thinks any service for the Lord proves to be so very, very nice.

Made it to Arkansas - not too long to stay - in Tulsa visited James and Flo,
Anxious to see Lillian's sister, May, who lives in Bentonville with
    her son, Bonneau.

Brother Paul's son-in-law was sick - a cancer - doctors were in accord;
The malignancy is in remission at present, and for this we thank the Lord.

Uncle Ed is in a Nursing Home in Plainview; his food and treatment are quite fair;
His bills are paid when they are due; he has nieces and nephews and
   for him they care.

All our family are happy to join us in sending CHRISTMAS GREETINGS
   your way;
We trust the Lord will be good to you and in 1980 give you many a pleasant day!

Bill and Lillian

A year later, Betty had another letter from Mason. It was from Vaughn, New Mexico, where "Pastor J. Wm. (Bill) Mason" was the minister at the First Baptist Church. His title and address were rubber stamped on the envelope.

The Christmas 1980 poetic letter follows:

CHRISTMAS 1980

Christmas time is approaching - it's just that time of year,
But for me without my Sweetheart, it is hard to have much cheer!
I can take comfort in the knowledge she's in heaven and devoid of pain;
She's singing Hallelujahs to Jesus and praising His holy name.

Some of you might not have heard, but she left for her heavenly home
December sixteenth last year, and just Jesus and I were left alone!
I know she's happy yonder, and has been the recipient of her crown,
And we would never call her back with sin so rampant all around!

We'll just be happy that she's with Christ Jesus on this Christmas Day,
So we too will be quite happy when at Jesus feet our trophies lay!
Until then we shall be busy trying desperately to serve our Lord,
Having great and untold happiness in attempting to preach His Holy Word.

I was quite unhappy in Plainview after my dear Sweetheart went away,
And I kept praying most earnestly for a pastorate each and every single day.
The Lord had called me into the ministry so many, many years ago,
And even at retirement age He has not revoked that call, I know!

Here I am in Vaughn, New Mexico, pastoring a church which is so good to me;
The Lord has given me much happiness for I'm as busy as I can be.
I have no time for looking backward, and I just will not fret and sigh.
I keep pressing on for Jesus for His coming is eminently very nigh!

Winning souls for my Saviour and serving otherwise in His glorious Name
Are reasons for pastoring First Baptist Church in Vaughn -that is why I came!
The Lord helped me write a pleading letter to the Missions Secretary of the State;
The good Christians here at Vaughn called me and I did not hesitate!

I've been in Vaughn since July seventeenth and happy beyond a single doubt,

Have had the pleasure of baptizing six converts and that's what it's all about!
The people have been refurbishing the buildings, and doing wonderful work;
And we've found none of them with duties they will attempt to shirk!

I hardly knew for writing the Christmas letter I could ever find the time,
But I had not taken into consideration this snowy New Mexico clime.
So here in late November, I'm really quite snow-bound at home,
And in these deep snow drifts I find it most difficult to roam.

When the church called me as pastor we had only twenty-six resident members;
Lost one by death, two were lettered out and now we have thirty-three
    in November.
The roofs have been repaired, the buildings painted - so much the people
    all have done.
But when we think of carpeting and new furniture, it seems we've just begun.

Our members are small in number, but all are so very good and sweet,
They are so fine and precious, you would find them most difficult to beat!
We attempt to have for every member some special job to do,
And we are amazed that so very much can be accomplished by such a very few!

I know that you are tired of my bragging about our congregation,
You'd have to meet and know them to realize there is no exaggeration.
So why not come to Vaughn for a while and pay us a great long visit,
And you will find that the things I've said are not at all illicit.

So, I'll quit raving about the church and some family news I'll write,
But right off you'll say that it doesn't sound so pleasant and bright.
On the morning of March the fourth Uncle Ed passed away while in his sleep;
 He desired to go because in December his ninety-fourth birthday he had reached.

His other nephew Bill and I had charge, the funeral could not have been better,
And we carried out Uncle Ed's written instructions absolutely to the letter.
The service was at Gaston in Dallas, the church he always loved so well,
And he was laid to rest by his mother's side in the cemetery at Terrell.

Brother Paul's son-in-law, Sid Stockwell has had cancer and has been so ill,
We've been praying oh, so fervently that God would make him well.
His wife, Nancy, and two daughters with him have had such worlds of fun,
And we can have faith in all our praying that God's will just must be done!

Tommy and Billie Claire are still in Plainview in Coca-Cola and farming
    making good,
To be sure they do not have to worry about how they'll buy their food.
They are quite successful seemingly in everything they try to do.
And they are so very good to me - such sons-in-law and daughters are
    so very few!

Hollis is still unmarried, he doesn't seem able to find the right one,
He's so engulfed in his law-practice he thinks the right one just hasn't come!

Granddad listened in when he was pleading for the culprit to indict,
And he brought all the stark evidence right out into the light!

Rick and Elizabeth are in Lubbock, they both seem from the same piece,
Elizabeth teaches at Monterrey High, and Rick is a teacher out at Reese.
They both are interested in church work and are very faithful too
The church keeps them quite busy and giving them enough to do!

Bill and Cathy are at Mexia - Bill managing the Coca-Cola Plant.
Cathy works in the School System giving teaching a different slant.
Bill at twenty-four was ordained a deacon on the bright Sunday eve.
Granddad was honored to preach the sermon since his church did grant
    him leave.

Lillian's only living sister lives in Arkansas with her son;
Bonneau takes such good care of her he is of a million number one!
May is in her nineties, and, with help around the house she gets about.
We believe she's aiming for a hundred, and that beyond a single doubt.

I pray for all the friends I have and for all those to whom I write,
I try to remember each and every one when I kneel to pray at night.
God bless you richly, precious friends, and each and every beloved one,
And may He use you in His glorious service until your crown you've won!

So "Merry Christmas" and "Happy New Year" to you at this special
    time of year;
And may we all look forward anxiously to the American hostages' release,
We pray that God in His infinite mercy will bring to all abiding peace!

Sincerely and lovingly yours,
Bill Mason

Hair Grew On Their Time

Once when Dad was working at a public job and things were a little slow, he left the premises and went to a barber shop for a hair cut. As luck would have it, his boss came in while he was in the chair.

"Carter, you getting your hair cut on the company's time?" he asked.

"Yeah. It grew on company time and I thought it would be O.K. to get it cut on company time," he said and the boss had no answer for that.

Dad, Mom, Betty, J.A. (standing) Me and Lucile kneeling with the infant Linda crying.

Dad's Candidate For Laziest Fisherman

Dad was never much of a fisherman although he went with Mitchell and me occasionally to the Great Pee Dee River where we caught black crappie from the bank.
Talking about fishermen many times, I pointed out to him that it took energy to be a real good fisherman and that anglers generally were not lazy people. They were people who worked hard at their jobs and were equally energetic when they fished. He took that kind of philosophy with a grain of salt. Most of the fishermen he knew didn't do much work. They maybe farmed a little, but spent a lot of time sitting on the river bank half asleep and hardly exerting any more energy than it took to bat their eyes. And I admitted there were some of those, but they were not the really good fishermen. The ones who caught fish had to move from place to place, change baits regularly, keep good lines on the poles, and be alert for strikes, otherwise many fish would get away.
"Well, I know one fisherman who was really lazy," Dad said, "and I think you will agree with me. I was walking along the river bank one morning going towards a sawmill site where a tractor had to be repaired and started. I saw this man sitting on the ground and leaning back against a pine. He had his eyes open but looked like he was trying to go to sleep. When I was within about 100 feet of him, I saw the cork on his long fishing pole that was set under a rock and sticking out over the water go under and his line tighten. I walked on up to him and told him his cork was gone. He had a bite. Without moving to get up the man said: 'Would you mind pulling it in for me!'
"I picked up his pole and brought in a three pound bass that was flouncing on the ground and I was kind of thrilled when I

showed him what he had caught. Again he didn't budge from his comfortable position. He just looked up at me and said 'Would you put the fish on a stringer and put him in the water?'

"I thought he was asking a right smart of me but I strung the fish on his stringer, stuck the metal needle in the ground, eased the bass in the water and started to walk away. The fisherman again softly spoke without moving. 'Would you bait my hook and put it back in the water before you leave?' he asked. 'Yeah, I'll do that too but man, you are the laziest fellow I ever saw. A man who has to have all the help you do ought to get married, have a bunch of children and let them take care of you.' The man thought a moment and came back with a question that convinced me he was the laziest man alive. 'That's a good idea. Do you know where I can find a woman that's already pregnant?' "

As Dad had said, he had met the laziest fisherman in the world, and indeed I believe he did have that encounter with a good candidate for that title.

The Wayward Shots

Dad listened to us tell about a county-wide 4-H Club contest that promised some financial rewards to youngsters in Stanly who would bring in the most rat tails one fall. The rodents were doing a lot of damage to field crops and also to the grain stored in barns and other outbuildings. In an effort to promote the trapping and poisoning of the vandals, we were given an incentive to bring the tails of the dead critters to school meetings for the count.

Keith Almond, a lifelong friend and hunting companion on numerous occasions, and I decided to pool our acumen and energies to kill a lot of rats. We shot and trapped them along ditch banks and in the barns where they were rampaging at night. We shot many of them in the beam of a flashlight with shot cartridges in a .22 caliber rifle. And we did kill quite a number but not enough to take home the cash prize.

One of those rat hunting events was in a clover field on his dad's farm. We were hunting the creatures with a BB gun. They were gathered under bales of hay that had been left in the field and one of us would turn over the bale, while the other tried to shoot the scampering rodents with the air rifle. Keith flipped over a bale and two big rats bounced off at full speed. I aimed and just as I pulled the trigger, Keith jumped right in front of me trying to escape the third rat that had come out of the hay and was staring him right in his face. It was too late. The BB went off and the lead pellet hit Keith squarely in the butt. He straightened up fast and grabbed his posterior while yelling bloody murder. Fortunately, the BB shot didn't have enough power to go through the tough blue denim overalls but it certainly burned awhile if Keith was telling the truth. It made us both thankful we hadn't been using the .22 caliber rifle that day. I'll never forget how fast Keith straightened up when that shot hit him.

Not long after that, Keith and I were hunting in a dense ravine along an old branch run with a fine little black and tan hound named "Queenie." We had borrowed the dog from Randall Burleson, another neighbor who taught us in school and was our scoutmaster for 27 years. Queenie jumped a cottontail and it tore out down the shoreline of the little stream with the dog barking just inches behind. Keith aimed his old shotgun and fired. Queenie instantly stopped the chase with a high pitched yelp. Keith had missed the rabbit and several shot hit the dog's stretched-out tail. The tail bone was broken and it dropped down at a 90 degree angle halfway to the end. The shot had severed the bone. A few days later Queenie was ready to hunt again, but the rest of her life she had that crippled tail from Keith's wayward shot.

Hitting a dog chasing a rabbit isn't unusual, at least not during our teenage years. I remember vividly a day along Little Bear Creek when a half breed collie jumped a rabbit and ran it right towards me. I was aiming diligently, trying to get a bead on the bouncing, swerving, cavorting cottontail as it scampered at break-neck speed through the gallberry bushes. Finally, it made a turn to the left and I thought my shot had arrived. I pulled the trigger just as the chasing collie left the trail and bounded after the rabbit from the other side. Collies conventionally will take short cuts to head off rabbits on the run. Unfortunately, I didn't suspect this dog was going to meet the rabbit at the same instant I shot. But that's the way it happened. The rabbit was shielded by the dog and my whole load of No. 6 shot went into the side of the dog. I was sad. It was an unfortunate accident. The young collie yelped a time or two and died. That's the only dog I ever killed and I lay awake at night for a week regretting my mistake.

In that era, many quail hunters shot dogs that disobeyed. They tried to do this at a distance so that the small bird shot would only sting and not do permanent damage. But I remember well a local bird hunter who was so angry with his pointer that had flushed a covey of quail that he shot a couple of times at the escaping flushed covey and then fired the last shot at his dog some 100 feet away. Nevertheless, the old dog picked up a dead quail and brought it back to the hunter. Blood was oozing out of more than a dozen spots where the shot peppered the pointer. Even that crusty old bird hunter had some pangs of compassion for a hunting dog so intent upon doing its duty that it retrieved the dead bird while hurting from many lead shot that had penetrated its hide that it died ten minutes later. That was a canine tragedy not easy to forget.

I have had some experiences quail hunting with birddogs when I had the urge to shoot my dog but didn't. I remember once when I had a huge old pointer named "Jack." He was a fine country birddog that we allowed to run loose. That differs from most city birddogs that are kept chained or fenced. But a birddog that runs loose has great stamina. You can hunt one of those all day and he'll have more energy at sunset than the hunter will. A penned birddog hunting in savannas where there is a lot of ground cover will often be totally fatigued by mid-morning and you'll have to pick the dog up and carry him back to the car. That's normal in Eastern North Carolina where the swampland is much more difficult to hunt than the relatively open woodlands of the Piedmont section.

But Jack made a lot of his living by catching rats and other wild creatures on his own and eating them. We never heard of such a thing as dog food until we were grown. Dog food for Jack was the scraps we gathered from the table and the residue from the birds, rabbits and squirrels that we shot. Perhaps that is some kind of excuse for Jack's despicable behavior.

I was hunting along a deep canal that ran through the woods and shooting a single that had settled on the ditch bank here and there. One bird fluttered up and crossed the canal just as I knocked it down with an accurate shot, often unusual for me. It fell 150 feet away on the other side of the canal. Jack was in hot pursuit, found the dead bird and trotted back to the canal holding it lightly in his teeth very professionally. There was a lot of fast water rushing down the canal and Jack looked at that torrent a moment, glanced at me, and seemed to say, "You want me to jump in there and bring you this quail?" Of course I did! I kept beckoning him to bring the bird, but he had other ideas. In a fraction of a second, he made one big gulp and that bird went down into his stomach without a single chew. Bones, meat, feathers and all, Jack had his lunch that day. But that's one of those times when you feel like shooting a dog. I didn't, but I thought about it.

Mitchell And The Game Warden

My brother Mitchell is what everyone who knows him calls a "good man." He has always been exemplary in his conduct and attitude and many times I have wished I could be of similar moral character. I doubt if he has ever even had a speeding ticket.

The fact that he is such a stickler for always being right, makes an incident that happened to him when he was growing up more memorable. He hunted quail regularly, often by himself, and was a good shot. Few quail escaped when he found them in fields or woodland clearings where he could get his gun to his shoulder.

Why it happened, I don't know, nor does he, but someone told the game warden that Mitchell was shooting more than his legal limit of quail and the law enforcement officer took it seriously enough to put him under surveillance. The next time he left the house with his pointer and gun the warden followed him. Later in the day, the officer confronted Mitchell and asked to inspect his kill. Mitchell had only three birds, and he showed them to the officer. While at the time it seemed to appease the warden and he left, apparently somewhat disappointed that he hadn't been able to issue a citation, he was really playing a cat and mouse game.

Mitchell went on his way after the search and a few minutes later, the dog pointed a covey of quail in a dense patch of honeysuckle vines. The birds flushed and Mitchell picked out a bird flying head high just over the thick growth. He fired! The bird fell and someone yelled. Moments later the game warden came walking out of the thicket. He had circled Mitchell, and hid in these thick vines hoping to catch Mitchell with too many birds. There was no way of knowing he was hiding in the bushes when the quail flushed and when Mitchell shot, several of the pellets buried in the game warden. That's when he hollered.

The game warden looked kind of sheepish. Obviously Mitchell had done no wrong and the officer had only himself to blame for getting shot. Sorry for the accident, Mitchell went back to the officer's car and drove him to a doctor to have the pellets removed. The warden had almost nothing to say.

Later Mitchell returned to continue his hunt and he didn't have to worry about that game warden hiding in the bushes again hoping to catch him breaking the law. Mitchell was embarrassed and he still doesn't like to talk about it. But it was nobody's fault but that game warden's.

- - - - -

We often had newly-hatched quail coveys come to the backyard in the summer time with their mother to get water from a pan that was always filled for the chickens. The little birds sometimes were no bigger than your thumb nail and were mighty fragile little creatures. The old quail hen had them trained better than Hitler's goose-stepping soldiers. In the short grass in the yard, she could make a clucking noise when apparent danger approached and instantly every quail chick disappeared. They could almost hide on a linoleum rug they were so well camouflaged. Then another safety cluck by the hen, and they all reappeared and scampered back into the cover.

Nature or God or both used great expertise in designing wild creatures. Only the drab colored female quail will set on a nest. The prettier, more colorful bobwhite male often hangs around the nest, but he won't set on the eggs. His job is to distract the predators. When danger is near, often he will make a chirping noise, make out like he has a broken wing and flap around on the ground, eventually moving away from the nest and drawing the predator toward him. The hen is so well hidden by her camouflage feathers that she is harder for the predator to see. But when danger gets real close, she too will leave the nest and put on that injured bird act to draw danger away from her eggs or offspring.

Wood ducks are another good example of coloration designed to save nests. Only the hen wood duck that is brown and drab sets on the nest. The beautifully colored male has the job of enticing danger away from the nest. The same is true of wild turkeys as far as color and camouflage is concerned. They nest on the ground.

Cardinals are similar. The male is red and pretty. The female is yellowish and brownish and not nearly so easy to see. Only the female sets on the nest in a bush or tree. English sparrows have the same traits.

Conversely, doves are exactly alike. Both the male and the female dove will set on the nest that is always in a tree, not on the ground like a quail, duck or wild turkey. Wood ducks like to nest in holes in trees or stumps. Both male and female doves will often play injured and drop off the nest to flutter and flap to attract attention to predators that get too close to their nest.

These were natural history facts that we learned growing up in a rural area where all small game species were plentiful and their harvest put protein on the table.

- - - - -

Dad wasn't much for hunting but once he went along to the Waccamaw River in Columbus County when he was visiting in Tabor City. He was amazed at the intelligence of a wild duck. The duck came swooping in from down river, and I shot the bird when it was almost overhead. It dropped to the water a hundred feet or so away, obviously hit but not dead. It dived and disappeared. We waited for half an hour. It still didn't come up. I paddled the boat to about where the duck went under. The water was shallow. You could see the dead duck hanging on to a blade of coontail on the bottom. I reached down, pulled the duck loose and put it in the boat. Even in death, that waterfowl was determined not to be captured.

There's another interesting duck fact about these waterfowl on the Waccamaw. Years ago when there was little hunting, the ducks always flew with the river. They would either come swooping in at a hunter from up the river or from down the river. This gave the hunter considerable time and distance to shoot. Today, ducks along the Waccamaw never fly up and down the river. They come in across the river. The stream is narrow. The trees are tall and thick on the shoreline and in many places there's only a little opening between trees on each side of the river. Ducks can be seen in the open only fractional seconds. You have to get most of your shots through tree limbs and leaves.

Maybe this cross river flying doesn't mean that the waterfowl are better educated, although sometimes you tend to suspect that. It probably results from the digging of canals and ponds along the river watershed where the birds do a lot of feeding and then return to the river.

But if you don't believe that wildlife does learn about the dangers from hunters, why is it that deer, turkey and other sought-after game are plentiful the day before hunting season opens and the day after it closes but are scarce when it is legal hunting time?

Betty's Determined Dog Bee Bee

Bee Bee was a bench-legged mongrel fice dog with more determination and confidence than intelligence and I'm sure if he had ever been given a canine IQ test he would have been graded retarded or worse. But if he had been inclined to attack the Hindenburg blimp he would have done so with enthusiasm and never relaxed until he had torn it to bits, or died trying.

A depressed look hung on Bee Bee's white and black face one afternoon when he slumped to the ground, looked around and licked his chops for a moment. He had just been outwitted by a tiny chipmunk that flitted its tail to the left while dashing off to the right when Bee Bee was giving chase and in hot pursuit. The tail maneuver sent Bee Bee sliding into the brier patch while the little squirrel scooted down a hole under a pine tree.

"Safe at last," breathed the chipmunk that was used to being chased by this dog that had nominated himself to be the guardian of our backyard regardless of what invader trespassed. But the little critter had not counted on the never-say-die temperament of Bee Bee.

Moments after Bee Bee righted himself from the tumble into the briers and collected his wits while lying calmly on his belly and day dreaming about the chipmunk that got away, he sauntered over to the big pine, looked down that hole where the rodent disappeared, made a final analysis of the situation, and then vigorously began digging with his front feet and rooting with his nose and mouth, piling the dirt underneath until his hind legs kicked it out of the way. The sanctuary of the chipmunk down that hole was being threatened, but not seriously at first. Bee Bee dug silently but later he began to mumble and grunt as the day dragged on, the hole getting bigger and bigger. He stopped occasionally for air and rest, but always he went back to his apparently hopeless task of going after the chipmunk in the hole. Darkness settled over the grove of pines. Bee Bee stopped work. Calmly he stretched out near his diggings and went to sleep.

When the first roosters crowed in the morning, Bee Bee shook the sleep out of his bones, eyed the deep hole under the tree and went back to pawing, rooting and grunting. His face was dirty from the previous day's work and his tongue wasn't long enough to get all of his face clean. He didn't seem to mind. That wasn't his problem now. He had one objective ---he must get that chipmunk that made a fool out of him the day before. He would get a few morsels of protein when he ate the critter too. He dug on and on in spite of what to most dogs and men would have seemed an impossible task. It's hard to beat anything at its own game and burrowing in the ground was a chipmunk specialty.

By noon on that second day, he had a hole halfway around the pine trunk and it was deep as your leg. Still no chipmunk and Bee Bee dug on. His paws were bleeding and his nose scratched and hurting. But so what! Confidence seemed to grow in the late afternoon. Perhaps that sharp, damaged nose was sniffing the nearby scent of the chipmunk in his den and the quarry might soon be in sight. Oh, how Bee Bee relished the thought of getting his teeth into that little striped squirrel. It would be both food and fun. His paws sent the dirt flying two feet in the air as he seemed to have renewed energy.

Then it happend. This little dog weighing no more than a dozen pounds but with the grit of a mountain lion, had so uncovered even the tap root of the big pine that it was loose in the ground. A gust of wind put a definite lean to the tree. Bee Bee was making progress.

Just before dark the wind increased and the pine crashed to the ground like thunder. Bee Bee was dancing all over the place, gleeful and happy. He looked like a four-legged cheerleader after a final goal won the league championship. He had won! That chipmunk hadn't escaped. His persistence had prevailed. The scared little rodent bounced out of the clayroot and headed for another haven. But Bee Bee was alert. He scampered after the chipmunk without any thought for tomorrow. His snapping jaws narrowly missed the squirrel's back as the predator and the prey reached a rock wall at the same time. Again the chipmunk dived for safety between two big boulders and Bee Bee couldn't stop his momentum, crashing headlong into the stack of stones, long years before laid here to make a pasture fence.

Bee Bee righted himself, shook his head and looked around. There was no way he could move those boulders even with great effort. He had already clawed down a big tree with his determination and energy but still he had failed to catch the chipmunk. He obviously had more brawn than brains but there would be another day and another chase. The swan song hadn't been sung in this episode yet, Bee Bee thought as he looked at the hole, glanced up at me and with chagrin in his every step, strolled back to the porch steps and stretched out for a well-earned rest. That squirrel would have to come out to eat sometime. Bee Bee would just wait. The battle wasn't lost.

This dog was obsessed with doing things no other canine would think about trying. Turkey buzzards were plentiful in that day when farmers and dairymen never buried an animal that died or was killed by accident. The cows, horses, goats, and hogs that died were simply dragged off a mile or so into the woods, and left for the vultures to eat. Big flocks of buzzards would then circle over the carcass for days as they became gluttons, scavenging the meat from the bones of the dead animal. With dead animals plentiful, buzzards were an expanding species. With the passing of laws that prohibited leaving animals on the surface, the buzzard population has steadily dwindled. Only wildlife fatalities on the highways now feed the vultures.

Bee Bee didn't like shadows of buzzards moving across the barnyard on the fair days. This was another invasion of his territory and from the time a shadow fell on the outskirts of the farm yard until it disappeared in the savannas and woodlands, he chased it on the ground, barking every breath and eyeing his nemesis in the sky. He was determined to protect the place from all such threats which he apparently considered potentially a danger for him and our family. He was the only dog I ever saw that chased buzzard shadows all his life.

We lived two miles from Canton Baptist Church where we attended Sunday School and preaching as regular as weeks rolled around. Mama cooked on a big wood-heated stove in the kitchen that had a twenty gallon water reservoir on the side next to the fire chamber. It was the hot water we had for taking a bath in a house with only an outdoor privy and a No. 2 galvanized tin tub for washing more than your face and hands on Saturday night before donning your Sunday best the next morning. Hauling up that water from a deep well a gallon or so at a time was a chore we were assigned. The reservoir must be kept full.

One winter morning Mama filled a big aluminum pot with some cubes of beef from a yearling we had recently butchered and she had canned in glass jars. It was before the day of refrigeration and deep freezers. Then she added some potatoes and onions. That beef stew would make our main course at lunchtime when we returned from church about 12:30 following the worship service. She chunked up the fire with the split pine blocks that we called "stove wood" just before we got in the Model A Ford and headed up some terribly muddy, slick clay roads to church. In winter often getting there was risky and uncertain and more than once we had to get some farmer along the way to pull the car out of a ditch when it slid sideways and backwards when we tried to spin our way up some of the wet, rolling hillside roads on the way to church.

On this particular fall Sunday morning, we made it to church and back without mishap, but alas! All was not tranquil on the home front. Bee Bee lay on the porch with a sly smile on his face when we arrived. He showed signs of over eating as his stomach was stuffed like a tight balloon. There were grease spots on his mischievous face. It was not explainable. That ne'er-do-well dog had opened the screen door that was still ajar, (we never locked a door to the house in those days even when we were gone overnight or on vacation) and had gone into the kitchen, hopped up on that stove, taken the lid from the beef stew and helped himself. He ate it all. Mind you, the top of that stove was still warm even when we arrived. It must have been much hotter an hour or so earlier when Bee Bee ate our lunch. Perhaps he knew that the top of the water reservoir was next to the firebox and was not as hot as the cooking top area of the stove itself. Perhaps, just perhaps, he stood on that warm portion of the stove, removed the lid and ate our lunch. That didn't exactly endear that mongrel to any of us, much less Dad. With Mama crying softly, Dad took his old 16 gauge hammer shotgun from the closet. He walked out in the yard with a shell in his hand to send that thriving hound to the Happy Hunting Ground. Betty was pleading for Bee Bee's life but Dad seemed not to notice. He called Bee Bee to the edge of the yard and inserted the shell. Without even a glance back at the family, stunned from the rapid developments under our noses, Dad pointed the gun at Bee Bee. He looked up, rolled those talking eyes and wagged his friendly tail. Dad lowered the gun, slowly uncocked the hammer, removed the shell, and walked back inside. He never uttered another word about that incident, but we read his thoughts that Sunday morning. This was 1934 and we were in the midst of the Great Depression. Grown men were walking into grocery stores, shouldering a bag of flour and walking out without paying for it. They were hungry and broke. Bee Bee was hungry too. He took what was available. Survival was his motive. Charity could wait. It is difficult to share when your stomach was growling. Dad read that in Bee Bee's eyes and wagging tail.

Bee Bee's demise wouldn't come from starvation. It would be more dramatic and some years away.

He Wouldn't Stay Dead

We always had a dog or two at our house. Some were supposed to be hunting dogs and others just pets but we carried them all into the woods and fields when we went after rabbits, sometimes squirrel hunting too. The only birddogs in our community back there in the '20's and '30's were owned by doctors and lawyers. Most other people couldn't afford them but some of the in-town professionals with no space to keep a dog, farmed them out to the rural families. The owners furnished the food and the farmer had the privilege of hunting the dogs when he wanted to and when they were not being run by the wealthy professionals. We didn't know we were poor until years later when some one told us, but we did know we couldn't afford $25.00 to buy a dog.

Land owners in that era hated bird dogs and many refused to let quail hunters on their land if they had pointers and setters. They believed good dogs would be able to sniff out every single bird from a flushed covey and thus destroy the population. Most of the birds then were the native bob white partridge that didn't fly as fast or as far as the exotic species later released in the Carolinas, and it was easy to shoot a covey down to extinction with well-trained birddogs. It was more difficult if you walked up birds without dogs.

This fear that bird dogs would destroy the quail led to the shooting of many innocent setters and pointers by hostile farm owners. I remember a sad moment at our house a few months after Dad brought home two high-priced, professionally-trained pointers that belonged to a county seat attorney. We were to look after them and let them exercise every day, but have them always available for the owner and his friends when he wanted to hunt. As a tiny tot, I can recall that bigshot coming to our house dressed in tan coveralls. That is what the wealthy hunters wore then as they slipped away from offices for a few hours and donned this protective dress over other clothing, hunted an hour or two and returned to work. I suspected it was a way of getting a little relaxation without wives knowing about it too. That practice by normally well-dressed doctors and lawyers is what prompted the invention of coveralls, thus its name.

The sad moment came one summer evening when we turned the two dogs loose, as we normally did, and they rushed out of the yard and soon out of sight, jubilant to be free to run and play. They scampered over a distant knoll and never returned. Searching everywhere for them the next day, we found them side by side with rifle holes through their midsections. A landowner detesting these quail sniffing dogs had killed them both. We never again kept bird dogs for any of the townspeople. Harmless, lovable, innocent, these creatures died from man's ignorance. They didn't comb their hair, wear shoes, or debate issues. They did live and love without prejudice. They lost their right to live because they trespassed. Maybe if they had been educated enough to read the "Posted" signs they would have been accepted in our community.

Someone did give us an English setter pup and we had visions of owning a real quail hunting canine. We loved that dog like it was family. Alas! Distemper came along and the dog was deathly sick. We pampered it day and night, even making it a bed in front of the open fire that heated the family room. We fed it milk with a spoon and covered it with a blanket to try to save it. Even though we had little money, we even carried it into town to the veterinarian for shots. It was all in vain. The little setter died and we never again had a bird dog of our own until we were married and had homes of our own..

What we really cherished were some beagle hounds. These flop eared critters would trail a rabbit better than any other species and if you knew what you were doing, you could almost always kill a cottontail when you had good trail dogs. They would stay in behind the rabbit and invariably the bunny would circle and return to almost the same spot he was jumped.

He would kind of slip back into the territory, moving slowly and was much easier to shoot with your shotgun on the return than when he bounced up from his nest and took off at breakneck speed. If you had the eye for finding a rabbit setting, you could, of course, shoot the cottontail in the bed even with a single shot rifle and be reasonably sure of success without damaging the meat with lead pellets from a shotgun used on running bunnies. But not everyone could see a rabbit setting. Perfectly camouflaged on ditch banks, in brush piles, around rotting logs and brier patches, a rabbit in Stanly County, North Carolina is usually safe if he will stay put as would most rattlesnakes if they didn't rattle. Most hunters would walk right past a setting rabbit and never see him. Of course, beagles would smell the still rabbit, pounce on him and make him jump and run for hunters. It was generally conceded that it was more sporting to jump the rabbit and give him a chance to escape rather than shooting him in the bed. But when you were hunting for meat, conservation in that era was often overlooked.

Those who do spot a setting rabbit usually see it when a mirror-like flash from the rabbit's eye reflects sunlight. When you first see such a flash, it is almost like a bolt of electricity struck you in the face and often it is a second or two before you are aware of what stunned you. You may have made one too many steps by then and the rabbit may dash off as you quickly try to get a shot at the fleeting ball of fur darting in and out of cover. It's not an easy animal to hit even with hundreds of No. 6 lead shot in a shell.

There were hunters then who were blessed with the uncanny ability of seeing setting rabbits. Every hunter in the community marveled at their prowess. They were so proficient that many killed enough rabbits to feed a family with an humble slingshot, made from two strips of rubber from a punctured innertube, the flexible leather tongue of a brogan shoe, a forked hickory stick you cut from a bush, and with a marble-size rock for a bullet. Occasionally you were lucky enough to find some steel ball bearings from same discarded machine for ammunition, but more often you used the slick native stones picked up from the creek beds or along the roadside. Spotting a setting rabbit that didn't jump and run when it was ten feet or so away, these hunters with the trained eye could shoot a stone into the head of a rabbit almost every time. They seldom missed the still target. It was an economical way to hunt in an era when shotgun shells sold for 75 cents for a box of 25. Often we didn't have the 75 cents nor the 25 cents that you could use to purchase seven shells. We often swapped two dozen eggs from the hen flock that ran loose around the barn for the partial box of shells. I wasn't very good at spotting the setting rabbits although I did see a few and understood that unusual sensation when the glint of the rabbit's eye reflected off my own. Dad said he never saw but one rabbit setting in his life and it jumped up just before he saw it.

Beagle hound pups sold for $5.00 even during the Depression and that might as well have been $500. We had to do our rabbit hunting with a border collie named Rex that wouldn't trail a rabbit but was good at jumping them and getting them out of thickets. He made it possible for us to carry home many cottontails that would have been safe without the help of that old pet dog that loved us as much as we loved him. Nothing hurt him as much as our scolding him to stay home when we walked out of the yard with our shotguns.

Then lady luck smiled. A neighbor's beagle had a litter of the prettiest little liver and white beagles you ever saw. He agreed to let us have two females that were close to being thoroughbreds and eligible for registration if we would raise some pups from them and give him two offspring in return the next year. We were elated. It was a deal and we brought the cuddly little animals home and didn't even bother to push them aside when they licked us all over the face and mouth. What a strange way to show affection! They must be part human.

The six-weeks-old pups lived under the house and came out whenever they were hungry for the bits of bread, milk and scraps that we fed them. I had never seen commercial dog food then and didn't know it was made. Maybe it was for sale somewhere but not in any of the stores I ever visited. We couldn't have bought it any way. I thought dogs and hogs were raised on table scraps until I was grown and left home.

The beagle pups were growing but then came another disaster. Both of them took distemper and died quickly. Like I suspected, these dogs were near pedigreed stock and it always was a strange fact that the highly bred dogs were susceptible to disease and death more than the mongrels that ran loose that you never even knew their ancestry. You couldn't kill one of them with a stick but the fine, expensive hybrids would die from just getting cold. It's like penned-up dogs that never roam free. They are exhausted after a few hours hunting while the yard dogs can run from daylight to dark and still go hunting on their own in the moonlight.

But Betty's half-breed fice Bee Bee defied distemper, attacks by bulldogs and big German Shepherds and every other threat to his safety for half a dozen years. He seemed to laugh at adversity and languished in activities that a more intelligent animal would have avoided. In time, his fate could no longer be postponed.

Dad was running a combination country store and an automobile garage a short distance from home at that time. It was a gathering place for loafers and soon became known as "Liar's Corner." Bee Bee started hanging out at the store, begging for scraps from honey buns, oatmeal cookies and crackers that customers munched. Perhaps hungry and chagrined one afternoon from man's lack of compassion for his plight, Bee Bee started back to the house and, in crossing the highway, was struck by a passing truck. He lay kicking on the asphalt with the blood pouring out of both nostrils. Luckily, none of us children were there to see the tragedy and Dad thought perhaps it would be best to just carry the carcass off and let the dog's mishap be untold. Bee Bee was such a pet that his death would surely bring too many tears. He picked the limp little critter up by the hind legs and walked a hundred yards into the woods to a myrtle bush thicket, and threw the bleeding Bee Bee into the heart of the dense undergrowth. He walked back to the store, a little emotional himself even though he was a tough man and it took a lot of tragedy to prompt any sign of tears.

Near dusk, Betty came to the store looking for Bee Bee. Dad couldn't lie to her. Eventually, he confessed that the dog had been run over and he had carried it off so she would not see her pet dead and bleeding. She shuddered with serious crying and insisted she wanted to go get the little dog and give it a decent burial. It didn't seem very practical, but Dad agreed to go with her to get the body and he would help dig a hole for the burial. They walked to the wooded spot and were startled. Bee Bee was sitting up on his haunches. His eyes were glazed and he wobbled when he tried to stand on all fours. He tried to wag his tail but it was a feeble attempt. Dad walked over the bushes, picked up the little dog in his arms and brought it home. A few days of tender loving care and

Bee Bee was as lively and mischevious as ever. He had only suffered a concussion from the blow on his head by the axle on the truck. He lived another four years before succumbing to the violent kick of an old mule that he was pestering in the pasture. That time he was really done in and Betty did bury the little rascal in a shallow grave with a cross from the staves of an old vinegar barrel nailed together. A few wild flowers adorned the grave.

If Bee Bee had a soul, I don't know whether his eternity would have been spent up or down. As the old saying goes, there's a little good in the worst of us and a little bad in the best of us. It certainly applied to Bee Bee's whole existence but that little critter never met a stranger. He loved life and basked in his energy and determination. He wouldn't even die easily.

He had two chances at life but his lifestyle after the resurrection was no different from his previous years. Few creatures have an opportunity to start out anew at middle age with a chance to wash away the mistakes of youth. It seems that such an opportunity by Bee Bee when he was so close to death would have changed his life. It didn't! As soon as he was fully recuperated, he was a predestinationist again. He died that way.

The New York World's Fair

When I didn't have the $50.00 needed to make an organized trip to the New York World's Fair in 1939 with the scout troop, I told Dad and Mama that I would go on my own. I had $15.00 and if I hitchhiked, I should be able to make it from North Carolina to New York and back with those three five dollar bills.

Obviously Mama screamed "No!" I was only eighteen years old and New York was so big and so far away that it just wouldn't work. But Dad disagreed. Perhaps his wanderlust days were in the back of his mind when he left for Texas, Ohio and Pennsylvania.

"Let him go. It will do him good. He needs to see some of the Yankee country," Dad came to my rescue.

A few days later, with my younger cousin Keith Carter, we picked up our little suitcases and pointed our thumbs toward the Big Apple, a monicker unheard of in that era. I wore my Boy Scout uniform, and we carried an amateurish sign that read, "New York's World Fair."

Keith's father, my Uncle Carl, carried us across the Pee Dee River and let us out on U.S. No. 1. It was the main thoroughfare to New York then. Before noon we caught a ride to Raleigh. There we saw a car with a Washington, D.C., license plate parked near the capitol building and we hung around until the owner appeared.

"Mister, we are bound for New York. Could you give us a ride to Washington?" I asked.

"Yeah, I guess so, I'm alone," the man answered and we piled in his automobile.

Late that evening we arrived in Washington and the generous motorist let us out at the Capitol steps. There were beggers all over the place and they volunteered a lot of information on how we could make five or six dollars a day by standing around, looking hungry and asking for money. They were real panhandlers. That's what most of those loafers were doing. That didn't appeal to us. We had money, humble amount that it was. What we wanted was a place to get some sleep. Fortunately, it was not the era of mugging and street robbers. We did not feel threatened or endangered.

We heard that there was a hotel a few blocks away that was cheap. We walked to it and found a double room for $1.25. We paid the lady, went to bed and didn't get up until the sun peeped through the shadeless, dirty windows in the morning.

We made our way to the northern outskirts of Washington and began thumbing again for Philadelphia. We waited for hours before two half drunk Negroes picked us up about dark. I have done a lot of hitchhiking but I never was as scared as I was on that ride to Philadelphia. The men kept drinking and asking a lot of questions. They got drunker and drunker. Finally, one said he was out of cigarettes. We didn't smoke but we quickly volunteered to buy him a pack of Luckies. We did and there went another 15 cents of our money.

After what seemed like an eternity, we entered Philadelphia and we asked to be let out. We were not sure they would let us out. We didn't know where we were but it was a relief to get out of that car. We slept a little that night and morning on a park bench, typical hobo style with newspapers for cover. That didn't cost anything. At daybreak we ate the last of the packed food that Mama and Aunt Mae had prepared, and we started searching for the road out of Philly for New York City. A policeman stood on the corner. I told him where we were going and asked how far we would have to walk to get to the northern side of town and the highway.

After one brief look, that officer knew we were from the country. "You can't walk through this town. That's miles and miles from here. You'll have to take a bus or subway. It'll only cost you ten cents each," he said. For the first time we realized this town wasn't like Albemarle or even Charlotte.

By mid-morning, we were on the outskirts of Philadelphia with our upraised thumbs. A nice old gentleman stopped. He once had been a Boy Scout. We jumped in his car, and later that day he let us off at the main gate of the New York World's Fair. We paid our 75 cent entry fees and started seeing the sights. By evening, we were tired enough to be walking around like zombies. An information desk gave us directions to a Brooklyn house that was available for overnight guests. We found the place and for 75 cents, rented a room. With the crackers and cheese we had bought for food the previous day gone, we had now exhausted the first of my five dollar bills and Keith had spent about the same amount. Breakfast cost us another 35 cents and we headed for the World's Fair gate again. That cost 75 cents for the second time, but we went in and observed everything that was free until early afternoon.

"Keith, we gotta get out of here. We are going to run out of money and not be back home. Let's go," I said.

He was agreeable and we walked out the gate, took a bus across town and hitched a short ride into Hoboken, New Jersey. It was night and we were hungry. A sign over the counter in a greasy spoon cafe said "Pea soup, all you can eat 10 cents."

"I'll have the pea soup," I told the man at the counter and he set a big bowl in front of me. There had been no other conversation.

"What part of North Carolina you from?" the waiter asked.

"Albemarle. How did you know I was from North Carolina?" I asked in amazement.

"Anybody can recognize another Tar Heel," he said, and smiled. "Eat up. I'll get you full before you leave here," and it was apparent we must have looked kind of puny from eating little or nothing for three days.

We spent the fourth night in Hoboken for another $1.00 apiece. Breakfast across the street from the room bit well into my second five dollar bill. We picked up our dirty suitcases in the cafe, walked back to the road and began thumbing. The very first car that we hailed, stopped. It was a man driving an A-Model Ford and pulling another one just like it. He was going to Florida to sell the cars. A buddy of his stopped behind and he, too, was driving one car and pulling another.

"Hi, mister, can we hitch a ride?" I asked.

"Where you boys going?" he asked.

"North Carolina," Keith said.

"Yeah, one of you get in here with me and the other one jump in with my friend back there. We need some one to talk to who will keep us awake. We got to drive all night but we'll get you to Carolina," the wonderful man said.

We rode all that day and all night. While we tried to keep awake, it wasn't easy and we had to prop our eyes open. At 7:30 the next day we got out of those Fords at Ellerbee, about a good hour's drive from Endy. We both plopped down in the grass in front of the Baptist Church and went to sleep. We awoke about noon on a warm pretty day and started thumbing for home. Our first ride carried us to Biscoe on Highway 27 with more traffic. There I spent the last nickel of my second five dollar bill for a Coke. An hour later, a trucker picked us up and we didn't get out of his vehicle until the Endy School building was in sight. I lived almost in the shadow of the school.

I walked up the dirt road to the house. My Boy Scout uniform was wrinkled and dirty. My little bag was worn out. I was tired and sleepy but happy. I had made it to the New York World's Fair and back. I had got a glimpse of the sights of the big city for the first time. It was my first journey on my own and I still had a five dollar bill in my pocket. I felt as successful as Columbus did when he discovered America. It was a Sunday afternoon. Mama grabbed me with a hug that made me feel a closeness never before enjoyed. Dad just smiled. His eldest son had kind of proven himself and he was proud.

"We're glad to have you home, son," was his only remark but I knew deep down he was ever so thankful. I hadn't failed him.

The Squirrel That Didn't Get Away

Dad's older brother was my Uncle Carl, the eldest child in the Tom Carter family, and he was one of the providers for the dinner table with his hunting prowess. On occasions, he invited Dad to go along with him, not to shoot but to scare the plentiful gray squirrels back on his side of the tree when they used their cunning to put a tree trunk or limb between the hunter on the ground and the body of the prey. They are experts at detecting by sound and sight the hunter with the gun and if you are hunting alone, it takes some innovative experiments to entice the squirrel around the tree so you can get him in your sights.

Finding a squirrel to begin with in early fall when a lot of foliage is still on the trees requires expertise as well as 20-20 vision. Most squirrels are picked out of the leaves and cover when an ear is exposed or, on occasion, the squirrel fails to hide his bushy tail. You can see an ear many times and it is out of character in a tree top so much that you know you have located your quarry. When there are two hunters, one can shake a bush or stomp in the dry leaves and often make the critter move so that his presence is discovered.

Dad was with Carl one cloudy, cold fall day when their big old red bone hound, Old Red, treed a squirrel in a tall hickory tree along the shoreline of a winding creek. Carl was having trouble seeing the squirrel and told Dad to go on the other side and shake a bush as violently as he could. Dad obliged and scampered to the other side. He began dragging the top of a bush over the leaves on the ground. Back and forth he dragged the bush top. Carl managed to see a tiny piece of the squirrel's side but the shot was not clean enough to bring the squirrel down.

"Try beating the trunk of the tree with a stick or something," Carl yelled.

Dad picked up a dead limb under the old hickory and began to frail the daylights out of the tree trunk. This kind of action often puts a lot of fright in the squirrel. He thinks, presumably, that some one is climbing up the tree after him. He will almost always give his position away when the trunk of the tree is being beaten. He hears the noise and feels the vibration.

This squirrel that had managed to stay in hiding for several minutes could not stand that racket below. He burst from his hiding place in a tree fork, ran to the end of the longest limb and jumped for the ground, as they will often do when scared out of hiding. The squirrel had not figured on the old red bone hound. The big dog was barking and baying with all the wind his lungs could produce, looking up and wondering why Carl didn't shoot and bring this squirrel down long before it began its hell bent run and jump. The squirrel's mad jump sent him squarely at Old Red and the open mouth of the dog was suddenly filled with the fur of a scrappy squirrel. It avoided the gnashing teeth and squirmed right on down the dog's throat in an instant. The squirrel and the hound were surprised. Obviously smothering and dying in the stomach of the hound, the squirrel was kicking and biting everything it could find in the dark. Old Red rolled on the ground in great pain until the last kick was gone from the squirrel. Only then did he get on his feet and look around as if to say, "This isn't what I call squirrel hunting."

The hunters didn't have any meat for the dinnertable but Old Red had his meal for the day.

Dad's Quail Hunting Experience

Dad worked so hard and regular that he never had much time for hunting, although my brother Mitchell and I grew up with guns in our hands and went after small game throughout the community from the time we were twelve or there abouts.

But on a rare occasion at Thanksgiving or Christmas, Dad would traipse with us through the woods and fields for a few hours. He was not a good shot, but he wanted to look good to us and some of the things that transpired still bring ear to ear smiles when we stop to think about them.

One winter day when we were hunting quail, or actually the old original bob white partridge that inhabited the county, a much fatter and slower game bird than the Mexican variety, we had flushed a number of birds. Each time a quail burst off the ground, Mitchell or I would shoot and often go pick up the dead bird. We were hunting without a dog, just jumping the quail and following them the best we could from sight and experience in the territory. While we were both shooting at the flushed birds, Dad was putting in his shots too, but in that bird hunters can generally tell whether they fired the shot that downed the quail, we were stuffing the birds in our pockets as we were positive of our marksmanship. Dad hadn't picked up a bird but you could see he wasn't entirely sure that all his shots were going awry.

Dad strayed off a few hundred feet from us and was walking down an old sawmill road that hadn't been traveled in years. A single partridge flushed under his feet and almost in a panic, Dad rushed the gun to his shoulder and pulled the trigger. The single shot rang out through the forests and we stopped to listen.

Which one of you kids got that quail?" Dad asked.

"I didn't shoot," I said.

"I didn't either," Mitchell said.

"Oh, you didn't shoot. Then I guess I killed this one," and he bent down and retrieved his harvest. That made his day. He had a bird all his own without an argument. But he always believed those we claimed were as much his as ours.

Once when we were hunting quail in the early fall along an old ditch bank, we saw that Dad was suddenly alert with his gun to his shoulder. There had been no covey flush and Mitchell and I stopped and looked right at him as he continued aiming at the ground mysteriously.

I walked a few steps nearer to him and realized what was going on. There was a covey of twenty or more quail in single file running along the ditch bank. Dad was drawing a bead on them.

"Wait, wait, Dad," I said, "You aren't going to shoot those birds running on the ground, are you?"

"Naw, I'm not going to shoot 'em running. I'm going to wait until they stop," he said.

For those of us imbued with sportsmanship and knowing that legally you can't shoot quail on the ground, his remark was hilarious. He wanted to make sure he didn't get skunked when hunting with us.

While I am not proud of it, as a youngster I once fired at a covey of quail on the ground. I was more than sixty feet from them and they were all chattering and scratching under a cedar tree. I had an old twenty gauge single barrel hammer gun and seeing a chance for some quail on the dinner table, I fired into the melee. It seemed I must have winged half a dozen birds. They fluttered off in every direction making strange noises that left me frightened and ashamed. I had killed a single bird but damaged the covey considerably. It was the last time.

Quail were plentiful in the 1930's and during a summer drought they would come up in our back yard and drink water from a chicken trough. You can't tame a quail regardless of what age you start trying. They will always be wild but those in the yard hung around enough that we almost considered them pets.

In the spring of the year, quail start looking for mates and in that we needed the meat and the partridges were all over the small farm, we learned to whistle the partridges to within shooting range. We were good enough whistlers to fool the birds. We would pick up an old .22 rifle, listen for a partridge beckoning his mate, and then we would whistle every time the quail did, mimicking the quail fairly astutely. Often within ten minutes or less, we could call the bob white right near our stand. We were pretty good shots and often popped the partridge with a bullet that put meat on the table. The few old bob whites we killed didn't reduce the population. They were plentiful in that era when lespedeza hay was being grown on every farm. The clover had small seeds that the quail loved and they had ample food supply for years with good woodland cover. Only when lespedeza was phased out and DDT and other chemicals came along did the quail population decline. Our hunting never caused a population decline. We were always careful to leave several breeding pairs in each covey we shot.

Stories of unusual quail experiences still come to mind from those days hunting at Endy.

Bernice Almond was accepted as the best slingshot marksman in the community. He often shot setting cottontails with his homemade weapon, putting a marble-size shot right between the rabbit's eyes many times. But late one summer afternoon, he saw a huge covey of quail settle in a thick cedar tree that grew along a fence line. He eased to within 50 feet or so of the tree, loaded his slingshot pouch with a half inch steel marble that he had kept for such a special opportunity, and fired it into the dark clump in the middle of the cedar. Even he was amazed. Three quail fell from the tree as the ricochetting steel bullet bounced through the covey. It was more lethal and accurate than the small stones he usually used for ammunition. He had a mess for the dinner table with a single shot, not unheard of when you fire a shotgun shell into a covey on the rise but rather unique with such an ancient weapon. It would have made David proud.

Grady Hunnicutt was another real Daniel Boone hunter in our community. One cold winter day when it had first snowed and thin ice had formed a hard crust on the surface, Grady was walking around looking for a rabbit to shoot. He was startled when he neared a big hump in the snow where a brushpile had been covered with the white, icy stuff and saw a quail's head pop up through a cup-size hole in the center of the hump. He dropped his gun, ran to the hole and plopped his cap over the entrance. In the next few minutes, he ran his arm down into the brush pile and plucked out seven quail, one at a time, wringing their necks and filling the pockets on his hunting jacket. He had a family-size meal without firing a shot. You didn't have to pick any lead shot out of the quail meat either.

The most unusual rabbit hunting experience I ever had was once when I was hunting with old Rex, our Collie dog, without a gun. A rabbit jumped up and headed down an old road bed. I threw a golf ball size rock in his direction. It hit the rabbit broadside and he fell over kicking his life out.

A 'Coon Hunter's Mercy Killing

Dad once told this true story about a 'coon hunting adventure that he remembered hearing some of his Endy neighbors recount shortly after he moved into the community in 1924. The eventful hunt reflects compassion and a moral message or two that have always intrigued me.

Spears of moonlight penetrated the palmetto patched sand dune on the west bank of a wide, shimmering lake on Rocky River when we threw open the doors of the hound dog box and let the barking mass of energy hit the dirt in full stride from the tailgate of the four-wheel drive pickup. The trio of anxious canines scampered down the rutted old sawmill road baying at the moon long before there was any need for noise when the exciting scent of a marauding, masked raccoon would swirl past their sensitive nostrils. That would come soon but right now they were just barking with delight at being free to run these woods speckled with gallberry bushes in search of that path where a hungry coon not long ago had meandered along the lake shoreline grabbing gambusia minnows and some nocturnal insects that made their gourmet supper.

The eldest of this pack of coon hounds was a rawboned old veteran named "Boss" and Jasper Hatley was as proud of that mongrel with questionable ancestry as if he had pedigrees a yard long. And it was Boss that first hit a trail that was obviously hot and fresh. His booming bellow sent tingles along Jasper's and Bernice Gore's spines. That 'coon would be treed pronto as the other hounds, Peegee and Gamma, joined in the barking chorus. It was a real symphony to Jasper and Bernice, prettier than any manmade music.

"That old Boss has the best nose in the world. He can smell 'coons that passed his way half a day ago and sometimes I have to put a bandaid over one side of his nostrils just to keep him from trailing two 'coons at the same time," Hatley laughed at his own joke and Bernice just grinned. He thought right much of his dogs too.

Boss, Peegee and Gamma all were in full cry now as that old coon carried them over a twisting route along the water's edge, finally deciding the noise was getting too close and scampering up a short, stubby old gnarled oak that had survived many a stormy year and the winds had deformed its limbs like man's joints after he has suffered decades of arthritis.

Jasper and Bernice trudged through the thick palmetto growth to the foot of the tree where the dogs were estatic with their success and were bounding up and down on their hind legs with noses pointed toward the heavens and their long mournful howls cast an eerie echo for miles among the wooded sand dunes.

The powerful beam of Jasper's five cell flashlight penetrated the darkness as he scoured each limb of the tree searching for those tell-tale pairs of mirrors that would pinpoint the where-abouts of the raccoon that was now safe from the jaws of the grounded hounds. Jasper and Bernice had hunted these critters for three decades, not for their pelts then were selling for up to $5.00 each, nor for the meat that some folks called "delicious," but for the pure pleasure of hearing their dogs trail and tree these people animals that have been hunted by Americans for 300 years.

"There he is in the forks, the first fork on the right side," Bernice said.

"He's a nice 'un for sure," Jasper remarked as he held the beam on the reflecting eyes.

"You know, that coon is in trouble. He's got a trap on his leg, the right front one. See it?" Jasper asked.

"Yeah, sure is something dangling from his leg. Maybe we better go back to the pickup and get the rifle. That old 'coon'll do a lot of suffering trying to make a living with that steel trap dragging along," Bernice showed compassion. He left in a fast walk for the truck and returned in half an hour with the gun.

"I'll try to hit him right between those eyes," Bernice said, and the gun fired.

The 'coon came tumbling through the limbs and crashed into a palmetto bush. Almost instantly Boss, Peegee and Gamma were upon the carcass but Jasper shoved them aside and picked up the dead old female. A rusty steel trap with two feet of chain attached hung from the 'coon's front foot.

"That trap has been on this foot for weeks. The whole leg is infected and this animal was hurting. It's a good thing we found its trail and the dogs put her up a tree. She's a big 'un too. Must weight about 20 pounds, about as big a 'coon as I have ever seen. I guess she was so big and strong that she just pulled the trap loose from its mooring when it clamped down on her," Jasper figured. "We'll take the 'coon on in and skin her. Might as well save the hide. As big as that 'coon is, she sure would have given our dogs a tussle in the water wouldn't she? Might have drowned them."

A mist hung over the farmyard where Jasper lived when he went out the next morning to get the coon from the pickup. Just as he opened the door, Ralph Hansen chugged up in his ancient, dirty pickup. He got out and strolled over to Jasper's vehicle.

"What you got there?" Hansen asked.

"Bernice and me got this old 'coon down at Rocky River last night. She had this steel trap on her front foot so we shot her out of a tree to get her out of her misery," Jasper said slowly, seriously.

Ralph took the 'coon from Jasper's hands and fondled the trap.

"You didn't get this 'coon out of no tree. You been raiding my traps. This is sure as shootin' one of my traps I had set on Big Bear Creek where I saw some big 'coon tracks last week. You and Bernice been stealing my catch," Ralph flushed with apparent anger.

Jasper was about as easy to get mad as Ralph but he fought for some control in this awkward moment.

"No! It ain't so, Ralph, this 'coon was treed by our hounds and we shot it. You know we don't usually kill coons. We sure as heck ain't going to rob your traps. But if that is your trap, you sure need to learn a lesson. Tie those traps down so you don't maim a 'coon and have her pull that weight around until she starves. And you ought to go to those traps every day, not wait for weeks while a trapped animal suffers and dies, sometimes even gnawing their legs off to get away. And you ought to be more careful where you set them too. My neighbor John found one of his hounds half dead in one of your traps a couple of weeks ago," and Jasper paused a moment while Ralph turned his eyes away a little sheepishly.

"But since you have a house full of kids and a wife and this is your trap, you can have this 'coon, Ralph. Just be a little more careful the next time and then don't be so fast to call me and Bernice trap robbers. We just saw a need for a mercy killing of this old 'coon and we did it. We would do it again too," Jasper said with a sternness in his deep voice that he meant.

"I thank you, Jasper. I shouldn't done said what I did. I'll take the 'coon and sell it and I'll not be so careless next time with fastening my traps down either. I don't know how to do much of nothing except hunt, fish and trap that I'se been doing since I was a boy growing up in Oakboro. It's the way I make a living. I obey the laws and try to live right but I make my mistakes too. I hope you won't hold it agin me," Ralph muttered and it was the first time Jasper had ever seen this old outdoorsman even slightly apologetic.

"That's O.K., Ralph. We're still friends. I just wanted you to know we saw a duty to that little bundle of wildlife and we did it. There's nothing wrong about trapping in season but all of us have the obligation to be as humane as we can be when we are harvesting the wildlife bounty in those woods and waters," and Jasper's philosophy lives on.

The Day We Caught The 'Coon

There were no raccoons in the Endy township that we ever knew of until one rainy day when Chad Efird, Mitchell and I spotted one's head sticking out of a hole in a huge blackgum tree in a swampy section of woods a mile from the house. We knew what it was from pictures we had seen, but neighbors who were veteran hunters had never actually seen a real, live 'coon before. We were determined to catch that critter. We couldn't climb the tall tree.

For hours we threw rocks from the nearby fields at the hole in the tree and several times put those stones in the hole. But that only served to keep the animal in hiding. He wasn't about to come out of that safe haven.

While we knew it was a chore, finally we went to Chad's house and got a crosscut saw. It was a lot of work and dangerous for kids our age, but we eventually sawed that tree, that was two feet in diameter, down. It crashed to the ground and that 'coon came out like he was hit by lightning. We had been there around that tree for half a day or more and by that time, we had a half dozen dogs of various species and sizes. The dogs had been barking and scratching up leaves around the tree as they smelled the prey in the den.

The dogs jumped on that coon, got it on its back in a ditch and amazingly, we got that vicious, struggling creature in a tow sack. I cut a hole in one corner and we got the 'coon's tail through it. While I held on there, Chad or Mitchell got the mouth of the sack and we trotted off toward home with that angry animal in the bag.

Mama hadn't ever seen a 'coon either, especially a wild, hostile beast like that one and she didn't offer any objection when we decided to dump it out of the sack on the screened-in back porch. If you have ever seen chaos, we had it as soon as that critter was out of the sack and his feet on the floor. It crashed into the screen, and finding it couldn't get through, it turned its attention toward the ceiling and ran up and down the screened walls for ten minutes. Finally, out of breath, it stopped to rest, looking at us with daggers in its eyes.

"How you going to get that 'coon out of here?" Mama asked with about the same amount of fright as we had as we marveled at it from the kitchen through a closed, half glass door.

We scratched our heads. An idea emerged. We would take one of Mom's heavy, homemade bed quilts and throw it over the animal. The idea was sound. Maybe we wouldn't get a hand eaten off in the process. Mama got the quilt, we cornered the 'coon and tossed the big quilt over it. The animal couldn't see to fight and we soon had it subdued.

There was a sturdy chicken coop in the yard. We got the 'coon in that coop and eventually it calmed down. It was an old 'coon, probably six years old or more, and it weighed about twenty pounds, one of the largest the hunters from down east where they were plentiful had ever seen. They surmised that this animal had perhaps been captured

219

somewhere else and released in the Endy community because none had ever been seen there prior to that capture.

In time, that 'coon was a pet of sorts. You can't completely tame an old raccoon but you can a captured kitten a few weeks old. This one adapted to the cage, and we fed it regularly for years. It began to eat from our hands but would bite the fire out of you if you tried to pick him up. We built a better cage and often climbed in with the animal, but it was never as peaceful as a house cat.

Like all such pets, we grew tired of feeding it, and Dad moved the cage to the store that he ran on the highway. For several more years it was an attraction for motorists who stopped by to gawk at this masked animal anxious to eat candy or apples that the tourists offered. Raccoons are people animals and even in the wild they thrive in residential areas, often getting cussed for raiding garbage cans.

One morning we went to the store and some one had unlocked the cage door. The 'coon was gone! We had kept it and fed it for so long we halfway expected it to return. It never did! Some one might have stolen it and carried it off for their pet. Or, it might have simply been released to go free again by some sympathetic observer. Certainly, it had given a lot of people a novel opportunity to admire a real live raccoon at close range for a long time. Maybe it deserved a chance at freedom again. But no longer would it have its food brought to it several times a day. It would have to work for the fish it trapped in the creek and must hunt for the berries in the brier patches. But it was strong and healthy and able to make a living for itself. Most able bodied creatures prefer to work for a living rather than be trapped by welfare handouts that sap them of their dignity and independence.

Dad remembered a story about a 'coon dog owner who declared his beagle was such a fine dog at treeing 'coons that his bark, even at a long distance, revealed exactly what the dog was baying. The listener was a bit skeptical and decided to go with the 'coon hunter the following night.

Soon after they were in the woods, the beagle began its long, mournful barks. It had something up a tree.

"Well what has your dog got this time?" the unbelieving hunter asked.

"That's a 'possum for sure. That's not the right sound for a 'coon," the dog owner revealed. And they walked to the barking dog and sure enough, there was nothing but a kitten 'possum up the tree. They called the dog off and set it out in another direction. Soon it was barking that baying sound again.

"That's a different bark, I'm certain this time the dog has run a house cat up a tree," the owner of the beagle said. Sure enough, when they got to the baying dog, there was an old marauding house cat in the forks of the tree looking down at the dog.

Again the 'coon dog was called off and directed to resume the hunt. Moments later it was barking again. It was no baying sound that the skeptical hunter had ever heard before.

"What's your dog got now?" the man inquired breathlessly. The 'coon dog owner just listened quietly another few moments and shook his head.

"Friend, my dog ain't got nothing. Something's got him," the man said and headed out of those woods at a fast trot.

Dad Wasn't Confident When It Came To Fishing

Over the last half century plus a few years I have caught about 300,000 crappies from lakes and streams all over the country and I still pull in a cooler full regularly in Florida. The changing world of crappie fishing is as distinct as that for the more sophisticated gamefish species and perhaps this generation of panfishers will drag more slabs over the gunnels on artificial lures, particularly crankbaits, than on the conventional Missouri minnows, once accounting for almost all crappie catches.

My first experience crappie fishing was in Little Bear Creek and The Great Pee Dee River (then known as the Yadkin) in piedmont North Carolina. It was the depression era when eggs sold for 15 cents a dozen, milk 20 cents a gallon and Cokes were a nickel. There was little money for spending on fishing tackle from a 50 cent a day wage for picking cotton or even the more inflated 30 cents an hour earned by adults working in the textile industry. We had to improvise to catch fish, any kind of fish.

My first fishing line was No. 8 black sewing thread off a big spool from my mother's old treadle style sewing machine. That line with a cork from a vinegar jug, a tiny piece of wrap around lead from a discarded auto battery, a store bought Eagle Claw hook and a pole cut from a limb of a popashe bush was the best fishing equipment we could muster.

Bait was easy. We ripped open a tow bag that was used for 200 pounds of fertilizer, tied some crooked limbs from a tree on each side, then we pulled the makeshift seine through the shallow, rocky waters of the creek and branches. It was easy to get several dozen two inch minnows in a matter of minutes in a period when pollution was unknown. Those wild, native gambusia, or whatever they were, impaled on a hook were the only crappie baits we had ever known.

Only doctors and lawyers had boats in that time frame. The rest of us fished from the bank, or the hill, as we called it. You baited the hook, stuck the pole in the ground, propped a rock under the butt and patiently waited for a fish to come along and pop the stopper under. Can you believe it, we still caught fish on just about every outing and seldom failed to fill the skillet with crappies at meal time. Of course, the fishing pressure was minimal and the habitat had not been consequently disturbed.

The world turns and my crappie fishing style changed with the evolution.

With the college days over and World War II history, I had a boat, good cane poles, factory made bobbers and lead shot that clamped on monofilament line perfected by Du Pont in Wilmington, Del., not long after the American women began attacking store clerks and counters for the few runless nylon hose that went on the market. Prior to that moment in history, well-dressed ladies wore cotton or silk hose that were not nearly as sexy as nylon and any slight snag caused an ugly run that ruined the stockings.

Fishing minnows hooked through the back or the lips and dangled in the grass, brushpiles, or around rocky bottom cover, you could catch a nice stringer of pound-size crappies any time after May 10. The North Carolina regulations at that time prohibited angling for gamefish in the rivers until that date. Opening of the fishing season was like July 4th and outdoorsmen flocked to the river banks for the first fishing adventure of the spring.

Like all fishing, every trip was not a bonanza. Crappies then and now sometimes are just turned off and I remember an observation made by my late father when we were sitting on the wooded bank of Mountain Creek in Stanly County with a half dozen baited poles protruding over the stream. It was a wide reservoir at that point and Dad looked out across the river after we had been without a bite for an hour or so. Never much of a fisherman, he made a classic analysis: "How on earth do you expect to catch any fish? They have all that water out there to live in and you think they'll come right up here to the bank to eat these minnows on your hook. The chances of them being here is mighty slim." Realistically that was astute but we caught fish.

Florida began attracting fishermen in winter when it was too cold in much of the country to fish anywhere else for crappies in comfort. The pattern for speckled perch back in the late '40's, '50's and even the '70's in the Sunshine State was to find them bumping lilies or other aquatic growth during the spawning months of January and February and dropping a live minnow on a line in their faces. When you located the nesting specks, you could fill a livewell in a few hours. They were plentiful and hungry and great gourmet food on the dinner table. Many Florida lakes are still great spawning season bonanzas for specks but fishermen have learned and throughout much of the state now, fine catches of crappies are made every month of the year.

To be successful at times other than when the specks are on the beds, anglers turned to drifting and trolling jigs, spoons and combinations of jigs and minnows a dozen years ago. They learned that the open water had crappies suspended in the deep holes and they didn't bite by the calendar. It didn't have to be cold weather and they didn't have to be full of eggs. When you pulled a minnow and jig across a hungry fish, the crappies struck and this system has been expanded to many states around the country. It has been extremely successful.

Other guides and crappie fishing experts started fishing for the species with rods and reels a couple of generations ago.

Mostly, they just used a long, limber rod with two or three hooks tied below a lead weight and they impaled minnows and lowered them on the fringes of natural or manmade structures in the deeper water. The system has been successful and when anglers can pinpoint the structure, they can come away with good catches reeled in on the natural baits and jigs.

The latest innovation in crappie fishing is the small crankbait or minnow-like lure. Bass anglers who have learned many of the secrets of bassing success by casting a variety of artificial lures for the large and smallmouths, were often surprised to find a slab-size crappie on the hook. Often the crappie were so active that the bass the anglers sought didn't get a decent chance to strike. The numerous crappies beat the bass to the bait.

Taking a lesson from the accidental strikes bass anglers reported, thousands of panfish anglers today have gone to ultralight and lightweight tackle with minnow-look-alike lures and they are dragging the fish to the boat.

Hundreds of small crankbaits are catching crappies today from Back Bay in Virginia, through Currituck Sound in the Tar Heel State, at Santee Cooper in S.C., Clarks Hill in Georgia, Center Hill in Tennessee, Kentucky Lake and all over Florida, among other states.

The crankbaits for crappies movement began in earnest in Central Florida in 1985. Many of the lakes were almost covered with dense hydrilla and trolling was impossible. Some innovators began flipping small crankbaits into the holes in the hydrilla. When they didn't get hung, they came in with fine fish. Then chemical treatments somewhat relieved the aquatic growth problem and the crappie casting sect began fishing the wildlife commission fish markers and natural cover in five to eight feet of water. The big specks could not leave the slowly retrieved crankbaits alone.

There are a few of the tiny artificials that are more successful than others. Among them are the 1/8 oz. Bass Track Shad Junior, the Wee-R, the Teeny Wee-R and Super Wee-R. The Wee-R crawfish by Rebel sometimes is a killer too. While these are true crankbaits with spoonbills that make it possible for you to determine the depth it runs by the speed you retrieve, the 1/4 oz. Rat-L-Trap chrome color that is a sinker and has no lip has been the most productive artificial minnow-like lure for the past three years. The big crappies can't leave it alone. It's most successful when fished with open-faced spinning tackle on a six or eight pound test line. Crappies often hit the Rat-L-Trap as it slowly sinks but they will also strike on the slow retrieve and you can make it run near the surface or almost on the bottom once you get the feel of the lure. The bream colors will catch some fish but nothing recently has been as attractive to the specks as the bright chrome.

Fishing with Betty Haire, of Charlotte, N.C., one of the leading Lady Bass and Bass 'n Gal professional bassers, at Chattanooga in a tournament, I tried this crankbait jigging in the spatter dock lilies and holes in hydrilla. The crappies found the system interesting and they bit viciously. The problem here was that the little bass wouldn't leave the lure alone. That's the opposite of the situation the bass anglers discovered when they caught specks accidentally when the more sophisticated species was their objective. Oh well, one man's trash is another man's treasure.

As some wag has said, "Time and tide waits for no man." Fishing for every species changes with each generation and the crappie fishermen have adapted to the change. The newest system is the small minnow-like lure and it is proving itself to hundreds of the crappie devout all over the land.

Years after I left home and was struggling to establish the weekly **TABOR CITY TRIBUNE** in Tabor City, N.C., Dad drove down from Stanly to go fishing. We would often drive about an hour to the coast to saltwater fish or else about half that time to the Waccamaw River or Lake Waccamaw to fish for bream, crappie or some other panfish species.

"It's strange but regardless of where you are going and are ready to put a bait in the water, it's always somewhere a long way off. No one seems to be able to catch fish at home," Dad said.

How right he was!

The Art Of Living Together

Dad never mistreated a black person that I know of but certainly he was prejudiced and never quite considered a Negro the equivalent of any white man. He saw thousands of this race emerge as great athletes in the latter days of his life, and while he didn't fully approve of their dominance in what heretofore had been white man's games, baseball, football and basketball, he had to admit that they had superior athletic skills.

Slowly he began to accept them for their abilities although his original reaction to their talents on the athletic fields was, "They are only a generation or two removed from monkeys and they should be able to run and jump better than we can." I don't know that he ever fully regretted that observation, but he did mellow some as the nation began to learn to live together with a little less hostility.

It was an era when frustration gripped the populace and people were unsure of the future. Some whites were jealous, some harbored hate. Some blacks were vindictive and determined to find revenge for generations of abuse. Some on both sides liked the status quo and would wait in the wings for transition without taking sides. The bulk of the citizenry was unsure of the future and simply knew people were going in a lot of directions at the same time. It seemed that it didn't make any difference what road you were on if you didn't know where you were going. Differences lessened and the races grew closer, eventually focusing on a direction that would make a better life for many. Both races changed ideas and conceptions and despite the unorthodoxy of the times, some harmony swept over the South before Dad's death.

A true story of a little gray fox and a couple of mongrel hounds that lived with the late Dr. John N. Hamlet, of

Beaufort, S.C., fits the pattern of the conflict between blacks and whites as the second half of the 20th century began.

Dr. John N. Hamlet died in the subtropical rain forest at Bayport, on Florida's Gulf of Mexico, five years ago. He was a great naturalist and a remarkable outdoorsman all his life. His experiences were myriad.

Dr. Hamlet headed the geographically secluded Primate Center at Prichardsville, South Carolina in 1946. There, 5,000 cynomolgus monkeys, which he had captured in the Phillipines, were kept for a worldwide research program which eventually led to the perfection of the polio vaccine. After he had captured the monkeys in Pacific jungles, the site of the remote South Carolina research outpost was sought out and purchased from "Lucky" Luciano by the National Foundation for Infantile Paralysis. Many diseases are communicable between the various primates, including man, so the location for the center had to be miles away from any concentration of people.

With only his wife, a few local assistants, some scholarly laboratory researchers and a couple of mongrel hounds for companionship, the project began. Dr. Hamlet cherished the closeness he had with the dogs. They "reminded him of his 14 years with the U.S. Fish and Wildlife Service (FWS)" before he was "loaned" to the foundation for the polio vaccine program, he said.

Dr. Hamlet had a trained wolf for a pet during his time with FWS. The dogs at his new home brought back memories of his early youth on a ranch outside Rapid City, South Dakota, where he grew up with the Sioux Indians after leaving a broken home. He and his Sioux playmates hunted all over the Black Hills, and by the time he was 14, he also owned some of the best wolf hounds in the territory.

He had missed having a dog during the years he relocated from place to place for FWS, and he missed having a dog later, while he was hunting the monkeys in the most remote sections of the Pacific Islands. But once he settled in South Carolina, at a base he could call home for awhile, he got an old red-bone hound and a little black and tan. The red-bone was named "Red" and didn't cost him anything. He received the old dog as a gift from one of the local hunters, after the dog hung a hind leg in a barb wire fence, mutilating a joint, and a veterinarian had to amputate the leg.

He had given a man $5 for the little black and tan hound. Old crippled Red and the little black and tan female became the very best pair of hunting dogs Dr. Hamlet ever owned.

"His nose was unbelievably sensitive. He had what swamp hunters at Prichardsville called a cold nose. That meant he could sniff an animal track from the night before and stay with it until it became a hot track and eventually flush his prey."

Red was not just a coon hound. He was equally adept at tracking and treeing opossums or baying foxes and minks in the holes along the river banks. A hunter had to let Red know what he was searching for, but he could do this by letting Red smell a hide of the animal sought. Put a raccoon skin to his nose, and he would hunt only for coons. Mink, fox, and opossum hides would have the same result. It was uncanny the way he could pick one animal scent from another, but Red proved this ability repeatedly.

The black and tan usually just followed alongside Red. She could bark and yelp and smell too, but not the same way old Red did. She was more of a follower; Red was a born leader.

One afternoon, William Pinckney, a Primate Center neighbor who had farmed and hunted in Beaufort County all his long life, brought a tiny gray fox to Dr. Hamlet's house. It was only a few weeks old and had probably been orphaned by some disaster. Pinckney had found it shivering in a meadow. Dr. Hamlet then as always, had a soft spot in his heart for every living creature. He had nursed countless wild things back to health. Pinckney knew about this, and that's why he brought the little fox to Dr. Hamlet. Pinckney figured correctly that the good doctor would pamper the critter until it was well, strong and ready to roam free in the swamp lands.

"I put the baby fox in a cage near the house and kept feeding and watering it every day," Dr. Hamlet explained. "It began to grow, and soon it would eat out of my hand. It wasn't long until it was as tame as the dogs and cats around the place. In a few months, it looked almost full grown and I figured it was time to let it loose so it could join its brothers and sisters in the swamps," he said.

"One day, I had to go into Beaufort for some groceries, so I put the little fox in a box, set it in my station wagon and headed for town. About five miles down the blacktop country road, I stopped at a particularly dense section of woodland, opened the cage and made the fox jump out. I then got back in the car and headed on to Beaufort.

"I shopped around for an hour or so, then drove back to the Primate Center. The first thing I saw when I got out of the car — carrying my bag of groceries — was the little gray fox. It was sitting on the front doorsteps, licking its front paws. My wife said the fox had come back to the house half an hour before I arrived," Dr. Hamlet recalled.

The Hamlets just smiled at each other and decided that if the fox didn't want to be wild, it could stay with them. They weren't going to cage it anymore, and it could walk out the front gate any time it wanted to leave. They continued to feed it and, for certain, it became a part of the household.

At first they tried to feed the fox in a bowl that was kept separate from the two hounds' bowls, but the fox would have none of that. The fox insisted on eating from the same dish with the hounds, and they would constantly growl and push each other around, scrapping for the food. While dogs and foxes are normally "mortal enemies," these grew to be "friends," and eventually would share the food peacefully until all three had a bellyful. As months dragged by, the three became like a family, and human visitors were surprised to witness this unusual alliance of wild and domestic animals.

"The building where my wife and I lived, at the Primate Center was known as the Foundation House. It was set on piers well off the ground, and the hounds slept directly under our bedroom. When the fox was nearly grown it decided to take up residence with the dogs and sleep with them at night. They had a kind of communal bed for a while," Dr. Hamlet explained.

"Fall arrived and the moon fulled in October that year," Dr. Hamlet recalled. "I went to bed as usual about 10:30 p.m. one night. I had not gone to sleep yet, but was dozing a little when I heard the fox get up under the house, shake itself a time or two and mosey out in the yard. It was strange behavior for the fox, before then, so I went to the window to look. The dogs hadn't moved or made a sound.

"Thirty minutes or so later, I heard old Red stand up under the house, shake himself and growl a little, then the black and tan arose too. Moments later, I heard them shuffling along through the yard. Again I went to the window. They still had not barked or shown any sign of excitement.

"Red looked at the moon, glanced around the premises, then put his nose to the ground — where the fox had trotted a half hour earlier — and let out a long ghostly, trailing bark as he headed for the gate. The black and tan joined in the music and they left the compound barking for all they were worth, right on the trail of the little gray fox. I listened until they were completely out of earshot, probably a mile or more away. Shaking my head in disbelief, I went back to bed. My wife and I laughed ourselves to sleep at such an unusual event," Dr. Hamlet said.

"At 1:00 a.m., I heard a slight shuffling under the house in the communal bed. I recognized the noise as that of the gray fox. He was panting as he lay down, and he quickly went to sleep.

"Twenty minutes later, I heard the hounds barking on a trail, coming closer and closer. At exactly 1:30, they came through the compound gates, barking at every breath, and trailed right under the house where the fox was already asleep. They shook off the dew they had gathered from the long chase, curled up together with the fox, then the trio slept peacefully for the remainder of the night. All three seemed satisfied with their adventure, and all were 'dog tired' after the long escapade.

"That 'cat and mouse' game between the two hounds and the fox took place nightly thereafter. It was always the same. They would go to bed together, then the fox would sneak out. Half an hour later, the hounds would emerge, find the trail, and off they would go on another three-hour escapade. It always ended back where it started — under our bedroom floor — where the three creatures curled up to rest and sleep together," said Dr. Hamlet.

Over time, that nightly routine got to be a little irritating to the Hamlets. Since it interrupted their nightly rest, they decided the fox would just have to go. So, when Dr. Hamlet had to make a trip to Savannah, which was a considerable distance from Pritchardsville, they built a little box cage and put the fox inside before he chugged off down the highway.

About 15 miles from the Primate Center, Dr. Hamlet stopped the car, set the cage on the shoulder of the road and coaxed the fox outside. Then the doctor put the box back in the car, shut the tailgate and started to drive away. For one long moment Dr. Hamlet thought about getting out, picking up the little animal, putting him back in the car and taking him home again. But remembering those nightly noises that interrupted his peaceful sleep, he drove on toward Savannah, looking back through the rear view mirror at the fox as it sat on its haunches watching the vehicle disappear.

Dr. Hamlet transacted his Savannah business and returned home later that afternoon. The fox was not waiting for him on the front steps this time. Dr. Hamlet was a little chagrined that at last he had gotten rid of this wild creature that had become so "at home" in their household. He was a little sad.

A half-hour later, Dr. Hamlet heard a scratch at the front door. It was the gray fox, panting and "smiling" as if to say, "you left me in the swamp, but I'm happy to be back home again."

The nightly chase game with the hounds continued that night and every night as long as the Hamlets remained at the Primate Center. Some months later, the National Foundation for Infantile Paralysis sent him back to the Far East on another monkey-trapping expedition. He had no baggage room for hounds or a fox on that trip. And he never saw them again.

"I left that strange trio in the research compound when I flew to Borneo and I suppose they kept up that behavior until they died of old age," Dr. Hamlet said.

There's a story for Americans in the way these different animals adopted to the circumstances and lived happily together.

Always there are some people who can't see the forests for the trees and that is perhaps illustrated in another way with the story that Dad often told in jest. He had been invited to go fox hunting one night and not long after the dogs were turned loose, they picked up a trail and the barking of a dozen dogs echoed over the Stanly County hills.

"Now listen to that music," one of the old time hunters said softly.

Dad listened and listened.

"I can't hear any music for them damn dogs barking," he said. And the old hunter didn't think it was funny.

KKK burned crosses to intimidate their victims

Robed and hooded Klansmen stood around burning crosses

Columbia University
in the City of New York
[NEW YORK 27, N. Y.]

GRADUATE SCHOOL OF JOURNALISM
OFFICE OF THE DEAN

May 4, 1953

Mr. W. Horace Carter
TABOR CITY TRIBUNE
Tabor City, North Carolina

Dear Mr. Carter:

    I take very great pleasure in confirming the fact that the Trustees of Columbia University have awarded the Pulitzer Public Service Prize to THE NEWS REPORTER and the TABOR CITY TRIBUNE for their successful campaign against the Ku Klux Klan.

    In accordance with that award the University has ordered the engraving of two gold medals, one will be presented to the TABOR CITY TRIBUNE and the other to THE NEWS REPORTER, as tangible evidence of this selection. This medal will be sent to you as soon as it is received from the engraver.

    With renewed congratulations, I am

                      Sincerely yours,

                      Carl W. Ackerman, Secretary
                        Advisory Board on the
                            Pulitzer Prizes

CWA:AD

This is the gold, engraved medalion awarded THE TRIBUNE for meritorious public service for the klan fight - award was made in 1953.

Me, Dad And The KKK

In 1953, seven years after I moved to Tabor City and founded the little weekly newspaper, **The Tabor City Tribune**, I won the prestigeous Pulitzer Prize for Meritorious Public Service for a long editorial fight against the Ku Klux Klan that ran rampant in the Carolinas. It was the first time any weekly newspaper had ever won the Pulitzer Prize and remains today the smallest newspaper to have been so honored. I was surprised and proud. Dad was confused and skeptical.

Dad could not understand why I was fighting the KKK. All he knew about the Klan was what Southern history books had taught and his generation had heard from their peers. It was in that desperate era following the Civil War, that an organized Ku Klux Klan, made up of vigilantes ready to oppose the scalawag leeches from the South who sought to take over politics in the ravaged land and who were supported by the Yankee Carpetbaggers, rose to save the natives from oppression. That post Civil War Klan was romanticized by writers and respected by virtually every red-blooded Rebel left alive who loved his country in the late 1800's.

I would have fought for that Klan myself. It served a worthy purpose, was made up generally of citizens with honor and character. Granted, it probably over-stepped its bounds and illegally intimidated some Negro communities, but its existence had some justification. It sought to restore the people's right and dignity.

Dad had deep feelings against Catholics, Jews and Negroes. He was conditioned to most of those prejudices, a word that he wouldn't have even known, from childhood. With his heritage, most of us would have thought like he did. He felt that Catholics were like Communists in one respect, determined to make everyone else accept their faith. It was an imperialistic philosophy. He believed that the Jews had cornered the market on the money of the world and other people couldn't pry it from them. He had a deep conviction that the Negroes were an inferior race that could and should never be considered equal in intelligence to the whites of the country. While totally unacceptable as a philosophy, many blacks today still are incapable of serious responsibilities. He would never have condoned abusing the Negroes, but his training and innate conviction was that he should not associate with them in any way that could be avoided. While he believed in the work ethic, he didn't believe any Negroes were capable of handling his job or any job that required more than minimal mentality. He was not alone with that concept in the '50's.

He was bitterly opposed to busing Negro children and whites all over the county to get them integrated in schools. Like he said in jest many times, "I don't believe in integration, I believe in slavery."

The KKK of the 1950's preached anti-Negro, Jew and Catholic messages everywhere they met. It's what drew much of the crowd. I reasoned with him on this subject several times. While religions have caused many unholy wars and indeed Catholicism has not always had lily white records of patience and understanding with competing denominations, neither have all Protestant religions. In America, everyone is supposedly free to choose and follow his religious beliefs. Catholics have that right, just as Baptists have. Jews indeed have been blessed with economic and financial success in America and in much of the civilized world. But their record of honesty, lawfulness and devotion to society and the country is unquestioned. It was the American way to work and get ahead if you could do it with integrity and the Jews I knew were wonderful people. Negroes, certainly in general, could not hold many positions in Dad's time frame that whites held. They had not had the training nor the education. But with equal opportunity, in time the minority could pull itself up by its bootstraps and perform work other than the most menial tasks. That is proving to be correct today. Maybe busing was wrong and certainly it doesn't make economic sense, but it wasn't right to bus blacks right by our white schools at Oakboro and Endy for decades to get them to an all-black school in Albemarle. Some rode twenty miles each way and more to segregated schools that was unnecessary. White schools were in walking distance of many Negro families then, but these facilities were off limits to the black race. The two wrongs didn't make a right but you couldn't oppose busing on economic grounds to achieve integration when we bussed to achieve segregation for a generation and more and considered it legal and proper. It's strange how we rationalize to fit our own narrow self centered idealism.

I agreed with him that ultraliberal politicians and the media many times distorted slavery in the South and the plight of the Negroes in his generation, before, and even today, but there were enough cases of abuse and dishonest association to command the passing of laws and issuing of supportive court decisions and decrees that would make the Negroes full-fledged citizens with equal rights. The status quo could not forever endure in a democracy like the one the United States lived with.

From the day I founded the **The Tribune** in 1946, I had tried to give blacks a fair shake with the news. **The Tribune** was the first newspaper in Southeastern North Carolina that ran the pictures of blacks on the front page of the newspaper when there was something good to say about them. Only black criminals made the front page in many Southern newspapers. In that era, the closest daily newspaper to Tabor City, was **The Wilmington Star.** It would not let the face of a black appear on its front page, even when a Negro was in a large group picture of charitable, civic or religious leaders. Printers were instructed to rout out the faces of Negroes in **The Star** in such pictures so there would be no integration in the newspaper's news coverage. Such blank faces appeared in **The Star** many times after I founded **The Tribune**.

I made a point when attending civic, promotional gatherings then that were sometimes attended by a few Negroes, to sit with those blacks. I wanted them to feel wanted and not rejected and ostracized. We needed unity and trust in a difficult period of our history. It may not have sold newspaper subscriptions for me, but it was what I considered right. I was proud to do my part toward welcoming Negroes into the mainstream of American life. In that objective, I believe I succeeded.

The 1950 KKK differed from the Civil War Klan in many ways. Few of its members were really community leaders. Indeed most were adventure-seeking local rednecks looking for excitement wherever they could find it. Flogging neighbors for sexual promiscuity and alleged immorality was a common nocturnal activity of the KKK in my community then. Klansmen dragged men and women from the sanctity of their homes, carried them to desolate areas, whipped them unmercifully, and ordered them to stop living un-Christian lives. Most of these floggings were KKK assaults upon Alglo-Saxon whites. But some were against blacks. Many victims were enticed from their homes late at night by strangers who pretended car trouble. Once the victims were out of the house, they were overpowered by robed hoodlums and the strangers disappeared.

Their public meetings were long harangues against blacks, Catholics and Jews with a smattering of warnings to the general populace living out of kilter with the guidelines of the hierarchy of Klandom. The KKK spokesmen often tried intimidating the audience by suggesting that the stranger at your elbow in the crowd could be a Klansman in civilian clothes and any derogatory statement you dared to utter might bring retribution with a buggy whip or worse. Klan spokesmen boasted of law officers on their rosters. Indeed, the only Klansman killed in that uprising in the Carolinas was a Conway, South Carolina policeman who died of gunshot wounds. He wore his police uniform under his Klan robe and hood.

I tried to impress Dad with my reasons for opposing this illegal, cowardly organization that was regularly threatening me on the phone, with messages under my printshop door, stuck under my auto windshield wiper, in hundreds of nasty letters and even with two daytime visits by the Granddragon, Thomas L. Hamilton, of Leesville, South Carolina.

"These people want to shut me up, Dad. They have openly stated that they would put me out of business by cancelling subscriptions and intimidating the few advertisers I have whose support is paramount to **The Tribune's** survival. I must fight them regardless of the pressure on me and my family. I know I am right. Vigilantes may be heroes in the movies, but it is not right in America for a handful of adventurers to beat citizens and intimidate them for being what they are in race and religion and whipping them for sleeping with someone else's wife. While I cannot condone that kind of immoral conduct, it is up to the law to bring punishment. Klansmen cannot be judge, jury and executioner but that's what they set themselves up to be in Tabor City and the Southeastern Carolinas now," I said.

"I am not saying this so that I might get a bouquet on my shoulder but I intend to fight them as long as I can pay my bills and get ink to stick to newsprint. There are not many free newspapers in America any more. Only two types of newspapers are truly independent, free to write what an editor really believes. Those two types of newspapers are the ones that are owned by a company that is independently wealthy and can survive regardless of the economic pressure, or the little newspaperman who has nothing and therefore can lose nothing. I have nothing of economic value to lose. I came to Tabor City with $4000 saved while in the Navy. I could lose my life and my family but **The Tribune**, be it ever so humble, and so tiny, will never give up a fight because of economic pressure or threatened physical abuse," I said to Dad frequently and he chewed on those ideals long enough to want me to win. Deep down, he knew I was right.

The Tribune did win. I was editor, advertising manager, subscription solicitor, janitor and everything else. The small mechanical staff in the printshop gave me wonderful moral support and for over three years **The Tribune** lambasted the KKK with strong words, often poorly written during lunch hour breaks, but displayed on the newspaper's front page as crusading editorials. It brought other newspapers into the fight and in the end, 62 Klansmen were convicted. The Granddragon, and many others went to prison or paid fines.

North Carolina's legislature passed an anti-mask law, outlawing Klan organizations as they were then. Little Klan trouble has been found in N.C. since those crucial years of the 1950's.

It was a long, difficult and scary crusade that Dad eventually applauded. Maybe it did a little good in the community. Certainly, it brought my Dad and me closer together.

He could scarcely write a simple sentence but he was vest button popping proud of his first born who dared to stand up and be counted even when his best Tabor City friends advised him to shut up....Maybe the KKK would go away.

Rise And Fall Of The Klan

Frequently the question arises as to why the Ku Klux Klan rose to such great power in Southeastern North Carolina and the adjoining South Carolina counties in the 1950's. There are a number of reasons.

It was the era in which the U.S. Supreme Court had decreed that equal but separate schools for blacks was unconstitutional and integration was soon to come in the South. Harry Truman was president and was pushing the integration, making him one of the most hated leaders the country had ever had, especially in the latter months of his second term. Perhaps as much of the cause as anything, the area had thousands of young men home from the battlefields of the Pacific and Europe who had been engulfed in violence and adventure. They could not settle down quickly to growing tobacco and produce crops. They were itchy for something to do and the KKK offered a change in the routine. While it is difficult to excuse an organization for vigilante lawlessness, many of those caught up in the klan floggings were sincere. They actually believed they were doing something good, some of this dating back to the school book training of KKK usefulness after the Civil War. The United Nations was in its infancy and in ill repute all over America. Klan promoters used the weakness of the UN as another reason why the people must ban together to enforce the rules outside of the law.

While little newspapers like **THE TRIBUNE** usually find that their crusades are for lost causes, this campaign was successful beyond the wildest dreams of anyone. It was successful for reasons I have often rehashed in public speakings for years, including 168 talks that I made in more than a dozen states in 1954. The **RALEIGH NEWS** and **OBSERVER'S** Jay Jenkins picked up the fight and he was a welcomed intruder in the campaign. It took some pressure off **THE TRIBUNE**. In Whiteville, **THE NEWS-REPORTER** and the late Willard Cole did an outstanding job of fighting the KKK in virtually every issue after they jumped into the crusade. The Pulitzer Prize was awarded to both **THE TRIBUNE** and the **NEWS REPORTER**.

Success for the crusade largely resulted from the backing we had from the FBI. In most crusades, the newspaper fights the establishment for corruption, inaction, favoritism, political shenanigans or other reasons. But the federal government was on the side of the newspaper in the KKK fight. While local and state law enforcement agencies sought to create the impression that they were going all out to eradicate the klan, it was the more astute investigation and action of the FBI that made the first arrests, broke the back of the organization and let local and state police pick up the pieces. It might have been a lost cause fight had we not had the support of Uncle Sam. It's hard to buck city hall as we have many times.

The convictions of dozens of klansmen, the first such success against the klan in history, brought great recognition and honors to **THE TRIBUNE**. In less than a year, more than a dozen national, state and regional awards were won by the little newspaper. I was as proud as the proverbial peacock. In addition to the Pulitzer, I was named "One of the Ten Most Outstanding Young Men in America for 1954" by the U.S. Junior Chamber of Commerce in Seattle, Washington. I had previously been named "North Carolina Young Man of the Year" by the Jaycees.

I won the President's Award of the National Editorial Association in Baltimore. Both the North Carolina and the Eastern North Carolina Press Associations gave me certificates of merit. B'nai B'rith presented me with its eleven state regional honor. There were others.

But perhaps nothing was more pleasing to me and my family than an event sponsored by the Endy Community in 1955. Promoted by Randall Burleson, my old scoutmaster who led me to be an Eagle Scout, and others, a "Horace Carter Day" was held at the school. I was pleased to be honored in my home community and I know that Dad and Mom could not have been prouder had I been governor of the state.

We were slow in our family then to say "I love you" to each other. But when Dad put his arm across my shoulder as the events of the day ended and the banquet dishes were being cleaned up in the school cafeteria, tears were in his eyes. He didn't have anything funny to say. And he didn't have to tell me he loved me and was proud. I could see it all over him.

I had tried to make a serious speech about the need for service above self and the desire of mankind to leave a legacy for future generations to envy, but my heart filled my throat. My remarks didn't truly reflect my thanksgiving for being so honored "a prophet is not without honor save in his own country."

Crusades And Threats Of Suits

Years after the Ku Klux Klan campaign that the tiny **Tribune** conducted and won in a strange mixture of accident and coincidence, we tackled another perceived evil in the community. We were alerted that the Horry County sheriff's department was being bribed by moonshiners throughout the rural areas and the gamblers of the much more metropolitan Myrtle Beach in the same county. There were weekly payoffs running into many thousands of dollars, or so said the informants, as the moonshiners were protected from arrest for selling non-tax paid, stumphole whiskey and beach gamblers were allowed to run gambling tables and slot machines of all sorts without being harassed.

We petitioned the federal government to investigate and two veteran Alcohol and Tobacco Tax Unit (ATTU) enforcement officers moved in quietly. Over the course of the next year, they gathered thirty-eight sworn and notarized affidavits from the law breakers admitting that there was a lot of corruption in the sheriff's department. They were admitting their complicity in the corruption because the squeeze on their incomes had grown so tight that they could not make a living. They didn't have anything left after paying the bribes.

The officers also brought in the FBI that gathered information charging the sheriff's force with violation of the civil rights of the blacks in a remote section of the county. That case finally went to Federal Court in Florence. It was the first case ever prosecuted under the new Civil Rights laws and **The Tribune** was credited with bringing this action. Unfortunately, the jury turned all the dozen defendants loose. The Horry County grand jury heard the evidence about the alleged corruption from me and studied the affidavits from the bribers for months but never returned a true bill as the wholesale lawlessness had crept into almost every political facet of the county government. Thus, it would appear that our intense crusade against this corruption was wasted. Not so, the sheriff and all his deputies lost their jobs in the next election. Some left the county quickly. Others died and the county government was at least partially cleansed for a time.

It was the most dangerous crusade of the dozens we promoted with the lively little newspaper. Threats by phone, letter, in person and second hand from friends who had been approached by my adversaries, indicated how desperately the deputies and sheriff wanted to hush us up. There was even a call from a Myrtle Beach doctor at dusk one afternoon who said he had overheard a conversation by one of the officials I had accused with a hit man in Tampa, Florida. They had made a picture of my house and the paid executioner was going to blow up the house, the doctor said. It was nerve wracking, especially for my wife and children. The Tabor City police department, a two man crew then, hired a substitute to be my body guard for a couple of weeks. The house didn't get blown up. The crusade ended with the change of personnel in the sheriff's department. It was a kind of back handed, indirect way of winning the war when we had lost the battles.

During these many months of this really dangerous crusade, Dad and Mama were worried sick. They visualized that some gangster type might blow us all up, kill us in a dastardly execution.

"Why do you get yourself in all these predicaments?" Dad asked during the campaign when the heat was really on us.

The answer was simple. As the only newspaper, be it ever so humble, in the town, I had the responsibility of trying to insure the best possible government for the people. I had to be the watch dog. It was a charge, a challenge, and I could not sit back and straddle the fences like most newspapers do just because it was risky to speak out. Idealism? Yes, and probably a little ridiculous, but that's the way it was in my mind and still is. Newspapers should be protectors of the common man in the populace, especially little newspapers where it is the only media close to the citizenry. The big papers don't give a whoop about an injustice in Tabor City.

But newspapers that speak out on what they really feel is justice and equity, have a hard time. The middle of the road newspapers are much more economically prosperous. When you crusade and say your piece regardless of where the chips fall, you will always be alienating a portion of your readership, a portion of your advertisers. A portion will side with your adversary. And you can only split this clientele a time or two in a small community before you have lost your financial base. Some will forgive and forget and eventually return to your subscription list and advertising manifest. Others mark you off forever. You have to be willing to sacrifice fiscal success for a clear conscience if you are the editor and write things as you really see them. Weekly newspapers are people. The editorials are the character and personality generally of one man, me in the case of **The Tribune** in those early years. If he has character and indepth ability, he can be of unusual value to the morality of the community. Where he is severely lacking, his newspaper will be lacking and nothing good will come from such an unfortunate marriage.

It was my hope that **The Tribune** would be symbolic and a mouthpiece for peace and serenity in a community castigated for its decades of lawlessness. **The Tribune**, and I, as the only editorial writer for many years, honestly wanted to help pull the community away from violence and tragedy to tranquility and prosperity. I think we succeeded to some extent in the 1950's and until today. The violence is reduced but economically the community still suffers.

And that's what I often tried to explain to Dad when he wondered why I was always getting into hot water by writing too boldly. I hope he eventually understood but there were many times when I didn't understand myself.

When you are outspoken in the news and editorial columns, you can expect some legal problems or at least the threat of such action. People whom you antagonize will threaten libel suits any time that they think you can be intimidated to stop writing about them. Their complaint and threat is usually for the purposes of intimidation and if you have not done your homework, you'll have some uncomfortable moments. If you have written the truth, the purist defense against libel, you can go ahead and get a good night's sleep.

After **The Tribune** had survived a few years, the late Al Harrison, of Spencer, North Carolina, went to work with me right out of UNC Chapel Hill as news editor. He wrote a popular column every week on the edit page. One week after having spent a few days at Carolina Beach, at Wilmington, he wrote,"Carolina Beach is the worst beach I have ever seen." The ink was hardly dry on the newsprint when the phone rang and Mayor Glenn Tucker of Carolina Beach was on the line.

"Horace, I read what Harrison said about our beach. I'm going to sue you for libel," he said in a near rage.

"Good, Glenn, just stand in line. Sue us when your turn comes up," I said.

Glenn laughed. The suit was never filed. Nor were any of the other 31 that have been threatened over the last 42 years. But I'm sure there have been some times that we would have lost. You aren't always right, even when you think you are.

But **The Tribune** has always been out-spoken, never timid.

HORACE CARTER DAY

April 3, 1954

BUILDING CITIZENSHIP
CHARACTER TRAINING

BOY SCOUTS OF AMERICA

Sponsored by

ENDY GRANGE, ENDY SCOUT TROOP, AND ENDY SENIOR CLASS 1939

ENDY SCHOOL CAFETERIA

April 3, 1954 — 7:30 P. M.

If The Shoe Fits

I was Mayor of Tabor City a couple of years back in the 1950's and was editing **THE TRIBUNE** at the same time. As Mayor, I was also judge of the local court and we tried the minor cases every Monday night.

One of the regulars in that court was an alcoholic by the name of Sam Hester (name changed to protect some survivors). Almost every week he was in court charged with being drunk and disorderly and many times I fined him $50.00 or put him in jail for 30 days, the maximum penalties I could invoke. It was kind of sad to punish him at all because it took food out of his children's mouths or locked him up a month, leaving the family with no means of support. But it wasn't practical to just dismiss his charges every week either. Just such difficult situations is why I chose to serve only one term.

On Wednesday following the Monday night sessions, the newspaper ran a list of the cases tried along with the case dispositions. Hester's name was an almost certainty every week in that column.

One of the most respected merchants in town came in the office one day and said, "Horace, would you please run a little note in the paper saying the Sam Hester who is always in Mayor's Court and charged with being drunk and disorderly is not the same Sam Hester who runs the big general store in town by the name of Sam Hester's General Store?"

"Sure I'll be glad to," I said, and the paragraph appeared the following Wednesday.

Almost before the ink was dry, the alcoholic Sam Hester came in the office and asked for me.

"Mayor, will you run a little note in the paper to clear up something for me?" he asked in his most serious tone while he wobbled and smelled of moonshine whiskey.

247

"Yes, what you want, Sam?" I asked, picking up a pencil and piece of copy paper.

"Run something next week that says the Sam Hester who is always in Mayor's Court charged with being drunk and disorderly is not the same Sam Hester who was convicted in Federal Court for selling loads of sugar to the bootleggers during the war from his Tabor City store," the alcoholic Hester said.

We ran it just like that. There was much comment around the town but none from the Hester store management. Alcoholic Sam had the last word. Dad thought it was the funniest item the newspaper ever printed. It sounded like some of his stories.

He Dug The Foundation

Our uncle Cyrus was a rough, tough brute of a man, a real physical specimen, but he never quite had both his oars in the water. He was a good worker, but he was kind of on the slow side when it came to thinking. One summer he spent a few weeks with us. Dad had some work that he needed to get done and Uncle Cyrus was never married and got mighty lonely living in a ramshackled house on the old Palestine home place.

Dad had him dig a long ditch at the bottom of a hill where a pasture fence separated our line from the Blalocks across the dell. He took the assignment seriously, and I never saw before or since any ditch 200 yards long or more that had perfect vertical sides and a smooth bottom from one end to the other. It was a masterful bit of craftsmanship and all of us applauded his expertise at ditch digging.

Regardless of your work in the world, it's great to do it well, even digging ditches.

With the ditch complete, Dad told him one morning to hitch up old John, a twenty-five year old mule that Glenn Efird had given to us, and to plow out the Irish potatoes in the garden in front of the house. Cyrus was agreeable and Dad went on off to work.

When Dad came in that night, Cyrus walked up to him slowly, puffing on his smelly corncob pipe that almost never left his mouth, when he was awake.

"Raleigh, I plowed out those potatoes like you said but there wasn't many. What I did plow out were no bigger than marbles," he said in his normal lazy tone.

Dad's mouth dropped open. He didn't know whether to cry, laugh, yell at Cyrus or walk away. The potato seed were only recently planted. They had barely grown a few inches from the ground. Dad had meant for Cyrus to "bust out the middle" with a plow to keep the crab grass under control. Cyrus thought he wanted them harvested and did his best. There was a serious flaw in the communications.

The professional appearance of the ditches Cyrus dug kept Dad from blowing his stack. He just replanted the seed potatoes and avoided an unpleasant argument. That was not characteristic of Dad.

Years later when Dad retired and I talked of building a home in Tabor City, Dad, who was still strong and healthy, volunteered to dig the foundation. He wanted to do it, so I offered no objection. A few weeks later, he came down to Tabor with his pick and shovel and started digging the eighteen inch wide, four inch deep ditches. Like Cyrus, his digging was straight, the sides perfectly smooth and vertical. A neighbor came by to kibitz with Dad, whom he had never seen and, of course, did not know.

"You sure know what you are doing. That's the best house foundation digging job I ever saw," the loafing observer said, "You must have a lot of experience doing this."

"Yeah, I spent ten years on the chain gang. Just got off a month ago," Dad said, ever so seriously and he didn't elaborate.

I didn't think anything about the job he was doing or that conversation until a man up town a few days later stopped to ask who the ex-convict was that dug my house foundation.

"Ex-convict?" I asked.

"Yeah, that's what he told a friend of mine who was watching him," the acquaintance said.

Then I knew. Dad had been pulling someone's leg again.

"I'm afraid that ex-convict isn't available. He's gone home. He is my Dad." I clarified the misunderstanding.

Today the story wouldn't have made much sense. Prisoners aren't allowed to do any strenuous work like ditch digging. That infringes on their rights and criminals have more rights than most other people. They mostly watch

249

television. But they once did useful work on the roads and some could dig good ditches when that wasn't considered demeaning.

The Egotism of Writers

I don't think that Dad ever really understood the thrill that I got from writing small talk in the **STANLY NEWS & PRESS** when I was in high school. As I remember, I first wrote the Endy School News and later a sports column called "Sport Shorts." I began it about 1938 and wrote the stuff for nothing at least two years. Later I did work for the semi-weekly newspaper a bit in the summer and the late John Harris paid me five cents per column inch. Then he complained because I wrote the stories so long that I sometimes earned eight or nine dollars a week, too much he thought.

Later when I went to UNC Chapel Hill, I was a stringer for the **CHARLOTTE NEWS** when Burke Davis was sports editor and for the **WINSTON-SALEM SENTINEL** when Nady Cates was handling sports. I remember that from time to time I got paid as much as fifteen cents per column inch.

While at Chapel Hill, I was elected editor of the **DAILY TAR HEEL**, the student newspaper, and that was profitable. I got $15.00 a week for working about 50 hours a week. In the Navy I wrote again for nothing for the base newspaper at Charleston, South Carolina called **AHOY!** When I was sent to Notre Dame University for one year by the Navy, I edited **THE CAPSTAN**, a 300 page yearbook. Again, it was done without pay, except the Navy was my employer then and giving me $50.00 a month.

The first magazine article I ever wrote was in the **AMERICAN JERSEY CATTLE MAGAZINE**. It was a story about a thoroughbred Jersey milk cow named Dream Noble Blanche Ixia, owned by P.E. Miller, Sr., my late father-in-law. The cow had set a production record. I didn't get paid for that either, but you have never seen anyone any more vest-button-popping proud than I was when that story came out with my name on it. That was in 1946.

Over the past fifteen years, after more or less retiring from **THE TRIBUNE**, I have written and sold more than 1,000 magazine stories, many paying more money than I used to make in a month. I have also written ten books. But that is not the real reward. All writers that I know are egotists. We want to see our by-lines on our creations and often that name means more than money.

I don't think that fact ever quite sunk in to my Dad who could see a thrill on my face that wasn't exactly rewarded in my pocketbook.

Things That People Read

Many times after I started the little newspaper in Tabor City, Dad would note when I came home for a weekend that it carried a lot of stories about cuttings, shootings and various forms of murder and death. He wondered why we had so much of the bad things in the news columns. He wasn't the only one. All my life readers have asked that question.

The reason is philosophical but accurate.

You can write about the good days, how they were enjoyed and the beauty of life. People will read or listen for a short while and then quickly it isn't much to listen to. But things that are gruesome, evil and threatening make good copy and the tale may interest readers or listeners for weeks. It's the unusual that makes the memorable news.

Once when a subscriber came into the office complaining that we had a lot of violence and lawlessness in **The Tribune** overlooking the statistics that proved more than twenty percent of our copy was always about schools or churches, I defended the reporting, explaining that it was bad news that the people wanted to read.

"But there is some good news that we do not write about that maybe we should. Suppose I run a story next week on the front page saying that you do NOT beat your wife?" I looked him in the face for his reaction.

"No, don't do that. Someone will think maybe I have been beating her," he said, and that ended the conversation.

Glenn D. Kittler Didn't Make The Anniversary Party

When the struggling **Tabor City Tribune** was in diapers and **The Loris Sentinel** was in its first year, a bright young man from Chicago wanted a job and started writing for the newspapers for $35.00 a week. He was an idealistic journalist who wanted only enough money to live on and he could live at Mary Todd's boarding house for the $35.00 a week, all we could afford to pay him in that time frame over 40 years ago. Sometimes he had to take a handful of invoices to advertisers on Friday afternoon and collect some money before he could get the $35.00. He was not an outdoorsman at all but sometimes he went fishing with us anyway. "It was the only time in my life that I had to go fishing in order to have something to eat," he often joked.

The young man was Glenn D. Kittler. Some of today's **Tribune** readers will remember him. He had a brilliant mind and could come up with some fine columns which he entitled **"Such Is Life"**.

He helped both with **The Tribune** and **The Sentinel** for about a year before moving on to Norfolk, Va., for a newspaper job and later to New York City where he launched his real writing career. He was on the staff of **Coronet**, now defunct, and for years was a contributing editor of **GUIDEPOST**, a position he held until his death which we didn't learn about until months after he died.

But we did suspect something. When we held the 40th anniversary of **The Tribune** in July 1986, Kittler had promised faithfully that he would be in Tabor City. He didn't show up and we didn't hear from him. As it turned out, he was deathly sick then but lived until May 31, 1987, when he passed away. We do not know the cause of his death. We simply read in **GUIDEPOST** in its 1987 Daily Preview that it had dedicated the '87 edition of that magazine to Kittler, "a long time contributing editor who died last May 31."

The following short item in that preview edition says much about the faith and mind of Glenn D. Kittler:

*Forbearing one another, and forgiving one another...*Colossians 3:13.

For years I've been unable to convince people that I am color-blind. Whenever I beg off making a color judgment and tell why, they look at me as though I'm kidding. Today, after hours of struggle at my typewriter. I relaxed and put my feet up on the desk. A secretary walked by and said, "Okay I believe you — you're color-blind."

"What finally convinced you?" I asked.

"Your socks don't match," she said.

"That's funny," I said. "I've got another pair at home just like them."

Sure, I can laugh at my own failings. But why should I have to? All right, so I can't hammer straight. I have no sense of direction. I am lousy at math. I don't finish everything I start... The list is endless. I don't pretend to be perfect. But why should people expect me to be?

If I have learned anything from living with these shortcomings it's to be more tolerant of others who also aren't so hot at everything. The Bible says we should forgive each other — seventy times seven. That's what I survive on, coming and going. I'm banking on God's forgiveness, too.

Lord, teach us Your divine mercy, so that we can forgive others' failings in the same way that You forgive ours. Glenn Kittler.

While writing literally thousands of magazine articles as a free lancer in New York, Kittler also wrote more than 50 nonfiction books. He turned them out quickly and astutely and made a good living with his typewriter all of his adult life.

Kittler never went to college. He tried it a few weeks and said they were not teaching him anything. He was a self-taught scholar with tremendous ability.

Glenn D. Kittler was a man with firm beliefs and great intelligence. All of us who knew him admired and loved him. It's sad to hear of his passing, alone, unmarried and in a cold place like New York City.

I'm seated on left and the late Willard Cole, of the News-Reporter is seated as the two of us won honors from the North Carolina Press Association.

End Of The Line

The funeral was over. It was the end of the line for my Dad. I drove along silently headed east past the muddy river, up and down mountains, over winding blacktop roads. I smiled at three small black children who waved along the roadside. Some skinny cattle grazed in a pasture on the banks of a tiny fish pond. Smoke curled up from a brush fire on a distant hillside. Rows of soybeans and corn covered farmlands in the valleys. Buzzards circled overhead where an opossum had been mutilated under the wheels of a passing car. Some old crows darted out of our path as they rushed in for bits of the dead animal. Then we passed through a village where we stopped momentarily for a red light before moving on to the east and the flatlands where tobacco yellowed in the sandy fields.

I was on a lonely trip back home. Solemn thoughts sneaked out of the crevices of my mind where they had been tucked away for a long time. An idyllic vision took shape. Life is a trip that we all must take. Good and bad dreams come true as we travel along toward a destination where we expect flags to be waving and fragments of our life miraculously merge into a finished product.

Sometimes it seems the trip takes forever. Life is so slow and painful and we curse the lonely hours and the days that loiter and make us wait, and wait and wait for the happy goal at the final destination. Then there are fast moving moments and events that we would like to freeze and relive forever and ever. But time and tide wait for no man. We must stay on the trip and keep moving, moving, moving.

You remember once when you became 21 and you had waited so long for that day. You recall the first new automobile you ever bought, the first house mortgage you burned, the day you knew your vocation was well chosen and you were a success. You smile with relief when remembering the year the last child finished college. You think about these jewels of the past and vow you will do nothing and live happily ever after once retirement time arrives. That's the part of the trip that you are on that grows nearer, nearer, nearer.

Then you stop and think more realistically. There is no one place, no one age or one time that you reach and keep forever. The joy of life is not just a dream that constantly is beyond our grasp and we never quite get there. The true joy of the trip is the life we hold in our hand today. Not tenable forever but not elusive forever either. We can't focus on the regrets of yesterday or the uncertainty of tomorrow. Regret and fear combine to rob us of today. Relish the moment at this stage of the trip. Joy is here and now. That's the real destination of life's rocky road and each of us can live happily with the truth of today or suffer with regret and fear until the end of the line overtakes us.

Joy of the trip comes when we quit packing the aisles and stop counting the miles. We must take more vacations, eat more candy, hug more loved ones, fish more lakes, climb more hillsides, wiggle our toes in the surf, bask in the midday sun, pause for the beauty of another sunset, admire another sunrise, laugh more and cry less. Life must be lived today when we first start the trip, reach the halfway mark or even when the end is near. The destination, the finale will come soon enough. Joy comes from the way we live as we move down the road exploring each moment, loving each mile and determined to smile until we at last reach the end of the line.

As the tightrope walker said, "Nothing counts but the time we spend on the wire."

An Eulogy To My Father...
I Remember

(Reprinted From The Tabor City Tribune, May 1969)

He had said he wanted to die with his shoes on. I remember him for that but much better for his sense of humor. I remember him for his other story about shoes. The one which he said, "I didn't know they made little shoes until I was 17 years old. I thought they were for grown people." And such was about the plight of his family as they struggled to survive in a time of depression, hardship and suffering around the turn of the century in a little biblical-sounding community known as "Palestine" — in Stanly County, N.C.

I remember him for the hard work he did. For the tractors he sold and maintained. Even the time he broke his arm cranking an old Fordson. He kept right on working every day with the arm in a sling and then had to pay for the aluminum splint that he wore a hole in during the six weeks he mechaniced with his arm in a sling.

I remember him for his hard-work true stories that intrigued me 40 years ago that must sound almost unbelieveable to the indifferent society of today that apparently resists all forms of work. You see, he went to work full time at the age of seven. There was no minimum wage law and no hourly restrictions, and he labored 12 hours a day Monday through Friday and ten hours on Saturday. His pay was 10 cents a day in a textile mill.

And I remember him for his work with a construction gang on the railroad where he walked five miles to get to the job, worked ten hours for $1.00, and then walked the five miles back home. And that was when he was a robust young man of 20.

I remember him for his answer to a question about his education. "What grade did you complete?" And his answer was a Will Rogers if we ever heard one, "I don't know what grade I got to. It was whatever you could get to in three months." That was the extent of his schooling, yet he could read, not fast, but read, and write enough to get by.

I remember him for his honesty. I never knew him to beat anyone out of anything, even though the effort was tremendous at times to keep his head above water, pay the household bills and try to get three children through school. And, too, for his soberness yet awareness that he wasn't perfect and his "I'll never punish a child for doing something I do."

I remember him for his outspoken opinion on any issue. He never minced words to please a listener. He was conservative, Christian, American. He was much of what the pioneers were who helped build a nation. I remember him as a man interested in young people who served 22 years as a member of the Endy Boy Scout troop committee.

I remember him for his adverturesome spirit as a young man when he left home with $1.00 in his pocket and headed for Texas. There with a grandfather cotton farmer, he lived a year. Then on to Detroit for a time, then Cleveland where he learned mechanics and obviously much of what all young men of any age learn.

Then came World War I, and I can remember his account of reporting for service. But he had been born with six fingers on one hand, and in that era few babies had corrective surgery that would have so easily removed the blemish. They turned him down but advised that he get into war production with his mechanical experience. He did and worked throughout the war as a boilermaker on the battleship Maryland. It cost him his hearing in one ear but he never seemed to mind it.

I remember his telling of the return to his native Stanly County in North Carolina and his marriage to a 100 pound blue eyed young lady 50 years ago, come December 24th, 1969. And, while all was not forever peaceable, I remember the love he had for that wife, three children and in recent years a bevy of grandchildren.

I remember the time I held his head for nearly 500 miles as we returned to Tabor City from a fishing trip in Florida where he had suffered from a heart attack and all but passed away.

I remember him for that time 12 years ago when at the age of 65 he retired from his public job, only to find he could not survive as a rocking chair elder citizen living off Social Security. He found a part time job, liked it and survived a decade more, growing interested again in living which he did until last Friday morning at a few minutes past nine.

Today I remember him as that white haired, square-jawed gentleman of 77 lying peacefully amid satin and flowers, ever so still. I remember what he said about hair as I look at that on his head, "I don't care what color my hair turns as long as it don't turn loose," he said many times.

I remember him for that last moment before the lid was closed and I knew he would tell no more stories, do no more hard work, express no more love for his family, community and the worldly things about us.

I remember him as another fatality of the highways of America that snaps out the life of so many, so often and so quickly.

I remember him as my father, Walter Raleigh Carter, Born March 24, 1892, Died April 25, 1969. And I cannot forget. W.H.C.

Dad's Last Day

If indeed the yardstick of success in the world is the happiness that you enjoy, then Dad must have measured several yards. He worked hard and didn't regret it. That was how he was raised, working, and always he believed that the American way was to earn a living and provide for your family by the sweat of your brow. He provided us with the necessities even in a period when many far more educated and blessed with much greater abilities had difficulty surviving. Always we had food, clothing and shelter. While we were poor by government standards, no one told us that we were poor and we were happy with what we had. Dad and Mama made a lot of sacrifices for us.

Their three children grew up, had families of their own, were economically secure and all were church goers with compassion for those around them. What more could parents want?

Mama needed a loaf of bread and Dad got in his old car and drove to the community store a mile away. With his purchase in hand, he got back in his car, cranked the motor and made a U turn from the driveway into Highway 27 that would carry him back home. He was not as observant at age 76 as he had been. A speeding car burst over the crest of a hill a hundred yards or so to the west. It plowed into the side of Dad's vehicle. He was thrown from the car and lay still on the grassy shoulder. There was not a bruise on him. One huge drop of blood gathered in the half inch deep scar in his right temple --all that remained of an old wound from the corner of a brick that had fractured his skull more than a half century earlier. His head had absorbed a blow then that was meant for some one else. Many men would have been killed from such a head wound. But he survived it as a young man. But now the highway accident apparently had pressed the bones from this old scar against his brain. He died after only three breaths. He had not suffered. It was instant death. That's the way he would have chosen for his last moments. He would never have died with dignity as an invalid and a burden to others in bed. It was almost as if he had made a deal with God and died with his boots on.

There were plenty of tears at the funeral. There were some sincere, kind words by those who eulogized him. But somewhere in the deep recesses of the brains of those attending, there were the vivid memories of his words and experiences so filled with humor that you smiled again inside.

He is gone now and we miss him. Dad was an uneducated Will Rogers who made life interesting and projected something humorous into almost every day of his life, even when beset with tribulations.

He was the kind of man, husband and father that you do not soon forget.

There never will be another Walter Raleigh Carter, "A Man Called Raleigh."

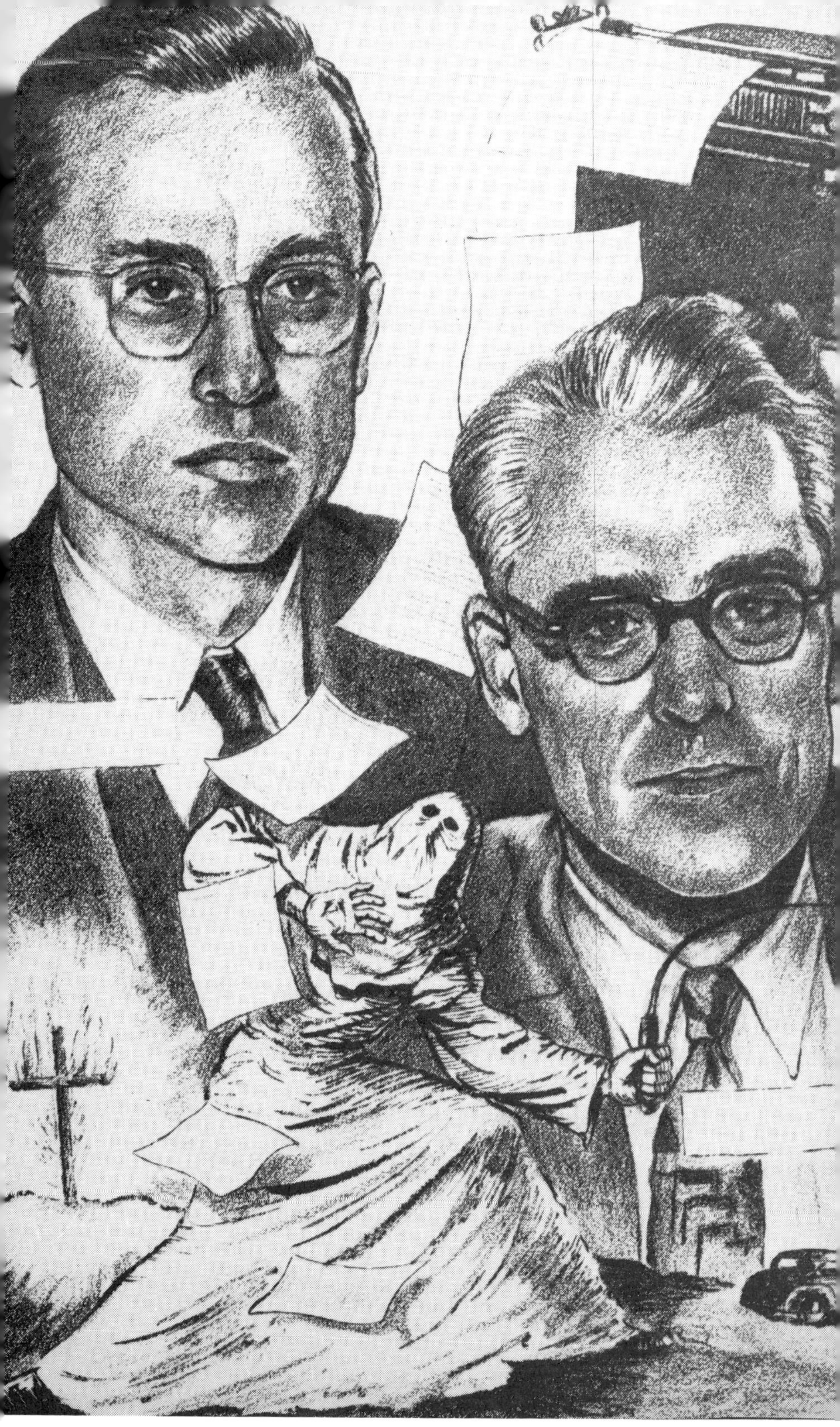

Convenient Order Form

I would like to have additional copies of this book,

A Man Called Raleigh

Please mail me _____ copies to the address below:

Name: _____

Address: _____

_____

Enclosed please find check or money order in the amount of $9.95 that includes postage, and handling, for each book.

Please mail to:
W. Horace Carter
Atlantic Publishing Company
P.O. Box 67
Tabor City, N.C. 18463

(Tear out & mail this sheet to publisher.)

Please ship me one copy of Atlantic Book checked below:

☐ **Hannon's Field Guide For Bass Fishing $9.30**
☐ **Creatures & Chronicles From Cross Creek $7.30**
☐ **Land That I Love (Hard Bound) $12.30**
☐ **Wild & Wonderful Santee-Cooper Country $8.30**
☐ **Return To Cross Creek $9.30**
☐ **Nature's Masterpiece at Homasassa $9.30**
☐ **Catch Bass $8.30**
☐ **Hannon's Big Bass Magic $13.50**